F. Scott Fitzgerald and the Art of Social Fiction

N. L. Terteling Library

Swisher
Memorial Collection

THE COLLEGE
of IDAHO
Idaho's Liberal Arts College

For my children, Nicholas Ieuan, Isabel Mair, Katharine Siân and Lawrence Caradoc.

F. Scott Fitzgerald and the Art of Social Fiction

Brian Way

St. Martin's Press
New York

ISBN 0-312-27950-7

Library of Congress Cataloging in Publication Data

Way, Brian.
  F. Scott Fitzgerald and the art of the social fiction.

  Bibliography: p.
  Includes index.
  1. Fitzgerald, Francis Scott Key, 1896–1940 —
  Criticism and interpretation.   2. Social problems in
  literature.   I. Title.
  PS3511.19Z95 1980   813'.52   80–105

  ISBN 0-312-27950-7

Printed in Great Britain

Contents

	Introduction,	vii
1	The artist and the milieu,	1
	Foundations — the making of a social novelist,	1
	Fitzgerald and the 1920s,	9
	Fitzgerald the artist,	15
2	Fitzgerald and the tradition — Henry James, Henry Adams and Edith Wharton,	22
	The moral sense,	25
	American civilization — 'a vast, vulgar, and meretricious beauty.'	30
	American civilization — the failure of the aristocratic principle,	33
	Social fiction as a mode of poetry,	38
	The history of manners,	43
3	Fitzgerald's early work — a study in development,	49
4	Fitzgerald's short stories — the shape of a career,	72
5	*The Great Gatsby*	98
6	*Tender is the Night*,	119
7	The crack-up and Hollywood,	149
	Select bibliography,	164
	Index,	167

Acknowledgements

The author and publishers would like to thank the Bodley Head for permission to quote from the works of F. Scott Fitzgerald.

The following abbreviations are used throughout:
BH1—6, for Vols. 1—6 of the *Bodley Head Scott Fitzgerald*.
Letters, for *The Letters of F. Scott Fitzgerald*, edited by Andrew Turnbull, London, 1964.

Introduction

When D. H. Lawrence reviewed William Carlos Williams's *In the American Grain* in 1925, he declared that 'all creative art must rise out of a specific soil and flicker with a spirit of place.'[1] Although F. Scott Fitzgerald has little in common with either Lawrence or Williams, this dictum applies to his work with a peculiar exactness and felicity. He was extraordinarily responsive to certain cultural elements in the American scene, particularly to the unique character of the places and historical periods in which he lived, so that, for him, growing up in the Middle West, sharing the life of the American rich in the 1920s and working at Hollywood during its most resplendent years were not merely marks on a calendar, but the conditions which helped to form his artistic vision. For this reason, a purely formalist approach to his fiction, one which occupies itself solely with patterns of language and structures of meaning, is bound to be sterile in the end. To read a Fitzgerald novel is to be led inevitably to an enhanced appreciation of certain aspects of American life, while, conversely, many of our impressions of that life attain their fullest clarity and definition only through an understanding of his work. These interrelations are generally so subtle and delicate as to give special point to Lawrence's metaphor of growth and flowering.

Fitzgerald is a social novelist, though not in the sense in which that phrase is usually understood. He does not borrow abstractions from the social sciences like Dreiser and Dos Passos, nor does he rely upon myth and symbol as Fenimore Cooper had done. The view that his main theme is the failure of the American Dream, though it has led to some stimulating criticism (particularly in Marius Bewley's work[2]), is ultimately harmful and misleading. This approach cannot provide an adequate basis for the appreciation of his art, since it reduces his novels to the status of a simplified version of American history. *The Great Gatsby* and 'The Diamond as Big as the Ritz' have been the worst sufferers: in academic criticism and undergraduate teaching they are often forced to serve a crudely illustrative function which obliterates every nuance of irony, wit and feeling.

For Fitzgerald, the most significant kind of reality is to be found in the

1   D. H. Lawrence, *Phoenix* London, 1961, p. 334.
2   See Bewley's essay on Fitzgerald in *The Eccentric Design*, London, 1959.

observed manners of the immediate social group. As he wrote in a letter of 1934, 'I always crystallize any immediate group in which I move as being an all-sufficient, all-inclusive cross-section of the world, at the time I know it (the group).'[3] From this living centre meanings radiate outwards so as to illuminate the whole society, just as the entire solar system is lighted and warmed by a single source of energy. This is not merely a way of looking at life, it implies a particular kind of novel, one in which the author depends to a very large extent upon a subtle dramatic sense of how people behave in their social relations — the rhythms of excitement and fatigue at a party, the patterns and inflections in the chatter at a dance, the ways in which men and women talk to each other, or the contrasted attitudes people have towards the spending of their money. Fitzgerald is not a novelist of manners in any limited sense, however: he is almost always interested in his characters' inner lives — their dreams, their processes of thought, their deeper psychology. But this concern invariably shows itself at the point where a character's inner life and his social life blend together, at the point where psychological analysis and social observation become virtually indistinguishable from each other. The centre of illumination provided by the immediate social group, in other words, lights up the dark interior of the human mind as well as the wide expanses of American social life. Gatsby's parties are a microcosm of Jazz Age America; they are also the dramatic language through which we come to understand the elusive nature of his dreams and his illusions, his comic vulgarity and his imaginative greatness.

The complex and subtle artistry which goes to the making of such fiction places Fitzgerald in a definite tradition. He is a successor to Edith Wharton and Henry James, both of whom brought a similar outlook and similar fictional methods to the observation of the American scene. Henry Adams, too, is an important figure in this connection, and his *Education* occupies a significant place in Fitzgerald's literary background. In trying to place Fitzgerald within this distinctive area of American literature, I am not concerned with mere influence hunting: my aim is to establish the nature of his deepest literary allegiances; to find out what kind of American novelist he is; and to determine the context in which it makes most sense to discuss his novels and stories.

It is impossible to write about Fitzgerald's work, especially in the way I have suggested here, without coming to definite conclusions about his life. There can be little doubt that there are vital connections between his fiction and his experience: the difficulty arises when one tries to decide which connections are the really important ones, and here I find myself in sharp disagreement with Fitzgerald's biographers and most of his critics. They have tended to stress the purely personal elements in the case, whereas it seems to me that there is far more to be learned from the intellectual and cultural factors. A biographer naturally wishes to tell a colourful and

3 *Letters*, p. 511.

moving story, and the events of Fitzgerald's life clearly lend themselves to this kind of treatment. The story indeed is so compelling that it gradually takes precedence, in the biographer's mind, over the very works of art which were presumably the only justification for telling the story in the first place. In Andrew Turnbull's biography, passages from the novels are used to conjure up pictures of what Fitzgerald was feeling at given moments in his life. In Arthur Mizener's *The Far Side of Paradise* the fiction and the life seem to become blurred alternative versions of the same story: the novels are valued as a fascinating though somewhat unreliable kind of biographical evidence, the life as a flawed work of art. The life story which emerges from these studies is a highly personal drama: it dwells on the peculiar family and financial circumstances of Fitzgerald's early years; it follows in minute detail the vicissitudes of his career at Princeton; it turns his marriage with Zelda into a uniquely romantic and unhappy tale of love; and it presents his crack-up and declining years as a completely individual descent into alcoholism, ill-health, loneliness and failure. This is a true story but an incomplete one: it is not the story of Fitzgerald the novelist. It gives a false importance to some aspects of his life and obscures others which are potentially more illuminating. Princeton is an interesting case in point: one's understanding of Fitzgerald's best fiction is not greatly advanced by the knowledge that he wasn't seriously considered for the university football squad, nor by a detailed grasp of the circumstances by which the presidency of the Triangle Club slipped through his fingers. These things mattered to Fitzgerald the undergraduate, but they ceased to occupy his mind once he began on his career as a professional writer: any attempt to see his best novels and stories in terms of such experiences, can only have a trivializing and sentimentalizing effect. It is true that he assigned a crucial role to these events in his crack-up essays, but this was at a moment of collapse when he had lost faith even in his greatest work and was casting back to half-forgotten humiliations in order to establish a consistent pattern of failure in his life.

Fitzgerald himself is undoubtedly to blame in part for the false image which hovers persistently in the popular and, all too often, the academic mind. He had a weakness for exhibitionism and self-display which he controlled in his best fiction, but nowhere else. In his autobiographical essays, particularly those he published with increasing frequency in the 1930s, he shows a propensity for turning his own life into an absurd and vulgarly romantic scenario, so that it reads like one of his own worst short stories. Less scrupulous writers than Mizener and Turnbull have restated the lush and sensational elements so insistently that they have finally acquired the force of legend. The Scott Fitzgerald story, as one may call it, resembles one of those showbiz extravaganzas in which Hollywood used to commemorate some vanished band leader, singer or romantic artist — and has as little to do with its ostensible subject.

The evolution of the legend has helped to make Fitzgerald a cult figure, but it has harmed his reputation as an artist and made it more difficult to discuss his work sensibly. The assumption that his fiction is personal, that it always deals directly with events in his own life, is false and limiting. He naturally wrote best about experiences and situations which were within the range of his own fullest consciousness, but, apart from that, his fiction is no more autobiographical than that of most other great novelists. The most harmful consequences, however, spring from the nature of the Scott Fitzgerald story itself. Even in the most sympathetic versions, it is a story of weakness and failure, of flawed or uncompleted work, of unrealized ambition, of energies and feelings wastefully expended. At worst, as in Budd Schulberg's *The Disenchanted* (a thinly fictionalized account) or Aaron Latham's *Crazy Sundays*, we are given a crudely insensitive portrayal of the drunken and anarchic behaviour of Fitzgerald's last years. In this atmosphere, it is not surprising that many critics should be reluctant to credit him with the qualities of intelligence, craftsmanship and conscious design which were obviously indispensable for the production of his best work; and that he should so often be thought of as a 'natural writer', with a marvellous gift for words, who wrote well because he couldn't help doing so. This, too, is the climate of opinion in which it could seem proper for Malcolm Cowley to rearrange the text of *Tender is the Night* — as if an experienced editor and literary journalist would necessarily know better than Fitzgerald himself what he was about; and this is why it would seem eccentric to most readers of American literature to argue that Fitzgerald is, at his best, a great writer of short stories.

His major novels and stories were created by a better self than the one which biography and legend alike have chosen to celebrate. If one turns aside from the flamboyant drama of his personal life, one encounters the hard-working professional author and the dedicated artist. One discovers a novelist more subtly responsive to the cultural and historical aura that surrounded him than any American contemporary save Faulkner, a social observer more intelligent and self-aware than any since Henry James. For the reader of Fitzgerald's fiction, it is these intellectual and cultural connections that really matter, and in my first chapter I attempt to give an account of their nature. In chapter 2, I discuss his affinities with the American writers with whom he had most in common — the specifically literary context in which his work can best be understood. In chapter 3, I consider his early writings up to and including 'The Diamond as Big as the Ritz' so as to put forward a theory of his development — the process of trial and error by which he discovered his true bent as an artist. Chapter 4 serves a dual purpose: it argues the case for taking his short fiction seriously and also makes use of the fact that he wrote good stories at every stage in his working life, in order to suggest the shape of his career. The next two chapters offer extended readings of *The Great Gatsby* and *Tender is the Night*, which are not simply self-contained critical essays, but grow out of the preceding discussion. The major phase of Fitzgerald's career ended with the publication of the latter novel, and so my last chapter acts to some extent as an epilogue. It gives me an opportunity to challenge the commonly accepted view that the crack-up essays are among his most important writings: despite a few brilliant aphorisms, they seem to me to be artistically inferior, besides giving a highly distorted and damaging impression of the author. This final chapter concludes with a discussion of the writing that came out of his association with Hollywood.

The present moment seems favourable for attempting the kind of reconsideration of Fitzgerald's work I have suggested here. We have just passed through a period of apparently limitless prosperity which has many obvious similarities with the Boom years of the 1920s; and its ending in the energy crisis of 1973 seems scarcely less abrupt than the Wall Street Crash of 1929. In both periods, many people adopted a completely hedonistic philosophy of life in which there seemed to be a simple and direct equation between money and happiness; and in both, there was a revolution in manners and sexual behaviour. We are still close enough to the affluent society to remember it as an agreeable and spacious time, but the psychological, even more than the economic effect of its sudden termination, has been to sharpen our awareness of the human problems it created and those it failed to solve. With this doubleness of vision we are well equipped to appreciate Fitzgerald's own complexity of attitude, his capacity to be fascinated by the collective adventure of Jazz Age America and at the same time highly critical of it.

1

The artist and the milieu

From his earliest years, Scott Fitzgerald began to acquire a framework of ideas, assumptions and values which were social in origin, and which, in turn, became an essential element in his understanding of the social life around him. Unlike the drama of his personal life, this material does not lend itself to being told as a continuous story. There are formative periods of intense significance in his development separated from each other by years of consolidation or stagnation. Three of these periods seem to me to be particularly illuminating: his childhood and adolescence, during which he absorbed, by a largely unconscious process, many of his fundamental notions about wealth, class and morality; the decade of the 1920s, when he participated in and observed the life of the American rich; and his last years at Hollywood, when he was brought into contact with new and unfamiliar forms of American wealth and power. I shall defer discussion of the last of these to the closing pages of my book, but the first two provide a large part of the subject matter of this chapter. Whenever possible, I document my account from Fitzgerald's own letters and essays, but I also make use of biographical materials (especially in the section on his early life) and for these I am indebted to the work of Arthur Mizener, Andrew Turnbull, Nancy Milford and Henry Dan Piper. In general, I disagree with their conclusions — the facts which seem most interesting to me are not, on the whole, the ones they choose to emphasize — but I have found their studies an invaluable source of reference.

There remains the general question of Fitzgerald's sense of his own role as artist and professional writer. This topic has been almost completely ignored, even though his essays and letters, particularly the latter, contain many interesting and intelligent remarks on the subject. In the final section of this chapter, I have tried to draw these together and to bring them into relation with certain biographical facts so as to present a picture of Fitzgerald the artist.

Foundations — the making of a social novelist

In 'My Lost City', Fitzgerald speaks of New York as an exciting but perpetually strange and disturbing place. Home, 'the warm centre', was back in

1

the Middle West where he was born on 24 September 1896 and passed much of his boyhood and adolescence. When their child was to be born, he and Zelda 'played safe' and came home to St Paul, Minnesota — 'it seemed inappropriate to bring a baby into all that glamour and loneliness.' The Middle West represents provincial comfort, solid domestic virtues and economic security (as it does for Nick Carraway in *The Great Gatsby*). Fitzgerald continued to think of it not simply as the place he came from but as a place he could return to, at least up to the mid-1920s.

As well as providing the basis of these emotional certainties, the Middle West contributed in the profoundest ways to his sense of class and his sense of morality. Most Middle Western novelists of his time — Dreiser, Sherwood Anderson, Sinclair Lewis, Hemingway — grew up in a predominantly rural or small town way of life. Fitzgerald was unusual in having an exclusively urban background. His family belonged, somewhat precariously, to the social élite which had thrust itself forward in the larger cities by the end of the nineteenth century. This class had some pretensions to aristocratic style and manners. Its richest members had a talent for exuberant display which Fitzgerald could observe in his native city of St Paul, where the railroad tycoon James J. Hill had built an immense mansion. But these aspirations were not matched by a corresponding sense of fitness and proportion. Henry James and Henry Adams, writing in the first decade of this century[1] — the period of Fitzgerald's boyhood — reflected despairingly on the American failure to create an aristocratic civilization out of the unparalleled wealth of the Gilded Age. Fitzgerald himself in two early stories, 'The Ice Palace' and 'The Diamond as Big as the Ritz', indicates that in his view colourful extravagance, reckless waste and a distinct vein of megalomania were the usual marks of Western display.

His own family were only moderately well-off, but even so there were ways in which they could aim at an aristocratic style. For the young, the main formative influence was the dancing class. The associations which a boy or girl formed there led to a wide range of social activities — formal balls and parties and the country club pursuits of skating and sleigh-riding, swimming and golf. To grow up in this setting was to acquire a rigid code of social conduct: good manners of a formal, rather old-fashioned kind, strict rules of dress, firm conventions of behaviour towards women and the presence of chaperones, at least in theory, during all meetings between persons of opposite sex. In this way, too, the upper classes of the big Middle Western cities expressed their sense of solidarity: a young person who conformed to this pattern belonged socially (the dynastic and financial business of marriage was a different matter), whether he came to dancing class in the family's chauffeur-driven limousine, or, like Fitzgerald, rode the street-car and trudged through the snow.

Nevertheless, this carefully acquired style was all surface, all

1   In *The American Scene* and *The Education of Henry Adams* respectively.

purchased — paid for with the new wealth, like the dancing lessons and the correct clothes. There was no 'spell of transmission' as James would have called it, nothing of that inherited conception of the aristocrat with; however dim, its Renaissance Platonic antecedents, which survived in the European aristocracies and even in Henry Adams's Boston and Edith Wharton's old New York. The Middle Western upper class was completely provincial in its lack of high culture and its total insulation from any standards but its own — 'built', as Edmund Wilson remarks, 'not on the eighteenth century but simply on the prairie'.[2] Its contradictory qualities are conveyed with great precision in another of Fitzgerald's early stories, 'Bernice Bobs Her Hair': he shows possibilities of excitement and pleasure dulled by a narrowness of outlook and an elaborate social ritual only half-concealing a lack of inner substance. At its most idyllic and benign, this phase of American life is vividly recaptured in the best of the Basil stories, 'The Scandal Detectives' and 'A Night at the Fair'. (In the cinema it is present in the beautiful sleigh-riding sequence from Orson Welles's *The Magnificent Ambersons.*)

Despite certain gestures and aspirations, this social group was not really an aristocracy at all: its way of life in all essentials was irretrievably middle class. It was not generally a rentier or leisure class; its men had occupations and its money was earned. The qualities it admired were epitomized in Fitzgerald's family by his maternal grandfather, who made a fortune in the wholesale grocery business, rather than by his father, whose exquisite Southern manners were joined with an unfortunate inability to make a living.

It was not a particularly exclusive class. Family and status were relatively simple things and, while there was a good deal of snobbery, wealth could always break the barriers. Anything as complex as Gilbert Osmond's Roman palace with its 'evenings', when the important question was not who came but who was excluded, was inconceivable. When lines were drawn they were simple to the point of crudity: Fitzgerald was rebuked in his courtship of the Chicago débutante Ginevra King with the remark, 'poor boys shouldn't think of marrying rich girls.' Even so, charm could guarantee a social success as considerable as Fitzgerald's own in St Paul.

The society he moved in was as strict in its attitude to morals as to manners. In externals, at least, it appeared to uphold the standards of American puritanism, though in fact it was largely a form of puritan decadence (a useful phrase which Stephen Spender employs in a somewhat different connection in his autobiography *World Within World*). Puritanism was no longer an energizing moral force, as it had been for seventeenth- and, in a secularized form, for nineteenth-century New England, or as it continued to be for the rural Mid-Western communities of the Bible Belt. Among prosperous city people it had degenerated into a largely mechanical

---

2 Edmund Wilson, 'Fitzgerald before *The Great Gatsby*', reprinted by Alfred Kazin, *F. Scott Fitzgerald: the Man and his Work*, Cleveland and New York, 1951, p. 79. (originally appeared in *The Bookman*, New York, March 1922)

set of social conventions. The apparently strict sexual morality included much hypocrisy and depended for its survival, predictably, on the brothel, the kept mistress, the double standard and the notion of the fallen woman. For people who were not hypocrites, puritan decadence had an almost wholly negative effect: it confined response and sensation without bringing the traditional compensations of spiritual intensity and the conviction that life is a moral drama, which had given colour and dignity to genuine puritanism.

Since Fitzgerald was a Catholic (his mother's side of the family were very devout), this essentially Protestant moral tradition might at first sight seem to have little to do with him. By this time, however, the tradition had become a diffuse cultural influence rather than a matter of religious practice. Besides, the predominantly Irish Catholicism Fitzgerald was brought up in was if anything more severe in its moral restraints — particularly where sex was concerned — than even Bible Belt Protestantism. Its atmosphere was close to what Joyce describes in *Portrait of the Artist as a Young Man*. Fitzgerald drew upon the atmosphere of his religious upbringing in one of his best stories, 'Absolution'. As an adult, he rejected the ritualistic and confessional aspects of his religion, but his ethical sense continued to be deeply affected by it. In 'One Hundred False Starts' he claims that he has 'a New England conscience — developed in Minnesota'.

The accepted standards of conduct were still outwardly intact and were not openly challenged in provincial Middle Western society until after the War. Young people of Fitzgerald's generation, however, as they grew up, were more and more aware of feelings and motives within themselves which were entirely at odds with what was supposed to be right. Since the current orthodoxy was merely conventional and lacked inner conviction, it did not command real respect. The result was a state of moral confusion which affected relations between children and their parents, and, even more, between adolescent boys and girls. Their social contacts were strictly chaperoned, and sexual relations between members of the group were rare — even girls who went in for petting in parked cars were considered 'speeds'. The boys were held back by an ill-defined puritanism, which acted more as a source of social and psychological uncertainty than as moral conviction. Girls remained technically chaste, but there was no relation — even symbolically — between virginity and innocence. Since they felt safe, they often turned falling in love into a series of daring emotional and social manoeuvres, played close to the edge of complete sexual involvement.

Young people wasted their energies in a frenetic contest for popularity: girls measured their success by the strings of beaux they had in attendance and by the number of men who cut in on them at dances, boys by the amount of attention they could get from popular girls. The system prolonged adolescence and made it more difficult to achieve sexual maturity. Fitzgerald's own romantic fascination with girls like Ginevra King was balanced by a deep sense of revulsion at the thought of physical sex. When he wrote *This Side of Paradise* at the age of twenty-three, he was still unable to control and analyse these contradictory feelings.

He believed that these psychologically destructive emotional games produced, especially in girls, a premature weariness and cynicism. This was still in his mind as late as 1937, when he warned his daughter that 'for premature adventure one pays an atrocious price' and went on to speak of her mother as a woman who was destined to 'wear out young'.[3]

In many ways the social life which was the setting for Fitzgerald's early development seems unattractive now — the puritan element particularly so — but Middle Western life taken as a whole still retained many of the traditional American decencies of friendliness, hospitality and domestic affection. It gave him a number of the images and experiences which concerned him most as an artist and helped to form his moral sense — his intense fastidiousness about personal relationships, particularly with women.

Fitzgerald felt he owed a more specific debt to his father, as he noted in an unfinished autobiographical essay:

> I loved my father, always deep in my subconscious I have referred judgements back to him, what he would have thought or done.[4]

Edward Fitzgerald was descended from a Maryland family which, though its fortunes were declined, had played a minor role in the making of American history between the Declaration of Independence and the Civil War. It had usually taken a reactionary position: one ancestor had fought on the British side in the War of Independence; another was Chief Justice Taney, whose ruling in the Dred Scott case was one of the final aggravations leading to the Civil War; and a third was the Mrs Suratt who was hanged as an accomplice to the assassination of Lincoln. Most of the romantic conservatism which is a frequent element in Scott Fitzgerald's writing came from the memories and family legends passed on by his father.

In a letter to his cousin Ceci, written on the occasion of a death in the family, he recalled these colourful associations, but also reflected on the more substantial virtues of his father's generation: 'What a sense of honor and duty they had — almost eighteenth century rather than Victoria.'[5] As the phrase 'honor and duty' indicates, the father transmitted to the son qualities which the Middle West lacked, qualities which belonged to an older and more stable society. Edward Fitzgerald was despised by his wife's side of the family for his failure as a businessman, but he never relinquished a quiet sense of quasi-aristocratic superiority. As Scott put it in another

3 *Letters*, pp. 15—16.
4 Quoted by Matthew J. Bruccoli, *The Composition of 'Tender is the Night': a Study of the Manuscripts*, Pittsburgh, 1963, p. 124.
5 *Letters*, pp. 419—20.

letter, there was a 'black Irish' side to his family which had all the money, and there was his father's side, the 'old American stock' which had 'that certain series of reticences and obligations that go under the poor old shattered word "breeding" '.[6] Edward Fitzgerald's breeding was expressed in dress, in manners; and through a gentlemanly style of moral disquisition which does indeed seem to come from the eighteenth century. Once, when he sent his son a dollar pocket money at a summer camp, he advised him to 'spend it liberally, generously, carefully, judiciously, sensibly. Get from it pleasure, wisdom, health, experience.'[7] Scott responded to his father's tone and style from earliest childhood with an imaginative intensity which led him ever afterwards to associate the finer possibilities of living with an aristocratic conception of civilization.

This tendency was strengthened in school and college by his friendship with Monsignor Sigourney Webster Fay, who became a kind of second father to him. He was a wealthy and sophisticated priest with social connections of a kind Fitzgerald had not encountered before. He was a friend of Henry Adams, and Fitzgerald met Adams in his company several times. He presented the Catholic church in a way which intensified the attractiveness of the aristocratic idea.

In St Paul, Fitzgerald had disliked the church on the whole. His word for it was 'muggy' — that is, drab, stuffy and plebeian. It was mainly the religion of the Irish, the Italians, the Poles, those immigrant groups who seemed farthest from any conceivable American version of the aristocratic idea. Fay, and another of his younger protégés, Shane Leslie, emphasized the historical and hierarchical aspect of Catholicism. For them it represented, not poverty and ignorance, but wealth, political power, and an unequalled splendour of ritual, architecture, music and painting:

> ... he [Leslie] and another [Fay], since dead, made of that church a dazzling, golden thing, dispelling that oppressive mugginess and giving the procession of days after gray days, passing under its plaintive ritual, the romantic glamour of an adolescent dream.[8]

The tone of the passage is itself sufficient to show how receptive Fitzgerald was to such influences and how much they must have strengthened his disposition to define social values in romantic-aristocratic terms. It is strange that there should be so little trace of this aspect of Catholicism in his fiction (it is not even present in *This Side of Paradise*, where there is a thinly veiled and quite detailed portrait of Fay). One reason is that Fitzgerald seems able to use only American experiences and materials. The Catholicism of Fay and Leslie was deeply coloured by the ideas of Henry Adams, for whom the church represented a culture and a principle not only European in its historical origins, but specifically opposed to the spirit of modern America.

6   *Ibid.*, p. 503.
7   Quoted in Henry Dan Piper, *F. Scott Fitzgerald: a Critical Portrait*, London, 1965, p. 11.
8   Quoted in Arthur Mizener, *The Far Side of Paradise*, London, 1951, pp. 42–3.

In the grotesque simplifications we find in the later chapters of *The Education of Henry Adams*, the Virgin is opposed to the dynamo, the Cathedral of Coutances to the St Louis World's Fair.

The most probable explanation, however, is that, for Fitzgerald, Monsignor Fay was mainly a social not a religious influence. What he valued most in the friendship was being treated as an equal by a cultivated man of the world, meeting important men and dining out at fashionable New York restaurants.

The contradiction at the heart of Fitzgerald's attitude to Catholicism helps to illuminate the larger conflict which is central to all his social attitudes. He inherited a middle-class outlook — a version of the Protestant ethic — from the middle West and a sort of aristocratic humanism from his father and Monsignor Fay. As a result, he felt he belonged to both and to neither, and was simultaneously admiring and critical of each. In actual social situations, he was nearly always uncertain of the right way to behave.

Fitzgerald found ways to dramatize this conflict in the images of success, failure and the hero which evolved in his mind during his formative years. In an interview he gave soon after his crack-up he said:

> There has never been an American tragedy. There have only been great failures. That is why the story of Aaron Burr — let alone that of Jefferson Davis — opens up things that we that accept the United States as an established unit hardly dare think about.[9]

For failures which were not 'great', Fitzgerald had an exaggerated horror and contempt, in which middle-class notions about the importance of success were reinforced by the romantic conviction that poverty meant squalor. Although he admired his father's aristocratic breeding, he despised him for his economic failure, and he always spoke of the day when the latter lost his job as the deepest shock of his childhood.

From an equally early age, he was convinced that a certain type of failure — the 'great' kind — was more romantic than success. His reference to Jefferson Davis, President of the Confederacy, gives one indication — Fitzgerald had a lifelong preference for the defeated South in the Civil War, fed both by boyhood reading and family memories. But there are two inter-related images that help to define what he felt with still greater precision. The first comes from a book:

> ... that was I think one of the big sensations of my life. It was nothing but a nursery book, but it filled me with the saddest and most yearning emotion. I have never been able to trace it since. It was about a fight the large animals, like the elephant, had with the small animals, like the fox. The small animals won the first battle, but the elephants and lions and tigers finally overcame them. The author was prejudiced in favour of the large animals, but my sentiment was all with the small ones. I wonder if even then I had a sense of the wearing-down power of big,

9 Quoted in Piper, *op.cit.*, p. 10.

respectable people. I can almost weep now when I think of that poor fox, the leader — the fox has somehow typified innocence for me ever since.[10]

When Fitzgerald came to analyse some of the reasons which led him to choose Princeton as the university he wished to go to, he returned to the image of the war between the animals, and linked it to another — that of college football. Princeton, in spite of courageous and often brilliant play, usually just failed to win the championship:

> Yale always seemed to nose them out in the last quarter by 'superior stamina' as the newspapers called it. It was to me a repetition of the story of the foxes and the big animals in the child's book. I imagined the Princeton men as slender and keen and romantic, and the Yale men as brawny and brutal and powerful.[11]

This kind of failure, in which there seemed to him to be an element of romance, was the gallantry, the stylishness, of not quite winning against impossible odds.

These images, both of failure and of success, penetrated the deepest levels of Fitzgerald's artistic awareness. Tom Buchanan in *The Great Gatsby*, 'one of the most powerful ends who ever played football at New Haven', is a Yale man and, figuratively, a big animal, who 'smashed up things and creatures.' So is Anson Hunter of 'The Rich Boy', even though his brutalities are of a subtler kind. The romance of failure, on the other hand, is clearly a most important element in the conception of both Gatsby and Dick Diver, Fitzgerald's two finest creations.

The football hero has a special value for him which the Confederate soldier could never have. However far his imagination travels in the process of creation, his best work is always rooted in the concrete particulars of the American middle- and upper-class life of his time. The college football star was a truly indigenous type of the hero, who embodied the ideals and wish-fulfilments of millions of Americans. This was equally true of the heavy-weight boxer and the baseball player, who were vitally important figures to Fitzgerald's friends and contemporaries Hemingway and Ring Lardner. His own preference for the football player was purely a matter of class: the champions of the other sports, especially boxing, were usually of proletarian or recent immigrant stock, while football between 1890 and 1917 was dominated by Harvard, Yale and Princeton.

A star player in one of these teams became during his brief career a national figure. He could be made the vehicle for an almost unlimited degree of romantic involvement. Fitzgerald recalls one such moment in his reminiscent essay 'Princeton'. Years after his undergraduate days were over he glimpsed a magnetic, familiar figure on the Champs Elysées: 'It was the romantic Buzz Law whom I had last seen one cold fall twilight in 1915, kicking from behind his goal line with a bloody bandage round his head.' At the same time, because of his intimate knowledge of the social milieu in which

10   Quoted in Andrew Turnbull, *Scott Fitzgerald*, London, 1963, p. 20.
11   *Ibid.*, pp. 44—5.

the game was played, Fitzgerald could use his doubts and reservations about the football hero as a point of departure for the most searching criticism of American civilization. In a story like 'The Bowl', he shows how much of the magic of achievement is produced by an empty and capricious mania for publicity; while in figures like Tom Buchanan, the brute muscle of the football star becomes an image of the overbearing arrogance of the American rich.

Malcolm Cowley sees the game in the same way in a vivid anecdote from *Exile's Return*, in which, by an uncanny coincidence, the image of the war between the large and small animals reappears:

> In those years [the later 1920s] the big college football games served as almost the only mass-demonstrations of the American upper bourgeoisie. The Harvard-Yale game of 1928 was the biggest of all, the hardest to get tickets for, the most be-furred, extravagant, silver-flasked, orchid-dotted and racing-car-attended. Between the halves a gray squirrel somehow got loose on the field and was pursued by a drunken man in an enormous coonskin coat; I remember that the scared animal seemed more human than the eighty thousand people who shrieked while it was being captured.[12]

Fitzgerald and the 1920s

In the careers of certain writers a comparatively short period of time acquires overwhelming significance — for Stendhal the immediate aftermath of Waterloo, for Turgenev Russia in the 1840s, for Joyce Dublin in the first decade of the century. For Scott Fitzgerald it was the 1920s, or, to use his own more precise definition, the Jazz Age which began with the May Day riots in New York in 1919 and ended with the Crash of 1929. This period aroused his sense of life as no other could; it gave him images of youth, romance, success, degeneracy, callousness, violence, madness and disaster; it provided situations of a social and moral complexity and centrality which the Middle West and Princeton had lacked. It was a time favourable to the arts in America. Novels and stories like *This Side of Paradise* and 'The Diamond as Big as the Ritz' could not have been published before 1920 even though they drew on earlier experiences, and no other phase of literary activity in America could have enabled him to mature so rapidly. The impetus of what he learned and experienced in the Jazz Age carried him far into the next decade, culminating in the completion of *Tender is the Night* in 1934.

All this has led many readers to take it for granted that Fitzgerald is the most completely representative writer of America in the 1920s. Perhaps he is — but if so, in a sense which has to be very carefully qualified. No writer contains within himself the entire life of his time, and from certain points of view Hemingway, Dos Passos, Sinclair Lewis, H. L. Mencken, Hart Crane

12 Malcolm Cowley, *Exile's Return: a Literary Odyssey of the 1920s*, London, 1961, pp. 273—4.

and E. E. Cummings are quite as representative as Fitzgerald. If he seems more so to us, it is mainly because he is a better writer (only Hemingway and Crane are comparable artists) and because he loved the role of spokesman, which Hemingway in his good years shunned and which Crane never had the opportunity to play.

In the act of naming the age, Fitzgerald was expressing not only proprietorship but a sense of the limits of his own capacity to experience and record. The two brilliant reminiscent essays 'Echoes of the Jazz Age' (1931) and 'My Lost City' (1932), to which I shall be making extensive reference, are quite clear on this point. The voices of 'Southern mill-workers and western farmers' did not reach him: he had no contact with rural and industrial America. Apart from his brief friendship with Mencken, he had little to do with the world of satirical and polemical journalism and still less with the puritans, philistines, provincials and boosters whom that journalism attacked. He had no interest in the artists and poets of Greenwich Village. But he was at the centre of the most striking manifestation of the Boom years — a reckless and extravagant attempt to follow up the possibilities of wealth, pleasure and freedom. In his own phrases, it was 'the most expensive orgy in history', 'a whole race going hedonistic, deciding on pleasure', 'the whole upper tenth of a nation living with the insouciance of grand dukes and the casualness of chorus girls'.[13]

Even here, one has to distinguish carefully between the different ways in which he was representative at different times. Initially he helped to create the Jazz Age by 'telling people that he felt as they did, that something had to be done with all that nervous energy stored up and unexpended in the War'. He did not invent entirely new modes of experience, but he wrote about current changes in behaviour, feeling and moral outlook as if they were accomplished facts. He brought social changes which had had, up to that time, only an unacknowledged, furtive or shamefaced existence, within the orbit of his contemporaries' everyday consciousness. He made the unsettling effect of the War clearer to them; he taught them to take a flippant and relaxed view of the decaying puritan restraints on drinking and petting in automobiles; he inspired them with contempt for the material worries of the businessman — as he recalled ironically in 1931, 'Even when you were broke you didn't worry about money, because it was in such profusion around you.' Through his portrayals of Isabelle and Rosalind in This Side of Paradise and through the heroines of his earliest stories, he defined a new social type — the flapper. Women had been steadily gaining more social freedom in America since about 1910, but Fitzgerald recognized, sooner than anyone else, that the nature of their advance had changed radically with the coming of the Jazz Age. For the pre-war generation, whose ideas were formed by such writers as Ibsen and Shaw, liberation was an arduous affair — when Nora Helmer closes the door of the doll's house behind her

13   'Echoes of the Jazz Age', BH3, pp. 337, 331, 337 respectively.

she enters a hostile world. Fitzgerald's young heroines assert their independent wills and exploit their sexual attractiveness with complete impunity: indeed their social success is in exact proportion to the daring and high-handedness they display in doing as they please.

These are some of the factors which made *This Side of Paradise* an overwhelming success, which brought Fitzgerald an enormous fan-mail when he published stories like 'Bernice Bobs Her Hair' and which, between 1920 and 1922, made him and Zelda national figures second to none in influence and notoriety. There was much that was superficial and adventitious about his success, however. He recalls the anomalies of his position in 'My Lost City': 'A dive into a civic fountain, a casual brush with the law, was enough to get us into the gossip columns, and we were quoted on a variety of subjects we knew nothing about.'

By the time *The Beautiful and Damned* appeared in 1922, this phase of Fitzgerald's career as a representative writer — when he not only reflected and recorded the age but helped to form it — was over, but its ghost was to haunt him for the rest of his life. He describes one such visitation with amusement in his notebooks:

> A young man phoned from a city far distant, then from a city near by, then from downtown, informing me that he was coming to call, though he had never seen me. He arrived eventually with a great ripping up of garden borders, a four-ply rip in a new lawn, a watch pointing accurately and unforgivably at 3 a.m. But he was prepared to disarm me with the force of his compliment, the intensity of the impulse which had brought him to my door. 'Here I am at last,' he said, teetering triumphantly. 'I had to see you. I feel I owe you more than I can say. I feel that you formed my life.'[14]

This strange guest resembles the hopeful reveller who drove up to Gatsby's house long after the party was over. The incident occurred at a time when *Tender is the Night* was nearing completion, and Fitzgerald's incredulous irony was aroused by the gap he felt between the image that remained in the popular mind and the artistic and personal maturity he considered he had attained. Later, he became too bitter about the disparity to be able to laugh at it. Replying in 1939 to a request for biographical information, he wrote: 'Sorry I have no picture but I may say that out here [Hollywood] I am known as the old "oomph man". So any haberdasher's advertisement will do as a portrait.'[15]

Once Fitzgerald ceased to be partial creator and semi-official spokesman of the Jazz Age, his relation to it became much more complex. There is certainly no simple equivalence between his career and the history of the time — any more than there is between his life and his fiction. It is true that he made money, drank too much and showed in his own behaviour much of the violence and nervous instability that had become a kind of national

14 Quoted in Mizener, *op.cit.*, pp. 223—4.
15 *Letters*, p. 591.

neurosis by the end of the decade. On the other hand, he developed powers of self-analysis and detachment and qualities of moral discrimination most uncharacteristic of the people he is generally associated with. Still more untypically, he was, by 1924, beginning to measure the significance of his life chiefly by the extent to which he could devote himself to disinterested artistic creation. By this time, his fascination with the age — and therefore his representativeness — was no longer that of the participant, but that of the observer: where he had once been a propagandist and spokesman, he was now a historian of manners.

Fitzgerald saw a clear pattern of development in the history of the Jazz Age. The specific nature of the two events which contained it — the May Day riots of 1919 and the Crash of 29 October 1929 — gave an additional sharpness of definition to the pattern. The riots occurred when recently demobilized soldiers tried to break up the usual May Day socialist meetings and demonstrations, on the grounds that the socialists had been pacifist and therefore un-American during the War. The authorities, imagining they saw Bolshevism and revolution everywhere, put down the disturbances with considerable brutality. The indignation provoked by this tyranny, however (as Fitzgerald notes in 'Echoes of the Jazz Age'), was short-lived. The War had made people tired of great causes: 'the events of 1919 left us cynical rather than revolutionary.' Even the corruption of President Harding's administration and the martyrdom of Sacco and Vanzetti could only arouse a momentary concern once this attitude had established itself. The steadily increasing prosperity of the decade, in which many soon began to share, turned people's minds to more immediate satisfactions.

Fitzgerald's analysis here shows how much of the chaos of the 1920s was due to confusion about the idea of freedom. The times were both repressive and libertarian: the Palmer Raids, directed against anarchists, socialists, Bolsheviks and labour leaders, were a monstrous infringement of democratic rights, but at the same time writers like Sherwood Anderson, Theodore Dreiser, Dos Passos and Fitzgerald himself were beginning to enjoy a freedom of expression American artists had never known before. Puritanism was about to achieve a grotesque legislative triumph in Prohibition at the very moment when its real power to control moral and social behaviour was crumbling away. In this situation, clearly, one did not need to risk martyrdom in order to experience certain kinds of freedom, particularly if one had plenty of money. Few people choose martyrdom at any time: fewer still will choose it when offered so attractive an alternative. Most of Fitzgerald's contemporaries chose the life of impulse, and it was their choice which gave the age its distinctive character.

The hedonistic impulses of the age gave birth to a new social form, the cocktail party, where men and women met to drink, to flirt, to dance to jazz and to gossip. Malcolm Cowley considers that it originated at the end of the War in the bohemian life of Greenwich Village. By the end of the decade it was a national institution. Fitzgerald constantly uses the party as a way of exploring character and society in his fiction: Gatsby's parties are an expression both of his vulgarity and of his Western gift for magnificence; Tom Buchanan's parties are coarse and brutal like himself; Dick Diver's parties are exercises in aristocratic charm and subtle corruption. In 'Echoes of the Jazz Age' Fitzgerald treats the age itself as if it were a party — the kind of party that starts marvellously, but gets steadily more and more out of hand and ends in disaster.

The younger generation were the first guests, and while the party belonged to them it had at least the virtues of youth — the quality of ecstasy and romantic excitement and a self-abandon which served to stimulate the imagination rather than to gratify the senses:

> We felt like small children in a great bright unexplored barn ....
>
> When bored we took our city with a Huysmans-like perversity. An afternoon alone in our 'apartment' eating olive sandwiches and drinking a quart of Bushmill's whisky presented by Zoë Akins, then out into the freshly bewitched city, through strange doors into strange apartments with intermittent swings along in taxis through the soft nights. At last we were one with New York, pulling it along with us through every portal .... And lastly from this period I remember riding in a taxi one afternoon between very tall buildings under a mauve and rosy sky; I began to bawl because I had everything I wanted and knew I would never be so happy again.[16]

Hart Crane evokes this New York atmosphere with the same sense of euphoria when he apostrophizes Brooklyn Bridge:

> Again the traffic lights that skim thy swift
> Unfractioned idiom, immaculate sigh of stars,
> Beading thy path — condense eternity:
> And we have seen night lifted in thine arms.
>
> Under thy shadow by the piers I waited;
> Only in darkness is thy shadow clear.
> The City's fiery parcels all undone,
> Already snow submerges an iron year ....[17]

Whatever the power of such images, youth and romantic exaltation did not remain dominant characteristics of the age for long. By 1923, as Fitzgerald noted, an older generation was taking over, just as the grown-ups sometimes take over a children's party. The younger generation had found much of the stimulation it needed in simply being young; their elders needed artificial stimulants and began the really hard drinking which became typical of the Prohibition era and gave it the character of orgy. With the move from ecstasy to self-indulgence, there was a marked coarsening of the quality of life:

16 'My Lost City', BH3, pp. 344—5.
17 Hart Crane, *The Bridge*, 'Proem to Brooklyn Bridge.'

> The city was bloated, glutted, stupid with cake and circuses, and a new expression 'Oh yeah?' summed up all the enthusiasm evoked by the announcement of the last super sky-scrapers.[18]

The deterioration was not only moral and social, it was psychological:

> The tempo of the city had changed sharply. The uncertainties of 1920 were drowned in a steady golden roar and many of our friends had grown wealthy. But the restlessness of New York in 1927 approached hysteria. The parties were bigger ... the place was faster — the catering to dissipation set an example to Paris; the shows were broader, the buildings were higher, the morals were looser and the liquor was cheaper; but all these benefits did not really minister to much delight. Young people wore out early — they were hard and languid at twenty-one ....[19]

The wearing-out process and the element of hysteria were intimately bound up with the psychological foundations of the Jazz Age. We have already seen that Fitzgerald felt its origins had something to do with the expenditure of the nervous energy stored up during the War. His definition of jazz itself points in the same direction:

> The word jazz in its progress toward respectability has meant first sex, then dancing, then music. It is associated with a state of nervous stimulation, not unlike that of big cities behind the lines of a war.[20]

This condition, prolonged and intensified through a whole decade, gave to the party in its final stages the character of mass neurosis.

Much of the hysteria erupted as violence, the characteristic American response to situations of instability and strain. The rise of the gangsters and racketeers — the inevitable underside to the farce of Prohibition — represented only the public face of violence. Private life was becoming equally explosive, and in 'Echoes of the Jazz Age' Fitzgerald gives a catalogue of the 'contemporaries of mine who had begun to disappear into the dark maw of violence' — victims of murder, suicide, madness or casual brutality.

Fitzgerald had used the image of a party to chart the progress of the Jazz Age. For the Crash of 1929 which effectively marked its end, he used another image — the city of New York, and in particular the city's most extravagant expression of its own nature, the Empire State Building. As far back as 1906 in *The American Scene*, Henry James had described the New York sky-scraper as the new American Beauty rose, the most spectacular flowering of America's overweening commercial confidence and vulgarity. The tallest of them all, completed only a matter of months before the Crash, is presented by Fitzgerald, in a passage of truly Jamesian irony, as a final act of hubris:

> Full of vaunting pride the New Yorker had climbed here and seen with dismay what he had never suspected, that the city was not the endless succession of

18 'My Lost City', BH3, p. 347.
19 *Ibid.*, p. 346.
20 'Echoes of the Jazz Age', BH3, pp. 331—2.

canyons that he had supposed that *it had limits* — from the tallest structure he saw for the first time that it faded out into the country on all sides, into an expanse of green and blue that was alone limitless. And with the awful realization that New York was a city after all and not a universe, the whole shining edifice he had reared in his imagination came crashing to the ground.[21]

In 'Echoes of the Jazz Age' and 'My Lost City', Fitzgerald was concerned not merely to evoke the atmosphere of the postwar decade, but to bring out its historical pattern. The pattern fascinated him because of its obvious dramatic possibilities, and it took up almost all his creative energies during the major phase of his career. In his view, it manifested itself wherever Americans gathered to spend their money. New York was the epicentre, but shock waves travelled outwards to the cities of the Middle West and the small towns of the Deep South. In the later 1920s, there was a mass migration of prosperous Americans to Paris and the Riviera, in which Fitzgerald himself took part, characteristically, both as reckless participant and dispassionate observer. The difference made by these geographical variations was small in comparison with the essential similarities he recorded in the behaviour of his compatriots. He at no time attempted to put the whole pattern into a single novel or story, not even *Tender is the Night*, because he evidently felt that this was unnecessary. For him, any part of the pattern implied the whole: even in the ecstatic delirium of 'May Day' (1920), he foresaw violence and disaster — not, of course, in the shape of an actual historical event, but in psychological and moral terms; while, conversely, stories of disaster like 'Babylon Revisited' contain haunting reminders of earlier possibilities of freedom and excitement.

Fitzgerald the artist

Fitzgerald was far more interested in the nature of the artist than his critics and biographers have ever been prepared to recognize. It is true that he did not approach this question with the self-conscious deliberation which one sees in novels like *Death in Venice* or *Portrait of the Artist as a Young Man*, but in his best fiction he often makes an oblique reference or follows a train of thought which show how keen his awareness actually is: he explores the workings of the romantic imagination in Gatsby's character; he uses the skills of the actor and entertainer as metaphors for understanding certain equivocal aspects of Dick Diver's personality; and in 'Crazy Sunday' and *The Last Tycoon*, he deals directly with the situation of the film producer. In his letters and essays, the reality of his concern is still more unmistakable.

During the 1920s, it was usual to think of the artist as an alienated figure: by dedicating himself to the religion of art, he automatically renounced the great prizes of wealth, power and popularity. This is an unquestioned assumption in Malcolm Cowley's *Exile's Return* and Edmund Wilson's *Axel's Castle*, the two best retrospective studies of the period published in

21 'My Lost City', BH3, p. 348–9.

America. Cowley describes how his friend Kenneth Burke used to walk at night on the New Jersey shore and look across the Hudson at the massed lights of New York City; and how in Burke's mind, as he contemplated his chosen vocation of poet and critic, these lights became a symbol of all he must give up. Fitzgerald was unwilling to accept this alienated position, and in 'My Lost City' he uses the same image to express a diametrically opposite view of his own role: he recalls how the ferry boat, carrying him towards the city at dawn, always seemed to be bearing him on an irresistible course of conquest and triumph. He believed that the great artist was a heroic figure, a conqueror, and when, in 1936, he felt compelled to relinquish the idea that he, personally, could achieve this kind of greatness, it was, in his eyes, the surest indication that he had really cracked up. To be a writer and nothing else, he bitterly concluded, was clear evidence of failure.

Fitzgerald's conception of the artist reflects the ideas of the nineteenth century rather than those of his immediate contemporaries. It owes a great deal to Romanticism: in 'Pasting it Together', he says that he began his career with 'the old dream of being an entire man in the Goethe-Byron-Shaw tradition'. Shaw is far too insubstantial a figure to carry such a weight of significance, but the examples of Goethe and Byron are well chosen. Each contains within himself a significant combination of qualities: he is artist, aristocrat, man of action and, at the same time, an ideal representative of the age in which he lived. This was the standard on which Fitzgerald tried, in part at least, to model his own career.

Another piece of evidence, pointing in the same direction, is provided by 'Tarquin of Cheepside', a very early short story which Fitzgerald wrote while he was still at Princeton. When it opens, a young man is being chased through the streets of Elizabethan London. He takes refuge with a friend and, though his pursuers trace him to the house, they fail to find him. While they carry out their search, they explain that the man they are looking for has committed a rape. After they have gone, he emerges from his hiding-place and asks for pen and paper. He writes all night and in the morning presents his friend with a poem: it is called *The Rape of Lucrece*, and he is the young Shakespeare. Fitzgerald, fortunately, did not write of the artist so naively again, but the view implicit in this story remains a persistent element in his thought. The story intimates that the artist's work and his experience are so important that they raise him above the ordinary demands of morality: he becomes entitled to what George Orwell disapprovingly calls 'benefit of clergy' in his essay on Salvador Dali. This view was a commonplace, almost an orthodoxy, during Fitzgerald's formative years, and several early influences which would have made him familiar with it, can be cited with certainty. At Princeton, he read Oscar Wilde's *The Picture of Dorian Gray* with enthusiasm. He encountered Nietzsche's ideas at about the same time, first, in diluted form, in Shaw's *Man and Superman* and, a year or two later, in the version popularized by H. L. Mencken. Later still, when he was engaged in the writing of *Gatsby*, he discovered *Madame Bovary*.

As the 'Tarquin' story itself suggests, however, there is one source of influence which was probably more important than any of these — the Romantic conception of the Renaissance which grew steadily in force throughout the nineteenth century. It is impossible to say exactly where Fitzgerald encountered this view, though it was certainly diffused through much of the poetry and prose he read under John Peale Bishop's tutelage at Princeton. He had, in any case, absorbed the picture of the age which was to be expected under the circumstances: a colourful pageant of worldly popes, Italian *condottieri* and Elizabethan sea dogs, among whom artist figures like Leonardo and Shakespeare reigned supreme. It was a view he never abandoned, and we find it expressed in almost identical terms as late as 1933. In a long letter of that year, he made an elaborate defence of his belief in the 'superiority' of the artist. He begins by quoting Ford Madox Ford's claim that 'Henry James was the greatest writer of his day; therefore for me the greatest man.' He develops this idea by maintaining that the conditions of an artistically creative life are so arduous that they can only be compared with the duties of a soldier in wartime. He reserves what he clearly considers to be his strongest argument for the conclusion of his letter. It is an appeal to the example of Elizabethan England: the only 'people of affairs' we remember from that age are the Queen herself and Drake; all the other great names are those of writers — Bacon, Sidney, Shakespeare, Marlowe, Jonson, Raleigh.[22]

Many writers of the early twentieth century held views similar to these: Hart Crane identified himself with Marlowe and Rimbaud; Thomas Mann's work is full of Dionysiac and Wagnerian strains; Yeats puts on heroic masks from a dozen different cultures; and Pound takes Odysseus as a *persona* in *The Cantos*. Fitzgerald's sense of the artist as hero differs from theirs in one significant respect, however. They are content to be heroes in imagination — to identify themselves with historical or mythological figures. Fitzgerald wished to conquer the actual world of his own time, to gain wealth and popularity, to be 'a leader of men'. As we have seen already, his brief period of popular success in 1920-22 convinced him that this was possible, and it continued to hover before him as a tantalizing mirage during the remainder of his working life.

One consequence of this was that he formed a definite picture of how an artist should live: he felt that his genius justified and was, in a sense, indicated by a capacity for display, reckless extravagance and, on occasion, violent and destructive behaviour. When his mother wrote at the time of Zelda's first breakdown, advising a more moderate style of life, Fitzgerald replied that 'these would be good rules for a man who wanted to be a chief clerk at 50.' He went on to assert that 'All big men have spent money freely. I hate avarice or even caution.'[23] The same attitude is apparent in a long letter

22 *Letters*, p. 435.
23 *Ibid.*, p. 496.

he wrote his daughter in 1938, where he gives a singularly bitter account of the failure of his marriage. He accuses Zelda of having let him down in every possible way, and in particular of failing to sustain her part in the public role they were called upon to play together: 'She didn't have the strength for the big stage — sometimes she pretended, and pretended beautifully, but she didn't have it.'[24] (The question whether Fitzgerald is being fair to Zelda here doesn't affect my argument, since it is only the nature of his point of view, not the accuracy of his recollections, which is at issue.)

Fitzgerald believed, too, in the artist's right to be ruthless: like a military conqueror, he could use other people in order to accomplish his design. This explains the nature of his interest in Hollywood. In his fiction, he does not take the directors, actors, writers and cameramen of the film industry very seriously as artists, though they often appear as characters (Rosemary, in *Tender is the Night*, is an interesting example). He concentrates instead upon the producer, who is not, at first sight, an artist at all. Nevertheless it was a film producer like Irving Thalberg (the model for Miles Calman in 'Crazy Sunday'[25] and for Monroe Stahr in *The Last Tycoon*) who became for Fitzgerald the fullest expression of the type of the American artist. Thalberg had creative flair and, at the same time, immense power: he controlled millions of dollars and thousands of employees; he took individual men and women and made them into stars, or discarded them when they no longer served his purpose. Jakob Burckhardt in *The Civilization of the Renaissance in Italy* (the definitive nineteenth-century account of that period) speaks of Italian princes who turned the state into a work of art, an opportunity for the creation of magnificence and beauty. Similarly Monroe Stahr, 'the last of the princes', treats the film corporation as a vehicle for the creative imagination, rather than a mere business enterprise. In this final work, Fitzgerald's Romantic-Renaissance conception of the artist as hero is fused with specifically American images of wealth and power.

This aspect of Fitzgerald's thought, however, is balanced by an equally important and seemingly contradictory tendency: there is a middle-class element in his thinking about the artist — an acceptance, indeed, of some of the most fundamental tenets of the Protestant ethic. Being an artist might mean being 'a big man': it also meant working for money and being a provider, an economically sufficient man who supported his family in substantial style and could not tolerate debt. More important still, he thought of writing as a middle-class profession, a commitment to an idea of seriousness and responsibility. I do not wish to pursue this argument any further for the present: the nature of Fitzgerald's moral sense is best considered as an aspect of his relation to the American literary tradition, and his attitude to writing as professional work has most relevance to the discussion of his short stories.

24 *Ibid.*, p. 32.
25 Calman, to be strictly accurate, is both producer and director: he is referred to as a director in the story, but since he is in charge of his own production unit, he has the powers and functions of a producer.

In order to give some evidence of the liveliness of his concern, however, I should like to refer briefly to a letter to the daughter of a friend who had asked for his opinion of one of her short stories. He replied passionately and at length: 'I'm afraid the price for doing professional work is a good deal higher than you are prepared to pay at present.' Her story is bad because it cost her nothing to write it. She thought she could make something light and witty out of the 'superficial reactions of three uncharacterized girls', without committing her own feelings and energies to the task. But the capacity even to be light and witty can be learned, Fitzgerald warns her, only through a long and hard apprenticeship. The neophyte, having nothing else to offer, must be ready to sell his heart: it was necessary for Dickens to put all the bitterness of his own unhappy childhood into *Oliver Twist*; Hemingway and Fitzgerald himself had to draw upon their most intense and private feelings in order to write *In Our Time* and *This Side of Paradise*.[26]

In all Fitzgerald's thinking there is a consistent pattern, a habit of mind which asserts itself in every situation. His ideas on any subject tend to arrange themselves into a system of opposed contraries. We have just seen how strongly this is reflected in his conception of the artist, but it is equally apparent in all the other matters discussed in this chapter: he regarded wealth and social status from both a middle-class and an aristocratic stand-point; he acted as spokesman for a new freedom in morals and manners and yet possessed a puritan conscience; and the Jazz Age fascinated him because he saw in it a capacity for delirious excitement balanced by equally strong potentialities for disaster. He was fully conscious of this tendency in his thought and assigned a very high value to it: as he remarks in 'The Crack-up', 'the test of a first-rate intelligence is the ability to hold two opposed ideas in the mind at the same time, and still retain the ability to function.' It is no exaggeration to say that this is the essential element in his gift as a social novelist, but it implies a creative tension which can only be maintained at the cost of an enormous and unremitting effort. It provides the ground for the most fruitful kind of complexity in art, but must often lead to uncertainty and disorder in actual living.

In this connection, some of the anecdotes which have been told about Fitzgerald's social behaviour may be found to yield a value: they help to define, in fairly simple terms, the processes by which he moved from the unresolved contradictions of life to the ordered dualities of art. Quite often, his life broke down into mere confusion, and he appeared to lose every trace of his instinct for a social situation. There is a special irony in one such incident — his calamitous meeting with Edith Wharton. As novelists, no two living Americans had a finer sense for the nuances of a social situation, a more delicate tact in understanding and portraying it, and yet they found themselves quite unable to go through the simple operation of having after-

26 *Letters*, pp. 577–8.

noon tea together. Mrs Wharton confronted her guest with the frozen rigidity of a nineteenth-century *grande dame*, while Fitzgerald arrived drunk and attempted to enliven the conversation by telling her a bawdy joke.

The situations in which he managed to avoid disasters of this sort were usually carried off with some elaborate theatrical gesture. On one occasion, when he was very late for an appointment at a Manhattan bar, he excused himself by saying, with an air of well-bred unconcern, that he had been run over by a bus. When his startled friends asked him how he felt, he dismissed the affair by replying, 'I just picked myself up.'[27] The prodigal expenditure of energy involved in such performances conveys a sense of strain, a feeling of radical uncertainty. Fitzgerald was not often wholly at ease with other people: he tried to conceal his insecurity by a trick of dominance, a constant effort to be brilliant, amusing and inventive, which often, though by no means always, charmed his acquaintances, but was invariably exhausting to himself.

His intense self-awareness and the complexity of his reactions made it almost impossible for him to be spontaneous and natural, and his social life had the character of a series of complicated manoeuvres or theatrical tableaux. Sometimes these were hasty improvisations like the bus incident: often they were contrived in advance with the forethought of an impresario or a film producer. Sheilah Graham, in *Beloved Infidel*, describes how he invariably had a plan when he gave a party. Once, when his daughter Scottie had to entertain two boys who bored her, Fitzgerald devised a scheme to ensure that the occasion wouldn't fall flat. First, he advised her to buy the latest dance records. Then, if dancing gave out, she should take them into the kitchen to make fudge, on the grounds that action creates conversation. Finally, if all else failed, she was to bring them to him so that he could show them his pictorial history of the War, with its photographs of horribly mutilated soldiers. One cannot overlook the somewhat sinister quality of the concluding item in this programme of entertainment: it shows how easy it is for an element of cynicism, contempt and cruelty to enter into a social life so carefully plotted and contrived. Fitzgerald's feeling for the right thing was matched by an uncannily precise instinct for the worst possible behaviour: the quality of insight which enabled him to charm and captivate, could also be used to devise peculiarly subtle punishments for people who bored or irritated him. In his portrayal of Dick Diver's equivocal social gifts, he shows how acutely he was aware of these dangers. For my present purpose, however, the incident which Sheilah Graham recalls has a somewhat different significance. It reveals a fundamental trait in Fitzgerald's understanding of social situations — his conviction that they are so complex that they cannot be controlled, either in life or in art, unless they are given dramatic form. The implications of this view, for a social novelist, are

27 Mizener, *op.cit.*, p. 118.

obvious, and they will be one of my main preoccupations in discussing Fitzgerald's fiction.

Another equally important characteristic of Fitzgerald's social sense is his capacity (which I have remarked upon already in my account of his progress through the Jazz Age) to involve himself recklessly in social situations and then review the results with complete detachment. However grossly he mishandled his life, he could always, after the event, analyse his blunders with an ironic precision. His meeting with John Galsworthy in London in 1921 is an amusing minor instance. Over dinner, Fitzgerald told Galsworthy that he considered the latter, Conrad and Anatole France to be the three greatest living writers. Galsworthy received this tribute coldly. 'I don't think he liked it much', Fitzgerald said afterwards. 'He knew he wasn't that good.'[28] This process of retrospective clearsightedness is a major factor in the creation of the great novels and stories. What appears as confusion and error in his life is transformed into an ideal clarity of vision in his art. While this is the case with many great artists, it is true of Fitzgerald to an unusually marked degree. It is the main reason why the critics and biographers who see his life and his work as alternative, almost interchangeable, versions of the same story are so completely misled.

28 Turnbull, *op.cit.*, p. 118.

2
Fitzgerald and the tradition: Henry James, Henry Adams and Edith Wharton

When T. S. Eliot wrote to thank Scott Fitzgerald for sending him a copy of *The Great Gatsby*, he said, 'it seems to me to be the first step American fiction has taken since Henry James.'[1] It is clear that Eliot is not merely turning a compliment but expressing his sense of a relationship and, still more, of a tradition. My purpose in this chapter is to attempt to define the tradition and to suggest the nature of Fitzgerald's relation to it, just as in the preceding chapter I tried to bring out the significance of his life and of the broader cultural experience of which it was a part.

His best writing belongs to a tradition in the most favourable sense: it is not obviously derivative, in fact it is highly original, but it does reflect a deep community of interest with the work of some of his American predecessors, in particular Henry James, Henry Adams and Edith Wharton. Fitzgerald worked necessarily in very different conditions and with different materials, but in his habits of thought, his patterns of feeling and moral response and his attitude to the art of the novel, he is remarkably close to these earlier writers. We are not concerned here with any question of a direct and obvious influence, like that of Hawthorne on Melville, or Pound on Eliot. Instances like these, in which the connection is both extensively documented and genuinely illuminating, are not very common. A demonstrable influence is often unhelpful and even misleading: there is plenty of evidence to show that Fitzgerald's earliest work was affected by the novels of Compton Mackenzie and Booth Tarkington, but a knowledge of these facts directs us only to immature and superficial aspects of his writing. His connections with James, Adams and Mrs Wharton seem more indirect but in reality go much deeper.

Before I proceed any further with this argument, however, it is necessary to indicate the nature of Fitzgerald's own awareness of these writers. Edith Wharton was certainly the one whose work he read with the keenest interest: at the very least he read *Ethan Frome*, and in all probability *The House of Mirth*, during the very early 1920s. (When he wrote to Maxwell Perkins on 19 April 1922 to suggest that Scribner's should bring out a library of popular American classics, it was these two novels which headed his list.)[2] Edith

1 Reprinted by Edmund Wilson (ed.), *The Crack-up*, New York, 1945, p. 310.
2 *Letters*, p. 156.

22

Wharton, in turn, recognized him as a kindred spirit and, like Eliot, wrote him a personal letter of congratulation on reading *The Great Gatsby*.

Henry Adams, too, was a writer with whom Fitzgerald had personal connections: he met him several times through Monsignor Fay, and had read *The Education of Henry Adams* by the time he wrote *The Beautiful and Damned*. Since the *Education* is not a novel, its presence in this chapter may seem somewhat questionable, but two considerations have led me to include it: in the first place, it contains many remarks on the social life of the American rich and the role of money in American civilization which show striking similarities with Fitzgerald's own opinions; and secondly, although its substance is autobiographical, its form and method are novelistic.

Curiously enough, it is Fitzgerald's relations with Henry James, by far the most important figure of the three, which are the most equivocal. The scattered references to James in his letters point to a mixture of attitudes. On the one hand, it seems clear that he did not enjoy reading James very much. He thanks Maxwell Perkins for sending him *The Art of the Novel* (R. P. Blackmur's edition of the prefaces to James's novels), which is 'wonderful', but 'difficult reading'.[3] At other times, he gibes at 'the questionable later stylistics of Henry James', twits Edmund Wilson with his enthusiasm for *What Maisie Knew*, and warns his daughter off *The Portrait of a Lady*, 'which is in his "late second manner" and full of mannerisms'.[4] (It is only fair to add, *à propos* of the last quotation, that his advice to Scottie, a seventeen-year-old girl with a cosmopolitan upbringing, to begin instead with *Roderick Hudson* and 'Daisy Miller', is thoroughly sensible.) On the other hand, he is well aware of the immense importance of James to any novelist of his generation who cared about the art of fiction. As we have seen, he noted with approval Ford Madox Ford's view that James, since he was the greatest artist, was also the greatest man of his time. When Mencken attacked *The Great Gatsby* for its supposed lack of substance, Fitzgerald accused him of having grown used to formlessness as a result of his uncritical enthusiasm for naturalistic fiction: he proceeded to defend his own concern for form in the names of Conrad and James.[5] Even if he did not warm to James himself, he gave full weight to current views of James's significance — views which were brought to his attention through his literary friendship with Edmund Wilson and, more indirectly, through his interest in Conrad.

Fitzgerald's first-hand acquaintance with James's work is only a minor factor in the transmission of the latter's influence. James affected him in a more general but no less pervasive way: he created certain working conditions which younger novelists could not ignore; he carried forward the form of the novel to a new stage of development; and by the force of his example he initiated strong new currents of literary fashion and opinion. To use a rough analogy, Fitzgerald worked in an atmosphere created by James,

3 *Ibid.*, pp. 254-5, and *Dear Scott, Dear Max*, New York, 1971, p. 209.
4 *Letters*, pp. 433, 333 and 59 respectively.
5 *Ibid.*, p. 480.

just as a young socialist might operate in a Marxist atmosphere without having read a line of Marx.

There are two ways of dealing with this complex situation: one is to concentrate on the actual process of transmission, to chart the network of influences by which Fitzgerald was drawn to accept a broadly Jamesian set of allegiances; the other is to leap over the process of transmission, and to emphasize instead the nature of Fitzgerald's deepest affinities with James himself. I have preferred to follow the latter course, partly because it has not been seriously attempted before and also because it has more to contribute to the understanding of Fitzgerald as an American social novelist. There are strong reasons, too, for rejecting the alternative approach at the present time. For one thing, the scholarly work involved has been carried out with exemplary thoroughness by James E. Miller in *The Fictional Techniques of F. Scott Fitzgerald*. He has documented in great detail the ways in which Fitzgerald's awareness of the possibilities of the novel as an art form expanded during 1922-4, the period which began with Edmund Wilson's *Literary Spotlight* article in *The Bookman*, the first serious appreciation of Fitzgerald's fiction, and culminated in the writing of *The Great Gatsby*. During these years, he worked in an almost exclusively Jamesian atmosphere, sustained by Wilson's criticism and advice and by his own enthusiastic reading of Edith Wharton, Willa Cather and Conrad.

It is unnecessary to follow Miller over this ground again and, as the case of Conrad indicates, the critical usefulness of tracing the immediate influences on Fitzgerald's writing has long since been exhausted. Critics have displayed amazing feats of ingenuity in order to bring out every possible link between Conrad and Fitzgerald. R. W. Stallman, for instance, finds a significant connection between Kurtz's obsession with ivory in *Heart of Darkness* and the fact that Meyer Wolfsheim's cuff buttons are ornamented by fine specimens of human molars in *Gatsby*.[6] This is admittedly an extreme example but, even in cases where the argument is more judiciously presented, one is left with much the same feeling — that in order to draw attention to one adventitious similarity, it has been necessary to ignore a score of differences. Conrad's exotic settings, and the importance in his work of the life of action, mean that in most ways he and Fitzgerald are very far apart. For this and other reasons, it seems to me, there is only a limited utility in bringing out the similarities between Marlow and Nick Carraway as narrators, even if we assume that Fitzgerald had read *Heart of Darkness* before writing *Gatsby*. (As Robert Sklar points out, there is no firm evidence that he had,[7] and if the case has to rest on 'Youth' then it is not worth arguing at all.) Both writers, it is true, had a deep interest in the equivocal nature of the romantic sensibility, but it is difficult to see what Fitzgerald could have learned from Conrad in this connection: of the three novels he undoubtedly

6 R. W. Stallman, *The Houses that James Built*, East Lansing, Mich., 1964, p. 151.
7 Robert Sklar, *F. Scott Fitzgerald: the Last Laocoon*, New York, 1967, pp. 151—2.

had read, 'Youth' is too slight to have taught him anything he didn't know already and *Nostromo* and *Victory* too remote. *Nostromo*, although it deals with one of his main concerns, the dubious romance of money, does so in terms which may well have interested him, but could not really have been accessible to him as an artist: in any case, American society itself provided him with such abundant material for the exploration of this theme that he did not need to forego his characteristic preference for specifically American images and experiences. Conrad was important to Fitzgerald not so much for the unique quality of his own work, but because he was one of the many channels by which a Jamesian conception of the art of fiction reached him.

As I have already suggested, the discussion of Fitzgerald's place in the American literary tradition depends far more on the recognition of affinities than the mechanical charting of influences. A number of the common concerns which unite James, Adams and Mrs Wharton are also central to Fitzgerald's fiction. All four writers inherited a moral sense which is, in various ways, a secularized version of American puritanism. They all share a similar preoccupation with the quality of American civilization: in general terms this leads them to take a consuming interest in the history of American manners and, more specifically, to ask why the privileges of wealth, leisure and freedom enjoyed by the American rich have not been used to create an aristocratic culture. Finally, in at least one respect, Fitzgerald has particularly close affinities with James — his consciousness that social fiction may become a mode of poetry. These are the themes which will occupy me for the remainder of this chapter.

The moral sense

The moral sense which pervades Scott Fitzgerald's best work and the fiction of Henry James and Edith Wharton has its origins in American puritanism. Fitzgerald speaks of himself as having 'a New England conscience — developed in Minnesota',[8] and I have already tried to show that there were enough residual traces in the culture of the Middle West to enable him to effect what amounts to a rediscovery of the tradition. When James began to write, the spirit of 'New England's silvery prime' was still not quite dead, and the force of Hawthorne's example, which showed how important the puritan inheritance could be for an American novelist, was still fresh and clear. The sharpness of James's sense of the cultural connections can be seen in a passage from *Roderick Hudson*, in which he describes Rowland Mallet's New England antecedents:

> He had sprung from a stiff Puritan stock and had been brought up to think much more intently of the duties of our earthly pilgrimage than of its privileges and pleasures. His progenitors had submitted in the matter of dogmatic theology to the relaxing influences of recent years; but if Rowland's youthful consciousness was

8 'One Hundred False Starts', BH3, p. 358.

not chilled by the menace of long punishment for brief transgression, he had at least been made to feel that there ran through all things a strain of right and of wrong as different, after all, in their complexion, as the texture, to the spiritual sense, of Sundays and week-days. His father, a chip of the primal Puritan block, had been a man of an icy smile and a stony frown. He had always bestowed on his son, on principle, more frowns than smiles and if the lad had not been turned to stone himself it was because nature had blessed him inwardly with a well of vivifying waters.[9]

James's analysis is perfect in its precision, economy and wit. He points first of all to the way in which the American moral sense has become secularized — has lost its theological underpinnings and, with them, any ideological character. It is a matter of cultural inheritance, fixed in the child's consciousness by historical, social and parental pressures. At the same time, through his ironic tone — indeed his broadly comic treatment of Rowland's father — James makes it clear that he does not regard it as an inheritance to be accepted blindly. The icy smile, the stony frown, the need for a well of vivifying waters within the self if one would not be turned to stone — these indicate, beneath the comic surface, the gravest reservations. The salient fact about the moral sense is not so much that it is an unqualified good, as that it is indelible. The feeling 'that there ran through all things a strain of right and of wrong' has been completely internalized: it does not require the support of faith or ideas, and it is seen to survive the isolation of exile and the decay of the social conditions which originally produced it, both in James himself and the characters he creates. It is one of those facts of nationality which Ralph Touchett invokes when Henrietta Stackpole accuses him of giving up his country: ' "Ah, one doesn't give up one's country any more than one gives up one's grandmother. They are both antecedent to choice — elements of one's composition that are not to be eliminated." '[10]

The uncompromising nature of the moral sense sometimes provokes the artist into gestures which suggest a leaning towards didacticism. In a letter to his daughter, in which he comments on her interest in the idea of writing musical comedies, Fitzgerald says:

> Again let me repeat that if you start any kind of a career following the footsteps of Cole Porter and Rodgers and Hart, it might be an excellent try. Sometimes I wish I had gone along with that gang, but I guess I am too much a moralist at heart and really want to preach at people in some acceptable form rather than to entertain them.[11]

There is occasional evidence of the urge to instruct in his fiction, most prominently perhaps in the celebrated opening page of 'The Rich Boy': 'Let me tell you about the very rich. They are different from you and me....' This

---

9   Henry James, *Roderick Hudson* (1875), Harper Torchbook, New York, 1960, p. 26.
10   Henry James, *The Portrait of a Lady*, Bodley Head Henry James, Vol. 5, p. 117.
11   *Letters*, p. 63.

is not typical of his method, however, and the story itself is not didactic in the least. On the whole, the American moral sense commits James and Fitzgerald to an exploratory rather than a didactic approach to experience — a search for the finest possibilities in life rather than the conviction that these have already been found and need only be reaffirmed. This exploratory attitude is strengthened by the novelist's feeling for the complexity of experience. The conviction that the difference between right and wrong is real and important does not mean necessarily that it is easy to draw the distinction in a given situation: moral decision is seen, instead, to involve an almost infinite series of interrelated scruples and considerations. In another letter, this time to Maxwell Perkins, Fitzgerald finds a particularly felicitous image for the kind of dilemma the artist may encounter:

> I certainly have this one more novel, but it may have to remain among the unwritten books of this world. Such stray ideas as sending my daughter to a public school, putting my wife in a public insane asylum, have been proposed to me by intimate friends, but it would break something in me that would shatter the very delicate pencil-end of a point of view. I have got myself completely on the spot and what the next step is I don't know.[12]

At first sight, he seems to be sacrificing his immediate projects as an artist to a rather gratuitous sense of middle-class obligations. There is something exaggerated and perverse in the feeling that giving his wife and daughter a position of luxury and privilege has become the field of moral endeavour. But, as he perceptively notes, he does not really have a choice: the delicate pencil-end of his point of view as an artist would be shattered by the abandonment of these duties. What is fascinating about the pencil-end image is that it renders so precisely a sense of the innumerable delicate interrelations entered into by the moral sense.

Almost any one of James's novels would show an ample awareness of the scope of these interrelations, but *The Europeans* will suit my purpose best. Not only is it one of the finest of the shorter works, but it deals directly with the liberated American moral sense in historical and cultural terms — in terms, that is, of its relation to New England puritanism. It tells the story of two cosmopolitans, a brother and sister, born in Europe but of American descent, who come to America to visit their Massachusetts kinsfolk, the Wentworths. The sister's motive is quite cynically to make her fortune — to engage herself to some rich man, and so extricate herself advantageously from the morganatic marriage she has contracted with a German princeling. She has brilliant manners and a consummate social sense, but her feeling for the separateness of right and wrong has been fatally compromised. Her brother Felix has led what Mr Wentworth considers 'an irregular mode of life': by his own account of himself, he has been a bohemian, an amateur, a vagabond, making a desultory living as fiddler, strolling player, portrait painter and magazine illustrator. But, unlike the Baroness, he has an

12   *Ibid.*, p. 269.

extraordinary natural goodness, and the intensest light is thrown upon the nature of the American moral sense by the interplay between this natural goodness and the moral rigidity of New England.

Both Felix and James accord the puritan tradition the deepest respect and affection. They see in the Wentworths, its representatives, people incapable of treachery, selfishness, cruelty, or using others for their own convenience. The Wentworths' virtues do not consist merely in abstaining from wrong-doing: they are unfailingly kind, generous and hospitable, and they show that unostentatious openness and friendliness which is the greatest charm of American social life. Even the Baroness responds to the beauty and goodness of their way of life.

Much as Felix likes the Wentworths, however, he strikes a fine balance between approval and reserve when he communicates his first impressions of them to his sister: 'A plain, homely way of life; nothing for show, and very little for — what shall I call it? — for the senses....'[13] If there is little food for the senses in their way of life, the moral rigidity of Mr Wentworth himself sometimes presents the appearance of a living death. Felix recognized with amusement, but also with sympathetic concern, 'that, the old man being infinitely conscientious, the special operation of conscience within him announced itself by several of the indications of physical faintness'.[14]

Although Felix is to some extent a vehicle for expressing certain doubts and reservations about American puritanism, his vitality and capacity for joy do not represent a revolt against the tradition, still less a rejection of it. Conscience does not produce in him the indications of physical faintness, but he has his own moral rigidities, no less severe in their way than those of Mr Wentworth. His eventual marriage to Gertrude is the clearest indication of this: she finds in him a quality of life which New England lacks, but he finds equally in her a moral purity which he has not encountered in the Europe where his sister the Baroness is so much at home. In his dealings with her father, he goes out of his way to convince the latter of his moral seriousness, conscious that his light and frivolous tone may be mis-interpreted. When Mr Wentworth on one occasion refers to his 'irregular manner of life', Felix informs him with some force that he dislikes 'improper things': 'You see, at bottom I am a terrible Philistine.... I mean, as one may say, a plain, God-fearing man.'[15]

New England had developed its notion of morality on the narrow ground of purely ethical considerations. The liberated and secularized moral sense exemplified in the character of Felix Young does not surrender any of the scruples of the older tradition, but on the contrary represents an ambitious extension of the idea of human excellence. It proposes for itself a scope so wide that the moral sense and the sense of life virtually coincide. James

13   Henry James, *The Europeans*, Bodley Head Henry James, Vol. 1, p. 44.
14   *Ibid.*, pp. 47—8.
15   *Ibid.*, p. 103.

expresses this conviction most explicitly in a celebrated passage from his Preface to *The Portrait of a Lady*:

> There is, I think, no more nutritive or suggestive truth in this connexion than that of the perfect dependence of the 'moral' sense of a work of art on the amount of felt life concerned in producing it. The question comes back thus, obviously, to the kind and the degree of the artist's prime sensibility, which is the soil out of which his subject springs. The quality and capacity of that soil, its ability to 'grow' with due freshness and straightness any vision of life, represents, strongly or weakly, the projected morality. That element is but another name for the more or less close connexion of the subject with some mark made on the intelligence, with some sincere experience. By which, at the same time, of course, one is far from contending that this enveloping air of the artist's humanity — which gives the last touch to the worth of the work — is not a widely and wondrously varying element....[16]

The image of growth, the idea of a 'projected morality', the spaciousness implicit in the admirable phrase 'this enveloping air of the artist's humanity', all suggest a movement towards the enlargement of the consciousness. This movement appears in James's fiction not only as a notion of morality, but as an organizing principle in the development of plot and character. Lambert Strether, in *The Ambassadors*, travels to Europe to rescue Chad Newsome from the clutches of an immoral woman — to enforce what Massachusetts considers to be the moral law. He finds, however, that the fallen woman, Madame de Vionnet, opens his eyes to a kind of moral beauty he had never even dreamt of in New England.

The same awareness is a vitally important motive in Scott Fitzgerald's fiction. It is the central concern of one of his best short stories, 'Absolution': the consciousness of its hero Rudolph Miller, a Catholic adolescent boy, is restricted at first to rather mechanical notions of purity and sin, but he gradually learns to take a more extended view of the possibilities of life. Similarly Nick Carraway, in *The Great Gatsby*, begins by disapproving of Gatsby because the latter outrages his puritanical Middle Western sense of right and wrong. By the end of his moral adventure, however, he has come to recognize in Gatsby a degree of sensitivity and idealism he had not conceived of before.

There remains, nevertheless, a lurking puritan severity in the artistic consciousness both of James and Fitzgerald, which shows itself in a number of ways. The capacity for a comprehensive view of life brings happiness to Felix Young, but not to most of their other fictional characters. It often makes the necessity for moral decision a harsher, not an easier affair. As Fitzgerald recognizes in his letter to Maxwell Perkins, one may have to relinquish what is most important to one's happiness in order to avoid shattering the delicate pencil-end of a point of view — disrupting the whole

16 *The Art of the Novel: Critical Prefaces by Henry James*, edited by Richard P. Blackmur, New York, 1962, p. 45.

series of delicate interrelations that make up one's moral nature. Isabel Archer's decision, at the end of *The Portrait of a Lady*, that she must return to Osmond, is all the darker because of her deepened awareness of what life has to offer. In a somewhat different case — that of Dick Diver in *Tender is the Night* — a similar awareness makes his feelings of moral failure and self-disgust the more bitter and unrelieved.

American civilization — 'a vast, vulgar, and meretricious beauty'

Fitzgerald's concern with the quality of American civilization places him in a clearly defined literary tradition. *The Europeans* represents a very early stage in the establishment of that tradition, and there is an episode near the beginning of the novel which provides a striking opportunity for suggesting some of its characteristic features. Felix and the Baroness find their first day in Boston marred by an unseasonable fall of snow, but in the afternoon the May sunshine bursts through, and they go out:

> They walked about the streets at hazard, looking at the people and the houses, the shops and the vehicles, the blazing blue sky and the muddy crossings, the hurrying men and the slow-strolling maidens, the fresh red bricks and the bright green trees, the extraordinary mixture of smartness and shabbiness. From one hour to another the day had grown vernal; even in the bustling streets there was an odour of earth and blossom. Felix was immensely entertained. He had called it a comical country, and he went about laughing at everything he saw. You would have said that American civilization expressed itself to his sense in a tissue of capital jokes. The jokes were certainly excellent, and the young man's merriment was very joyous and genial. He possessed what is called the pictorial sense, and this first glimpse of democratic manners stirred the same sort of attention that he would have given to the movements of a lively young person with a bright complexion. Such attention would have been demonstrative and complimentary .... He kept looking at the violet blue sky, at the scintillating air, at the scattered and multiplied patches of colour.
>
> '*Comme c'est bariolé*, eh?' he said to his sister ....
>
> 'Yes, it is *bariolé* indeed,' the Baroness answered. 'I don't like the colouring; it hurts my eyes.'
>
> 'It shows how extremes meet,' the young man rejoined. 'Instead of coming to the West we seem to have gone to the East. The way the sky touches the house-tops is just like Cairo; and the red and blue sign-boards patched over the face of everything remind one of Mahometan decoration.'
>
> 'The young women are not Mahometan,' said his companion. 'They can't be said to hide their faces, I never saw anything so bold.'
>
> 'Thank heaven they don't hide their faces!' cried Felix. 'Their faces are uncommonly pretty.'
>
> 'Yes, their faces are often very pretty,' said the Baroness. ... Superficially, she was conscious of a good deal of irritation and displeasure; the Baroness was a very delicate and fastidious person. Of old, more than once, she had gone, for entertainment's sake and in brilliant company, to a fair in a provincial town. It seemed

to her now that she was at an enormous fair — that the entertainment and the *désagréments* were very much the same. She found herself alternately smiling and shrinking; the show was very curious, but it was probable from moment to moment that she would be jostled. The Baroness had never seen so many people walking about before; she had never been so mixed up with people she did not know. But little by little she felt that this fair was a more serious undertaking.[17]

James makes brilliant use of the contrasted reactions of Felix and the Baroness in order to bring out his own complex response to the American scene. Both observers see American life as social chaos; for one this is the ground for a striking and novel kind of success, while for the other it is an expression of failure. Felix's vivid appreciation establishes the quality of charm, the element of success, in American civilization — the liveliness of 'democratic manners', the colourful 'meeting of extremes' and the diverting atmosphere of 'an enormous fair'. As well as this gaudy, flamboyant vitality, there is a genuine freshness and spontaneity, expressed mainly in the figure of the American girl, her face boldly but innocently exposed. The Baroness, on the other hand, brings European aristocratic standards to her observation of social life, and she sees little in Boston but a disagreeable mixture of elements, an indiscriminate jostling, a lack of distinction and order. (Although she is a largely discredited figure by the end of the novel, there is no reason to dismiss her opinions here.)

One is hardly in danger of forgetting the many occasions on which James, Adams, Fitzgerald and Mrs Wharton record the failure of the aristocratic principle in American life. But their equally clear perception that American talents have produced a compensating success out of the conditions of democratic manners is almost invariably ignored. Even the life of the streets often has more to offer than any producible version of the grand style. American social life succeeds best when it provides an arena for that tumult, colour, diversity and profusion which make Felix feel that he is in an oriental bazaar rather than a city of the West. In Scott Fitzgerald's fiction, the fairground, the big hotel, the party and Hollywood perform this function on innumerable occasions, both as dramatic settings and as images. They are the images of that 'vast, vulgar, and meretricious beauty' which Gatsby served and, in the balanced attributes of that phrase, Fitzgerald conveys perfectly the sense of creative genius co-existing with garish emptiness.

I have already examined the significance of the cocktail party in chapter 1, and a discussion of Hollywood would clearly be out of place here; but since the fair and the hotel are important images for Henry James and Henry Adams as well as for Fitzgerald, they deserve some further attention. Much of the social mixing of the Jazz Age takes place, in Fitzgerald's fiction, in great New York hotels like the Plaza and the Biltmore. James's impressions of the Waldorf-Astoria, recorded in *The American Scene* a generation earlier, provide an interesting parallel. The Waldorf represents opulence and

17 *The Europeans*, pp. 24—5.

power, but also a social gregariousness which the rich in other cultures had always sought to avoid. The only requirements for admission are money and 'the condition, for any member of the flock, that he or she — in other words especially she — be presumably "respectable", be, that is, not discoverably anything else'. The resulting social life is a 'whole immense promiscuity':

> It sat there, it walked and talked, and ate and drank, and listened and danced to music, and otherwise revelled and roamed, and bought and sold, and came and went there, all on its own splendid terms and with an encompassing material splendour, a wealth and variety of constituted picture and background, that might well feed it with the finest illusions about itself.[18]

In James's view, 'the American spirit' has made the hotel into 'a social, indeed positively an aesthetic ideal ... a synonym for civilization, for the capture of conceived manners themselves, [so] that one is verily tempted to ask if the hotel-spirit may not just *be* the American spirit most seeking and most finding itself'.[19]

There is a sombre irony in these reflections which is very different in quality from the genial and joyous spirit of appreciation in which Felix walked the Boston streets — James's view of American civilization had become very much more pessimistic in the thirty years between the writing of the two books. Nevertheless, there is an air of bewildered concession in his response to the Waldorf-Astoria: it is a complete success on its own terms, while the palaces of the rich on upper Fifth Avenue and their summer shore places at Newport can only represent abject failure.

The most potent and suggestive of all these images, however, is that of the fair. We have already seen how James uses it in *The Europeans*. For Henry Adams and Scott Fitzgerald, it came to have a far wider meaning, just as the fair itself had become, by the end of the nineteenth century, one of the major phenomena of the national scene. As a manifestation of 'the whole enormous promiscuity', it was more spectacular even than the Waldorf-Astoria. It dispensed with the demand for respectability and, purely as spectacle, it could be enjoyed even without money — as Father Schwartz and Rudolph Miller contemplate it in imagination at the end of 'Absolution'. If it demanded nothing, it appeared to offer everything. Basil Duke Lee sees it in this way in 'A Night at the Fair':

> The two cities were separated only by a thin well-bridged river; their tails curling over the banks met and mingled, and at the juncture, under the jealous eye of each, lay, every fall, the State Fair. Because of this advantageous position, and because of the agricultural eminence of the state, the fair was one of the most magnificent in America. There were immense exhibits of grain, livestock and farming machinery; there were horse races and automobile races and, lately, aeroplanes that really left the ground; there was a tumultuous Midway with Coney Island thrillers

18 Henry James, *The American Scene* (1907), edited by W. H. Auden, New York, 1946, p. 103.
19 *Ibid.*, p. 102.

to whirl you through space, and a whining, tinkling hoochie-coochie show. As a compromise between the serious and the trivial, a grand exhibition of fireworks, culminating in a representation of the Battle of Gettysburg, took place in the Grand Concourse every night.[20]

The detail of the scene is carefully organized towards a climax which epitomizes the spirit, not merely of the fair, but of the whole society — a society which commemorates the most significant single event in its history by a firework display.

Henry Adams was fascinated by the same combination of the trivial and the serious in the Chicago Exposition of 1893 and the St Louis World's Fair at the turn of the century. In the bewildering multiplicity of the former, he believed he had found, paradoxically, 'the first expression of American thought as a unity'. In the latter, the whole amazing and doubtful adventure of American creativity lay exposed:

> One saw here a third-rate town of half-a-million people without history, education, unity, or art, and with little capital — without even an element of natural interest except the river which it studiously ignored — but doing what London, Paris, or New York would have shrunk from attempting. This new social conglomerate with no tie but its steam-power and not much of that, threw away thirty or forty million dollars on a pageant as ephemeral as a stage flat. The world had never witnessed so marvellous a phantasm; by night Arabia's crimson sands had never returned a glow half so astonishing, as one wandered among long lines of white palaces, exquisitely lighted by thousands on thousands of electric candles, soft, rich, shadowy, palpable in their sensuous depths ....[21]

When Nick Carraway returns to West Egg late one night and sees Gatsby's house lit up from top to bottom, he exclaims, 'Your place looks like the World's Fair.' For Fitzgerald as for Adams, the image of the fair has conflicting implications: in *The Great Gatsby* it is used to convey the mixture of feelings — ironic disapproval and wondering admiration — which Gatsby's entertainments arouse; in 'Absolution' and 'A Night at the Fair', it serves to objectify an adolescent boy's romantic sense of the limitless possibilities of America.

American civilization — the failure of the aristocratic principle

When the Baroness expresses her dislike of certain aspects of the Boston scene, she appeals to an explicitly aristocratic standard of value. This standard is invoked more frequently than any other by Fitzgerald and his predecessors in the tradition when they wish to assess the quality of American social life. It is therefore important to determine why they felt it was appropriate to apply aristocratic values to American conditions, and

20 'A Night at the Fair'. BH6, p. 36.
21 Henry Adams, *The Education of Henry Adams*, (privately printed 1907, first published 1918), Modern Library, New York, pp. 466—7.

why they believed that the failure of the aristocratic principle in American civilization was something to be deplored.

The aristocratic ideal, as an image of human excellence, has a class basis, but it clearly has little to do with the actual conditions of aristocratic life in any historical period. It is a bold imaginative extension of possibilities glimpsed fragmentarily in the best men of the type. Historically, it is a product of Renaissance Platonism, and finds its fullest statement in works like Castiglione's *The Courtier*. But its most characteristic expression is in works of art, especially in the images of man familiar to us in Renaissance painting, poetry and drama. These are the images W. B. Yeats turns to in a remarkable passage in the *Autobiographies*:

> The men that Titian painted, the men that Jongsen painted, even the men of Van Dyck seemed at moments like great hawks at rest. In the Dublin National Gallery there hung, perhaps there still hang, upon the same wall, a portrait of some Venetian gentleman by Strozzi, and Mr Sargent's painting of President Wilson. Whatever thought broods in the dark eyes of that Venetian gentleman has drawn its life from his whole body; it feeds upon it as the flame feeds upon the candle — and should that thought be changed, his pose would change, his very cloak would rustle, for his whole body thinks. President Wilson lives only in the eyes, which are steady and intent; the flesh about the mouth is dead, and the hands are dead, and the clothes suggest no movement of his body, nor any movement but that of the valet, who has brushed and folded in mechanical routine. There all was an energy flowing outward from the nature itself; here all is the anxious study and slight deflection of external force; there man's mind and body were predominantly subjective; here all is objective, using those words not as philosophy uses them, but as we use them in conversation.[22]

It is most apposite to the present discussion that Yeats should see failure epitomized in the figure of an American president. The ideal, on the other hand, is a commanding expression of 'personality', of 'Unity of Being' — all the energies and resources of an individual human being brought fully and harmoniously into play.

This ideal had a long and important history in Europe, extending from its Renaissance origins to its eventual disappearance in the collapse of the old order at the end of the First World War. Even now, it continues to haunt the imagination, and Giuseppe di Lampedusa's masterpiece *The Leopard*, published as late as 1958, is a tribute to its undying power. Lampedusa, in the process of creating his aristocratic hero, virtually re-invented the fictional style of Stendhal — a fact which is scarcely surprising, since Stendhal, together with a few French contemporaries like Balzac, played a crucial role in making the aristocratic ideal available to novelists. It was undoubtedly these writers, more than anyone else, who turned Henry James's mind in this direction; and Lionel Trilling has indicated the significance of the con-

22   W. B. Yeats, *Autobiographies*, London, 1956, p. 292.

nection between Fitzgerald's main characters and 'the youthful heroes of Balzac and Stendhal'.[23]

In Europe, the aristocratic ideal, though primarily the product of artistic creativity and philosophical speculation, was nevertheless sustained by, and helped to give direction to, the life of actual aristocracies: Castiglione's courtier was a Platonic vision, but the vision reflected his experience of the actual court of Ferrara and was addressed to the Italian nobility with a practical political end in view. Americans, on the other hand, while they inherited a European consciousness of the value of the ideal, never developed those institutions which in Europe attached it, however tenuously, to some kind of social reality. Only two isolated groups, neither surviving for more than a few generations, seemed capable of evolving an aristocratic way of life on American soil. These were the landed gentry of the Hudson Valley in the early national period and the Southern planters of the pre-Civil War years. The failure of the one is recorded by Fenimore Cooper, the disappearance of the other by William Faulkner; and this utter extinction of the aristocratic principle as a living social fact, serves to emphasize how much the aristocratic ideal in America has taken on a purely visionary, purely theoretical character. It was in this spirit that Thomas Jefferson, while rejoicing that the young Republic was free of an aristocracy of birth and privilege, looked forward to the emergence of an aristocracy of virtue and talent.

One need hardly say that no such class ever appeared, but if it had, it might not have been unfairly represented by Christopher Newman, the hero of Henry James's novel *The American*. James places Newman in this light — with obvious humorous overtones, and yet seriously enough for all that — when he is told of the favourable impression he has made on the young Marquise de Bellegarde: ' "Madame de Bellegarde said that if she had not been told who you were, she would have taken you for a duke — an American duke, the Duke of California." '[24] The fanciful notion of Christopher Newman as a possible Duke of California not only gives the idea of an American aristocrat a purely hypothetical existence, but significantly alters the way in which the value of the idea may be regarded. Yeats's Venetian gentleman, however vividly present, possesses a kind of ideal anonymity, and is interesting primarily because he epitomizes a class, a historical type. Newman cannot do this since there is no class for him to represent: he is, rather, a pre-eminent individual in whom qualities traditionally associated with a social class have been brought to a fine point of concentration. James brings out the importance of this distinction most fully in *The Portrait of a Lady* at the point where he contrasts the attitudes of Isabel Archer and Gilbert Osmond:

23 Lionel Trilling, 'F. Scott Fitzgerald', *The Liberal Imagination*, London 1961, p. 249.
24 Henry James, *The American*, Dell Books, New York, p. 170.

... they attached such different ideas, such different associations and desires, to the same formulas. Her notion of the aristocratic life was simply the union of great knowledge with great liberty, the knowledge would give one a sense of duty, the liberty a sense of enjoyment. But for Osmond it was altogether a thing of forms, a conscious, calculated attitude. He was fond of the old, the consecrated, the transmitted; so was she, but she pretended to do what she chose with it. He had an immense concern for tradition; he had told her once that the best thing in the world was to have it, but that if one was so unfortunate as not to have it one must immediately proceed to make it.[25]

In Osmond's view, the aristocratic life is entirely a question of forms and externals, but for Isabel it is primarily a quality of consciousness, an impulse springing from within. The impulse cannot fulfil itself without the support of external conditions — wealth and leisure, and the personal freedom they bring — but it is the impulse and not the conditions which finally matters. Wealth, leisure and freedom are important only because they release the individual from material burdens and necessities and give him scope to realize the potentialities of his own nature. The rarity of the opportunity and the extent of the privilege, as Isabel recognizes, impose a correspondingly heavy responsibility.

Fitzgerald cared no less intensely than James for this ideal of personal excellence and was always fascinated by men and women whose lives seemed in any way to suggest that it had been realized. His father and Monsignor Fay, as we have already seen, were vital formative influences; and Gerald and Sara Murphy, whose civilized expatriate existence impressed him so deeply, seemed for a time almost to redeem the chaos of the Jazz Age. In his fiction, Gatsby and Dick Diver are committed to the same vision, even though they are condemned to pursue it through distorted or corrupted forms. Fitzgerald was, however, in the last analysis, less preoccupied with the aristocratic ideal itself than with the failure of the class that might have made it a reality.

By the last decade of the nineteenth century, the American rich had emerged as a distinct social group. Their wealth, drawn from the exploitation of the West and the industrialization of the country in the years after the Civil War, was unparalleled: no European aristocracy had ever possessed so lavish a material basis for the creation of a style. The American rich even appeared dimly to recognize the nature of their opportunity and set about acquiring the machinery of the aristocratic life with the same energy and organizational skill they had displayed in amassing their fortunes: they built replicas of French châteaux and German castles; they hired English butlers and French cooks; they gave formal balls and dinners and conscientiously imitated the country sports of the English gentry; they collected paintings and established libraries. The result was not a new civilization, but a grotesque and vulgar charade, a ludicrous burlesque of forms and manners which had been mimicked without being understood. Henry

25   *The Portrait of a Lady,* p. 462.

James reflected on the full magnitude of the failure when he revisited America in 1904-5. After attending a banquet in one of the palaces on upper Fifth Avenue, he spoke of 'the foredoomed grope of wealth in its conquest of the amenities'; while the immense shore places at Newport were, he felt, a 'reminder to those concerned of the prohibited degrees of witlessness, and of the peculiarly awkward vengeance of affronted proportion and discretion'.[26] Henry Adams, attempting to place the same problem in a wider perspective, believed that it was an aspect of the general American failure to understand the uses of wealth. He wrote with passionate despair of the America of 1892:

> ... the American people ... were wandering in a wilderness much more sandy than the Hebrews had ever trodden about Sinai; they had neither serpents nor golden calves to worship. They had lost the sense of worship; for the idea that they worshipped money seemed a delusion. Worship of money was an old-world trait; a healthy appetite akin to worship of the gods, or to worship of power in any concrete shape; but the American wasted money more recklessly than anyone ever did before; he spent more to less purpose than any extravagant court aristocracy; he had no sense of relative values, and he knew not what to do with his money when he got it, except use it to make more, or throw it away. Probably since human society began, it had seen no such curious spectacle as the houses of the San Francisco millionaires on Nob Hill. Except for the railway system, the enormous wealth taken out of the ground since 1840, had disappeared. West of the Alleghenies, the country might have been swept clean, and could have been replaced in better form within one or two years.[27]

Edith Wharton understood the mechanisms of this society as well as Adams did and had as sharp an eye for its absurdities as James, but in one respect at least she had a deeper perception of its deficiencies than either. She recognized that certain kinds of failure (like dullness in Pope's *Dunciad*) do not merely imply the lack for some quality or other, but contain an active principle of destruction. In *The House of Mirth*, the best of her novels of New York upper-class life, she shows how a gross and vulgar society is not merely a society lacking refinement, but one possessed with an irresistible tendency to destroy the fine and the beautiful. Lily Bart, its exquisite heroine, is first compromised by the corruptions of the rich and ultimately crushed by their callousness and indifference. There is a great deal in Fitzgerald's own work which is particularly close to the spirit of this novel: he had almost certainly read it at the beginning of his literary career, and in any case the American rich as he first encountered them were virtually the same people as those portrayed by Mrs Wharton. The social habits of the Gilded Age lingered on into the early 1920s; and the great changes which took place during the postwar decade confirmed rather than altered his conviction that the American rich were a class who had been given the opportunity to become an aristocracy and had failed. Like Edith Wharton, he appears to have felt that the worst aspect of their failure was their capacity to

26 *The American Scene* pp. 164 and 225 respectively.
27 *The Education of Henry Adams* p. 328.

obstruct or injure the very manifestations of life towards which they should themselves have been aspiring: Gatsby experiences nothing but harm from his association with the Buchanans; the Warrens help to ruin Dick Diver; and Anson Hunter in 'The Rich Boy' brings unhappiness if not disaster to almost everyone he meets.

Social fiction as a mode of poetry

On two separate occasions in his later years, Scott Fitzgerald distinguished between what he felt to be the two kinds of novel he had written. To one correspondent he wrote that, whereas *Gatsby* was a 'dramatic novel', *Tender is the Night* was a 'philosophical, now called psychological, novel', and that to compare them 'would be like comparing a sonnet sequence with an epic'.[28] Three years later, he returned to the same point, to say that *The Last Tycoon* (which he had begun to block out), *This Side of Paradise* and *Gatsby* were 'selective', while *The Beautiful and Damned* and *Tender* were 'full and comprehensive':

> The difference is that in these last two I wrote everything, hoping to cut to interest. In *This Side of Paradise* (in a crude way) and in *Gatsby* I selected the stuff to fit a given mood or 'hauntedness' or whatever you might call it, rejecting in advance in *Gatsby*, for instance, all of the ordinary material for Long Island, big crooks, adultery theme and always starting from the *small* focal point that impressed me — my own meeting with Arnold Rothstein for instance.[29]

Of these two kinds of novel, one draws much of its vitality and power from the richness, the diversity, the detail of social observation (in the old-fashioned sense of the word, it is a history), while the other uses a method which is dramatic and, above all, poetic. Structurally, it is written in scenes; as an act of creation, it is conceived in images. Like the sonnet sequence, it relies upon concentrated moments of emotion and meaning; from the welter of social detail it takes 'the small focal point' which, by its power of sugges- tion, can act as a metaphor for a character, a relationship, a class. The one meeting with Arnold Rothstein, transmuted into Nick Carraway's two brief scenes with Meyer Wolfsheim, is made to tell us everything we need to know of Gatsby's underworld associations.

It is always in this way that Fitzgerald introduces a poetic dimension into his novels and stories, and from this point of view his work bears a striking resemblance to that of Henry James: indeed the affinities between the two writers are nowhere stronger than in their preference for this method. Here is may help to clarify the nature of their fictional technique if we make use of the distinction which F. O. Matthiessen draws between James and Melville. Melville, as Matthiessen finely expresses it, takes the reader 'ever farther into the multitudinous seas of speculation', whereas James uses symbol and

28 *Letters*, p. 363.
29 *Ibid.*, p. 551.

image strictly 'as a novelist'[30], to bring out the essential quality of character and incident. He often employs arresting images, highly evocative language and large effects of poetic patterning in order to give added precision and force to his observation of social life. So does Fitzgerald, and one might begin a comparison of their methods by juxtaposing two short passages from *The Portrait of a Lady* and *Tender is the Night*. In each, an image is used to give definition to the way in which a particular character behaves towards other people. The first comes from the scene in which Isabel tells Osmond that she must go to England to see Ralph before he dies. She finds Osmond in his study, engrossed in an antiquarian book:

> This volume was open at a page of small coloured plates, and Isabel presently saw that he had been copying from it the drawing of an antique coin. A box of water-colours and fine brushes lay before him, and he had already transferred to a sheet of immaculate paper the delicate, finely-tinted disk.[31]

In the second, we see Dick Diver come into the garden of the Villa Diana in order to consult Nicole about arrangements for the dinner-party at which Rosemary is to be a special guest:

> Presently Dick came out of his one-room house carrying a telescope and looked east toward Cannes. In a moment Nicole swam into his field of vision, whereupon he disappeared into his house and came out with a megaphone. He had many light mechanical devices.[32]

The image of Osmond copying the coin is masterly in its economy and range of suggestion. His task, like his taste, is highly skilled and finely controlled, but the actual result is trivial; in his studied self-absorption, he shows a remarkable capacity for subordinating the deepest emotional needs of others — Isabel is in deep distress at the news of her cousin's impending death — to the demands of his own aestheticism; and yet he has a striking power to make himself felt, to make an impression. There is great force in the sense in which he has transferred the disk to an immaculate sheet of paper: it reminds us of the impression he has just made on Pansy's sensibilities by imprisoning her in the convent and of the paralysing degree of displeasure he is about to convey to Isabel herself. The Fitzgerald passage works in much the same way. The pointless charade of Dick's use of the telescope and megaphone — we see a moment later that Nicole is able to answer him without even raising her voice — help to indicate how much, for him, the arts of social life have become a set of amusing but empty tricks, 'light mechanical devices' indeed.

Both these images point to qualities of behaviour which are social — Osmond and Dick Diver behave in these ways not only towards their wives but to all the world — and it is precisely at such moments that we see social

30 F. O. Matthiessen, *American Renaissance*, New York, 1944, p. 304.
31 *The Portrait of a Lady* p. 567.
32 *Tender is the Night*, BH2, p. 97.

fiction rising to the level of poetry. Both images, too, are dramatic in a very obvious sense: they work through characteristic details of gesture and action. Virtually all the poetic effects in the novels of James and Fitzgerald are dramatic in one way or another. This is true even of a passage as different on the face of it as Fitzgerald's description of the valley of ashes in *The Great Gatsby*. It would be perverse to argue that it has no symbolic overtones, but its most important effect is that, in strictly theatrical terms, it sets a scene: it is not so much an atmosphere, as a place where things happen, where people meet in unattractive relations, where ugly, unacknowledged emotions find their appropriate setting. Without wishing to press the analogy farther than the immediate point at issue, one might say that the Boar's Head Tavern in Eastcheap does not symbolize anything in particular, but it is certainly the right place in which to find Falstaff.

These local scenic effects, these moments of poetic and dramatic intensity, are a fundamental element in the narrative styles of both James and Fitzgerald, but their novels and stories often contain much larger effects of poetic patterning, upon which the structure and meaning of an entire work may depend. The importance of these patterns in *The Wings of the Dove* and *The Golden Bowl* has often been noted, but a shorter novel such as *What Maisie Knew* offers a much closer parallel to Fitzgerald's fiction and, in particular, to *Gatsby*. James often expresses a great fondness for 'the shapely *nouvelle*' (as he calls it in the Preface to 'The Lesson of the Master'), and by the time he reached his final period, the *nouvelle*, in his hands, had acquired a set of well defined formal characteristics: its brevity meant that it was a 'selective' novel, to use Fitzgerald's own phrase; it was written almost exclusively in scenes, with the absolute minimum of narrative; for handling local effects, it used a method of rapid poetic evocation; and it tended to develop its larger structures of meaning through correspondingly more elaborate poetic patterns. In all these ways, it is the most striking precedent in the American literary tradition for the form and method Fitzgerald mastered in *Gatsby*.

For this reason, I should like to examine briefly some of the more ambitious poetic effects James uses in *What Maisie Knew*. (My choice of this novel is influenced not only by its general suitability to the argument, but by the fact that Fitzgerald actually read it, on Edmund Wilson's recommendation, during the formative period which preceded the composition of *Gatsby*.) James's portrait of Maisie's mother, Mrs Ida Farange, is a remarkable instance of how poetic suggestion can be employed to build up a cumulative sense of a character's moral nature and dramatic force. From the start, he emphasizes certain details of her personal appearance. She is extraordinarily tall and chooses clothes and jewellery with a full sense of the visual effect her height creates: she dresses herself in immense draperies, adorns herself with 'a wilderness of trinkets' and paints her face until her huge eyes seem 'like Japanese lanterns swung under festal arches'. The purely comic effect of her 'violent splendour' is gradually modified and complicated as the novel progresses: the extravagant vulgarity of her appearance becomes an image of the effrontery with which she tries, quite literally, to put a good face on her cruel and selfish neglect of Maisie, her scandalous private life, and her precarious position in society. It is in this spirit that she brazens out the accidental meeting in Kensington Gardens, where her second husband surprises her walking with her latest lover. The cumulative force of these developing associations enables James to give her last appearance a dramatic power which he could have achieved in no other way. This is the scene in the hotel garden at Folkestone, where Ida finally casts off the burden of her unwanted child. What she is doing is infinitely base, and so her desire to look well is correspondingly strong. In particular, she wants to extract from Maisie some assurance that the latter does not reproach her or despise her:

> She turned this way and that in the predicament she had sought and from which she could neither retreat with grace nor emerge with credit: she draped herself in the tatters of her impudence, postured to her utmost before the last little triangle of cracked glass to which so many fractures had reduced the polished plate of filial superstition.[33]

The way in which James uses the detail of Mrs Farange's appearance to create a sense of her character is an exact parallel to Fitzgerald's method with Gatsby. Her moral nature is made visible and dramatic through a consistent pattern of images: in the same way, much of the absurd and yet gorgeous quality of Gatsby's imagination is conveyed through the detail of his clothes, his cars, his parties, his characteristic oddities of phrase and gesture.

At other times, James uses the poetic suggestiveness of a particular scene in order to draw together the moral implications of an entire novel. He does this towards the end of *What Maisie Knew*, when he attempts to clarify the nature of Maisie's relationship with her governess, Mrs Wix. When Maisie finally chooses to live with Mrs Wix rather than Sir Claude, one feels that she makes the right decision. There could be no decent future for her in any ménage set up by Sir Claude and Mrs Beale and, on the positive side, Mrs Wix offers solid virtues — uprightness, maternal affection and dependability — which have been in very short supply during Maisie's childhood. In drawing this conclusion, however, one is confronted by a difficulty which James is too honest to ignore: that doing right often results, not in a sense of fulfilment, but in a feeling of emptiness and sterility. This is the paradox he has in mind when he speaks of Mrs Wix's 'ugly honesty'.

The extent of the problem Maisie faces, and the difficulties of the personal and moral choice she has to make, are made vivid by the contrasted physical appearances of Mrs Wix and Sir Claude: the former is extravagantly ugly, while the latter possesses, not mere handsomeness, but great personal beauty. Furthermore, Mrs Wix lacks all Sir Claude's good qualities — his gaiety, amenity, generosity, sociability and sense of fun — precisely those

33 Henry James, *What Maisie Knew*, Bodley Head Henry James, Vol. 6, p. 178.

human traits which make life something more than a dreary pilgrimage. James has many resources for exploring these contradictory impulses, but nothing in *What Maisie Knew* is more effective to that end than a little scene, rich in poetic suggestiveness, which takes place during the final sequence of incidents at Boulogne. It is evening, and Maisie, leaning over the balcony of her hotel room, gazes down into the attractive bustle of the street, while Mrs Wix, with her moral insistences, lurks inside (the 'crime' referred to near the end of the quotation is the adulterous liaison between Sir Claude and Mrs Beale):

> She [Maisie] hung again over the rail; she felt the summer night; she dropped down into the manners of France. There was a café below the hotel, before which, with little chairs and tables, people sat on a space enclosed by plants in tubs; and the impression was enriched by the flash of the white aprons of waiters and the music of a man and a woman who, from beyond the precinct, sent up the strum of a guitar and the drawl of a song about 'amour'. Maisie knew what 'amour' meant too, and wondered if Mrs Wix did: Mrs Wix remained within, as still as a mouse and perhaps not reached by the performance. After a while, but not until the musicians had ceased and begun to circulate with a little plate, her pupil came back to her. 'Is it a crime?' Maisie then asked.
>
> Mrs Wix was as prompt as if she had been crouching in a lair. 'Branded by the Bible.'[34]

Maisie has to turn her back on the colour and animation of the entire sensuous world if she is to heed the moral demands of Mrs Wix. The latter, at this moment, appears to have little to offer in exchange for the sacrifice: her lair is constricted and dark, a kind of spiritual mouse-hole.

Everything James has to say in this scene is evoked by the two contrasted images of the unlighted room where Mrs Wix crouches and the flickering movement and freedom of the street; the language he uses becomes unusually concentrated and intense, and it acquires a power to suggest and imply which is specifically poetic. Such scenes are more than merely self-sustaining: they bring to a point of focus energies diffused throughout the work; and conversely, like brilliant sources of light, they illuminate the whole fictional world in which they have their being. Fitzgerald's own account of the genesis of the Meyer Wolfsheim episodes shows how much he was aware of the value of this method. He uses it on many occasions in order to give a decisive ordering to the meaning of a novel or story. Nick Carraway's impressions when he enters the Buchanans' drawing room for the first time; the afternoon when Nicole and Rosemary go shopping in Paris; the shipboard gala dinner in 'The Rough Crossing'; and the moment of chaos on the flooded studio lot in *The Last Tycoon* — these are only a few of the many examples which could be cited. In all these scenes, we see how Fitzgerald, like James, discovered his strongest and truest poetic impulse in the complexities of social life.

34 *Ibid.*, pp. 225—6.

The history of manners

I began the preceding section of this chapter by drawing attention to two strongly contrasted tendencies in Fitzgerald's fictional method: his reliance upon an art of poetic concentration which in his view is especially exemplified by *The Great Gatsby*; and his sense of the importance of an art which is 'full and comprehensive', represented most completely by *Tender is the Night*. His fascination with the mass of social detail was no less keen than his feeling for the possibilities of the poetic image, and he succeeded in developing an art which could express the former quite as effectively as the latter. These two kinds of writing are not mutually exclusive — there is much poetry in *Tender is the Night*, and abundant social detail in *Gatsby* — nevertheless it is convenient to distinguish between them, and having already discussed the one, I should like to devote the rest of this chapter to a consideration of the other.

Fitzgerald was not particularly interested in the kinds of social detail which preoccupy the naturalistic writer: he had little of Dreiser's passionate concern for the mechanisms of economic power or the intricate structures of industry (though in *The Last Tycoon* he showed that he could handle these materials superbly when he chose to). His real subject was the observation of manners in the sense defined by Lionel Trilling in his classic essay 'Manners, Morals and the Novel':

> What I understand by manners, then, is a culture's hum and buzz of implication. I mean the whole evanescent context in which its explicit statements are made. It is that part of a culture which is made up of half uttered or unuttered or unutterable expressions of value. They are hinted at by small actions, sometimes by the arts of dress or decoration, sometimes by tone, gesture, emphasis, or rhythm, sometimes by the words that are used with a special frequency or a special meaning.[35]

As a recorder of this multifarious social activity, with all its 'hum and buzz of implication', Fitzgerald becomes, in a certain sense, the historian of his own times. 'All painters of manners', Henry James remarked in his essay on Balzac, 'are historians, even when they least don the uniform.'[36]

James's dictum is valuable in several ways — not only because it gives an added sanction to the term historian of manners, but because it suggests indirectly the special meaning which the phrase acquires in the context of the American novel. Balzac could play the role of historian with a certain informality — without having to 'don the uniform' — simply because he could take so much for granted. As a novelist, he responded most deeply to the spirit of permanence in French life: he wrote at a time of relative social stability, during which he could assume that manners would not change very much from year to year — would remain much as they had been since before the Revolution of 1789. The American historian of manners, by con-

35 Lionel Trilling, 'Manners, Morals and the Novel', *The Liberal Imagination*, pp. 206—7.
36 Henry James, 'Honoré de Balzac', *Henry James: Selected Literary Criticism*, ed. Morris Shapira, Harmondsworth, 1968, p. 231.

trast, could count on nothing permanent, indeed the only normality he could expect to find in American conditions was the normality of constant change. To extend James's metaphor, he was never out of uniform, but perpetually on duty, condemned to a specially acute consciousness of the nature of his *métier*. Balzac's American contemporary Fenimore Cooper noted as early as 1829 that 'to see America with the eyes of truth, it is necessary to look often'[37]; while James, almost a century later, recorded his own bewildered sense of the changes which had occurred during his thirty years absence in Europe. This is his main preoccupation in *The American Scene*, and, still more interestingly, in 'The Jolly Corner', one of the finest of his short stories. Its hero Spencer Brydon, like James himself, returns to New York after a prolonged period of exile, and is at once assailed by the sheer unfamiliarity of everything he sees about him:

> The great fact all the while however had been the incalculability; since he had supposed himself, from decade to decade, to be allowing, and in the most liberal and intelligent manner, for brilliancy of change. He actually saw that he had allowed for nothing; he missed what he would have been sure of finding, he found what he would never have imagined. Proportions and values were upside-down.[38]

The feeling of dislocation Brydon experiences is so severe that for a time his very identity is threatened. He comes to believe that a kind of second self — the self he might have been had he stayed in America — haunts the house on the jolly corner where he was born; and it is only after a psychic struggle of extraordinary violence that he recovers some sort of wholeness of being. Fitzgerald responded in an equally characteristic way to the chronic instability of American life when he maintained in a newspaper interview of 1935 that there had been six separate generations since 1914. Each of these was a distinct emergent group of young people with their own manners and their own attitudes, who displaced their predecessors, and were themselves in turn rapidly superseded.[39]

The American historian of manners, then, is compelled to write in an atmosphere of constant social change: all his problems and all his opportunities as an artist are determined by that fact. At times he is motivated by a desire to fix the moment — to catch the evanescent manners of a particular time and place before they vanish into oblivion. Both *The Europeans* and *The Bostonians* are novels of this kind: in each, James attempts to put on record a significant stage in the evolution and decline of New England culture. Fitzgerald, with an even greater emphasis on the importance of historical precision, singles out the summer of 1922 as the precise date of Gatsby's adventure, and May Day, 1919, as the exact point in time when the

37   James Fenimore Cooper, *The Wept of the Wish-ton-wish*, Leatherstocking Edition, London, 1895, p. 209.
38   Henry James, 'The Jolly Corner', *Americans and Europe: Selected Tales of Henry James*, Riverside Edition, Boston, 1965, p. 412.
39   Sklar, *op.cit.*, p. 306.

Jazz Age began. Alternatively, as we have seen in 'The Jolly Corner', a novelist may concentrate upon the sense of disorientation produced by sudden exposure to the reality of social change. This is the situation which Henry Adams takes as the central theme of his *Education:* he frequently describes his autobiography as 'a story of education', but he might just as well have called it a story of dislocation. The rapid and yet insidious processes of social development which transformed America between 1840 and 1900 left him like a ship aground: he had, he complained, been given an eighteenth-century education, and then been called upon to lead a twentieth-century career.

Fitzgerald is fully aware of the importance of these disconcerting shifts in perspective, but he is generally more interested in subtler, less obviously dramatic manifestations of change. A striking example of his success in conveying this kind of situation is to be found in an otherwise very minor commercial story, 'Majesty' (1929). The heroine, Emily Castleton, is a rich and beautiful, but imperious and wayward New York girl, who jilts her fiancé in a manner so outrageous that she is condemned to an apparently permanent social eclipse. However, after a period of obscure and rather disreputable adventures on the Continent, she marries the dubious Prince Petrocobesco, and re-emerges triumphantly as the queen of a minuscule Central European state. The story is slight, and the writing of the European scenes is very poor, but in one place it comes brilliantly to life. Emily's wedding is an immense social and dynastic occasion — the whole of fashionable New York assembles for the ceremony — so that when Emily fails to arrive at the church, the scandal is correspondingly spectacular. Mr Castleton and the older guests fall into ludicrous postures of outrage or collapse, but in the behaviour of the younger people (seen through the shocked eyes of Emily's cousin Olive) Fitzgerald identifies a significant shift in manners. Olive, after ministering to Emily's maudlin and somewhat drunken father, gradually becomes aware of the faint but unmistakable strains of a jazz band. She runs out to the marquee set up in the garden for the reception, and finds the younger generation, unabashed by the absence of the bride, cheerfully dancing and drinking champagne. She expostulates with Emily's brother:

'Harold, what in the name of — '
'Emily's crazy,' he said consolingly. 'I always told you Emily was crazy. Crazy as a loon. Always was.'
'What's the idea of this?'
'This?' He looked around innocently. 'Oh, these are some fellows who came down from Cambridge with me.'
'But — dancing!'
'Well, nobody's dead, are they? I thought we might as well use up some of this — '
'Tell them to go home,' said Olive.
'Why? What on earth's the harm? These fellows came all the way down from Cambridge — '

'It simply isn't dignified.'

'But they don't care, Olive. One fellow's sister did the same thing — only she did it the day after instead of the day before. Lots of people do it nowadays.'

'Send the music home, Harold,' said Olive firmly, 'or I'll go to your father.'

Obviously he felt that no family could be disgraced by an episode on such a magnificent scale, but he reluctantly yielded. The abysmally depressed butler saw to the removal of the champagne, and the young people, somewhat insulted, moved nonchalantly out into the more tolerant night.[40]

Olive identifies herself with the standards of an older generation, and there is a comic disparity between her sense of the situation and that of her contemporaries as represented by Harold. Unawares, they have been carried apart by the subtle drift of social change, so that they do not even understand each other's language: Olive's implied notions of propriety are a closed book to Harold; his assumptions about current behaviour an incommunicable mystery to her. He is callow enough, but she is in a more serious predicament, since she is an unconscious exile in her own times. It is not that she judges and rejects what she sees — she simply does not see. She moves through the Jazz Age like a somnambulist: her eyes are open, but she observes nothing. Or, to change the metaphor, that culture's 'hum and buzz of implication' are forever inaudible to her.

As a historian of manners, Fitzgerald had more in common with Edith Wharton than with any other of his predecessors, and in this respect her three great novels of New York life, *The Age of Innocence, The Custom of the Country,* and *The House of Mirth,* offer the closest parallels to his writing. Both novelists showed an incomparably detailed and intimate knowledge of the manners of the American rich. Both observed the constantly changing surface of American social life with the same mixture of curiosity and delight. The spirit which permeates Fitzgerald's account of the comic *débâcle* of Emily Castleton's wedding, is often present in Mrs Wharton's fiction. In *The House of Mirth,* she notes how the variations in New York fashion reflect the fluctuations on Wall Street: if the stock market is buoyant, society aims at splendour; if the market is falling, fashionable people discover the charm of simplicity and the intimate occasion.

At a deeper level, both novelists are fully aware of the complications which the ephemeral character of American manners introduces into the problem of moral and social navigation. This is Edith Wharton's concern in *The Custom of the Country,* particularly in the episode of Ralph Marvell's divorce. Ralph, a member of one of New York's oldest families, marries outside his class. His wife, a Middle Western girl of obscure social origins, seems to him an innocent and untutored beauty, but is in fact a ruthless and vulgar adventuress. He undoubtedly loves her, but his marriage is, to some extent, a gesture of defiance. He has a great affection for his family — he respects his mother's ladylike reticences, and the quiet good breeding of Mr

40 'Majesty', BH5, pp. 456—7.

Dagonet, his grandfather — but he enjoys shocking them a little, proving to them that he belongs to a more modern world than they. The idea of his marriage pleases him because it seems a decisive step forward from the spectral past into the invigorating present, but he fails utterly to take account of what is involved in so violent a transition. The crisis of his divorce forces him to realize that he has neither disengaged himself from the manners of his ancestors, nor succeeded in joining his contemporaries: his marriage has alienated him from the values and assumptions of his family without making him a citizen of that modern world he thought it would be so easy to enter. The tragi-comedy of his predicament is most apparent in the way in which his relatives respond — or, rather, fail to respond — to the true nature of his personal disaster:

> The time involved in the 'proceedings' was viewed as a penitential season during which it behoved the family of the persons concerned to behave as if they were dead; yet any open allusion to the reason for adopting such an attitude would have been regarded as the height of indelicacy.
> Mr Dagonet's notion of the case was almost as remote from reality. All that he asked was that his grandson should 'thrash' somebody, and he could not be made to understand that the modern drama of divorce is sometimes cast without a Lovelace.
> 'You might as well tell me there was no one but Adam in the garden when Eve picked the apple. You say your wife was discontented? No woman ever knows she's discontented till some man tells her so. My God! I've seen smash-ups before now, but I never yet saw a marriage dissolved like a business partnership. Divorce without a lover? Why, it's — it's as unnatural as getting drunk on lemonade'.
> After this first explosion Mr Dagonet also became silent; and Ralph perceived that what annoyed him most was the fact of the 'scandal' not being one in any gentlemanly sense of the word. It was like some nasty business mess, about which Mr Dagonet couldn't pretend to have an opinion, since such things didn't happen to men of his kind.[41]

Ralph is a victim of the complexities of rapid social change, and his feelings of isolation and helplessness are a striking example of the difficulties Americans experience under these conditions. Much of Fitzgerald's best writing deals with similar situations. Nick Carraway, after growing up in the values and assumptions of the prewar Middle West, has to find new bearings among the postwar Eastern rich. Anson Hunter, in 'The Rich Boy', has an unshakable confidence in the solidity of his social position — to understand the manners of his class and period is his birthright: nevertheless, the evolution of the Jazz Age leaves him behind, and he awakens at last to the discovery that he is an alien in the society he once dominated. Most interesting of all is the case of Dick Diver, who finds himself increasingly confused and lost in subtle processes of change which even his fine intelligence cannot

41 Edith Wharton, *The Custom of the Country*, Constable Edith Wharton, London, 1965, p. 239.

fully grasp. Fitzgerald's resources as a historian of manners grew steadily throughout his career: he had the ability to capture the distinctive atmosphere of a particular phase of American life from the very beginning — virtually all the good writing in *This Side of Paradise* is of this kind; he rapidly acquired the power, as I have just suggested, to dramatize the dilemma of characters caught in the bewildering flux of changing circumstances; and by the 1930s, he had learnt how to place these situations within the context of a broad historical pattern. The culmination of this process of development was reached in *Tender is the Night* — a completely satisfying synthesis of the literary possibilities and social insights which we have been considering.

The conclusion of this chapter is a point of transition in the development of my book. So far, I have put forward a series of propositions about Fitzgerald's career and writings which seem to me to be generally applicable. These arguments have now reached a stage where they can only be extended and completed through a detailed examination of his actual novels and stories. In addition to this, there are important questions which arise only in the context of specific works, and in order to do justice to these, it is essential to discuss his writings individually and in their integrity. This will be the principle concern of my five remaining chapters.

3
Fitzgerald's early work — a study in development

The popular success of *This Side of Paradise* in 1920 tends, even now, to obscure the fact that, as an artist, Scott Fitzgerald made a slow start. His first five books — *This Side of Paradise, Flappers and Philosophers, The Beautiful and Damned, Tales of the Jazz Age* and *The Vegetable* — are little better than a succession of failures and false starts. A few of the short stories have great interest (one, 'May Day', is an undoubted masterpiece) and there is good writing here and there in *This Side of Paradise*, but, on the whole, these early works have little intrinsic value. Nevertheless, with the benefit of hindsight — from the vantage point afforded by his mature writings — they provide a fascinatingly complete record of his early development. Since he was a professional writer, relying on fiction to provide a livelihood as well as the creative satisfactions of the artist, he tended to publish his mistakes instead of destroying them; and since he was slow to find himself, the evidence of his progress towards artistic maturity is correspondingly rich and full. This chapter, therefore, will be a study of Fitzgerald's development, rather than a critical discussion of his early works.

This Side of Paradise is formless, pretentious, sentimental, self-indulgent and intellectually weak: at the same time, it contains a few passages of true poetic intensity, some isolated moments of keen perception, the first signs of a capacity for acute social observation, and occasional gleams of an exquisite comic sense. It is the kind of bad first novel which nevertheless gives promise of future achievement. It represents the creative effort of almost three years — from early 1917 to September 1919 — and Fitzgerald put into it almost everything he considered valuable in his earliest writings. He salvaged what he could from *The Romantic Egotist* (the unpublished novel he worked on at weekends in army camps), and he incorporated several episodes which had first appeared as stories in the *Nassau Literary Magazine* at Princeton. This accounts for the novel's chaotic and inconsistent nature, but it is also the reason why one finds indications in *This Side of Paradise* of most of the kinds of excellence which characterize his mature fiction.

Like many first novels, *This Side of Paradise* is a story of education and youthful initiation, with a large element of autobiography in it. It is divided into two parts by the War, and these two parts have strongly contrasted atmospheres. In the first, for which he retained the title 'The Romantic Egotist', his hero Amory Blaine is full of youthful enthusiasm and idealism. The most important experiences during this period of Amory's life are his residence at Princeton, his relationship with a middle-aged Catholic priest, Monsignor Darcy, and his various sentimental adventures — in particular, his affair with the capricious débutante, Isabelle Borgé. The setting for the second section, 'The Education of a Personage', is New York in the year following the Armistice — the chaotic period of transition out of which the Jazz Age was born. Amory finds that he cannot settle down after the upheaval of the War: he makes half-hearted attempts to write and to start work in the advertising business, and from time to time he gets drunk in the style which was to become typical of the Prohibition era. All these experiences have a disillusioning or destructive effect upon him, but it is his disastrous affair with Rosalind Connage that brings him to his lowest point. She is a rich spoilt New York girl who at first returns his love, and then breaks off their engagement because he has no money. In this condition of uncertainty and confusion, believing he has lost all the ideals and illusions of his youth, Amory sets out on a pilgrimage to Princeton where he intends to take stock of his situation.

This Side of Paradise helps us to understand Fitzgerald's development in three ways. He already shows, in certain scenes, the complex attitude to the American rich which is so characteristic of his best work. He is preoccupied — particularly in the first part of the novel — with finding ways in which the language of fiction can take on the dimension of poetry. And, finally, he is already interested in the history of manners: this is reflected not only in the detail of the novel — the many vivid observations of social change — but in its structure. Fitzgerald's decision to make the War the pivot on which the action turns is his only discernible attempt to impose a sense of form upon the chaos of his material.

One June night, Amory Blaine and his friend Thomas Parke D'Invilliers cycle out from Princeton into the sleeping countryside. During the course of their conversation, Amory describes himself as 'a cynical idealist' a phrase which brings out sharply the two sides of Fitzgerald's own creative intelligence — the capacity for intense romantic involvement, and, at the same time, for acute and disenchanted observation. In this episode, Fitzgerald does not succeed in establishing a satisfying dramatic relation between these conflicting attitudes: the Amory who declaims Keat's 'Ode to a Nightingale' to the bushes they pass has little connection with the Amory who makes a shrewd and somewhat hostile analysis of the Princeton social scene. But what is unskilfully blended here is nearly always brought to a point of concentration when Fitzgerald writes about the American rich.

This is true even of the early fiction, although his social experience is too limited and his artistic sense too undeveloped for his treatment of such material to have much intrinsic value. He knew only Middle Western adolescents and Princeton undergraduates, and while he was able to infer a surprisingly large amount from these areas of American life, they were clearly not enough to sustain a mature social fiction. Besides this, he was not clear enough about his attitudes: his sense of excitement could carry him too easily into self-indulgence, and his feelings of disappointment or revulsion could result in melodramatic extravagance.

Nevertheless, in the figure of Amory's wealthy friend Dick Humbird we find Fitzgerald's first conscious attempt to make sense of these contradictory reactions. Amory begins to observe Humbird during the course of a three-day spree: in company with half-a-dozen other Princeton undergraduates, they drive over to the coast in a borrowed car. As the group develops a definite character, Amory notices that though a kind of 'spiritual tax' is levied on each member, each contributes in a different way. For most of them, this contribution is made through some form of activity — through conversation and wit, through finding entertaining ways of keeping the party going, or thinking up the ingenious tricks by which they get free meals and cinema tickets. Humbird seemingly contributes nothing, and yet, by a quiet trick of dominance, remains at the centre of the group:

> Dick Humbird had, ever since freshman year, seemed to Amory a perfect type of aristocrat. He was slender but well-built — black curly hair, straight features, and rather a dark skin. Everything he said sounded intangibly appropriate. He possessed infinite courage, an averagely good mind, and a sense of honour with a clear charm and noblesse oblige that varied it from righteousness. He could dissipate without going to pieces, and even his most bohemian adventures never seemed 'running it out'. People dressed like him, tried to talk as he did ... Amory decided that he probably held the world back, but he wouldn't have changed him...
>
> He differed from the healthy type that was essentially middle-class — he never seemed to perspire. Some people couldn't be familiar with chauffeur a without having it returned; Humbird could have lunched at Sherry's with a coloured man, yet people would have somehow known that it was all right. He was not a snob, though he knew only half his class. His friends ranged from the highest to the lowest, but it was impossible to 'cultivate' him. Servants worshipped him, and treated him like a god. He seemed the eternal example of what the upper class tries to be.[1]

When Amory says that Humbird is 'Like the pictures in the Illustrated London News of the English officers who have been killed' he is disconcerted to learn that Humbird's father is a grocery clerk who made a fortune in real estate, and came to New York only ten years before. Not long afterwards, Humbird is killed in a motoring accident caused by his own stubbornness and irresponsibility, and Amory finds the circumstances of his death 'horrible and unaristocratic'.

Fitzgerald's tone in this scene is hysterical and unconvincing but his attempt, confused as it is, to use Humbird as a way of clarifying his feelings

[1] *This Side of Paradise*, BH3, pp. 83–4.

towards the rich, is of great interest in the light of his future development. The actual description of Humbird which I quote shows acute, if limited, powers of observation. In it Fitzgerald is concerned to isolate the quality which makes Humbird a gentleman, an aristocrat, in a way which is not true of most his contemporaries at Princeton. Little survives in him of the Renaissance Platonic conception of the aristocrat as complete man. The sole characteristics which remain as distinctively aristocratic are the assumption of social superiority, and the exercise of an unfailing pose of personal dominance. Humbird has a wonderful way with servants, and he can carry off dubious activities with a sense of style. His consummately successful manner clearly isn't the outward expression of an inner fineness of nature: it is partly a triumph of style, in the most superficial sense, and partly a state of psychological well-being — the happy faculty of never doubting the rightness of what one does. Dick Humbird is, in however imperfect a way, a forerunner of Fitzgerald's two finest portraits of wealthy young Americans — Tom Buchanan in *The Great Gatsby* and Anson Hunter in 'The Rich Boy'.

From this earliest childhood Fitzgerald had an intense feeling for poetry. His father introduced him to Poe and Byron's *Childe Harold's Pilgrimage*. At Princeton, under the influence of John Peale Bishop (the Thomas Parke D'Invilliers of *This Side of Paradise*), he read Keats, Swinburne, the poets of the nineties, and Rupert Brooke. He came to admire the kind of prose which is most closely associated with this strain in English poetry — Walter Pater's *Marius the Epicurean*, Oscar Wilde's *The Picture of Dorian Gray*, and the purple passages in such Edwardian novelists as Compton Mackenzie. For all these writers except Keats and Byron, poetry tends to be a self-validating ecstasy rather than a way of saying something. It is not so much a mode of communication as a state of mind — the exaltation of the senses produced by the self-absorption of day-dreaming rather than the keen incitements of passion. More often than not, it is an expression of the euphoria of youth, or of regret for its passing.

The kind of verse and prose which Fitzgerald admired and often tried to imitate in his Princeton years, may be represented by the two following quotations: part of the first chorus from Swinburne's *Atalanta in Calydon*, and an excerpt from the rhapsody on youth which Lord Henry Wotton addresses to Dorian Gray at their first meeting:

> For winter's rains and ruins are over,
>   And all the season of snows and sins;
> The days dividing lover and lover,
>   The light that loses, the night that wins;
> And time remembered is grief forgotten,
> And frosts are slain and flowers begotten,
> And in green underwood and cover
>   Blossom by blossom the spring begins.

'... I must tell you something about yourself. I thought how tragic it would be if you were wasted. For there is such a little time that your youth will last — such a little time. The common hill-laburnum will be as yellow again next June as it is now. In a month there will be purple stars on the clematis, and year after year the green night of its leaves will hold its purple stars. But we never get back our youth. The pulse of joy that beats in us at twenty, becomes sluggish. Our limbs fail, our senses rot. We degenerate into hideous puppets, haunted by the memory of the passions of which we were too much afraid, and the exquisite temptations that we had not the courage to yield to. Youth! Youth! There is absolutely nothing in the world but youth!'[2]

Writing such as this chimed in with Fitzgerald's own state of youthful romantic excitement. It also served to reinforce his conviction that the language of literature, whether verse or prose, should have a specifically poetic quality. He applied this principle to his own work, and in his last year at Princeton put as much effort into the writing of poetry as of prose. At this period, Shane Leslie's view — for what it is worth — was that Fitzgerald might become the American Rupert Brooke.[3]

In *This Side of Paradise* he made a conscious effort to give the language of the novel a poetic quality. The resulting prose is usually extremely bad — especially the dreaming spires effusions on the beauty of the Princeton campus, and the Gothic extravaganza of Amory's affair with Eleanor. Occasionally, however, there are passages which affect one in the same way as the quotation from Wilde — which combine a certain kind of power with a suspect quality that makes one unwilling to say unequivocally that they are good. The most striking example is the evocation of Amory's moods of ecstasy in his last year at boarding school.

In the spring he read 'L'Allegro', by request, and was inspired to lyrical outpourings on the subject of Arcady and the pipes of Pan. He moved his bed so that the sun would wake him at dawn that he might dress and go out to the archaic swing that hung from an apple-tree near the sixth-form house. Seating himself in this he would pump higher and higher until he got the effect of swinging into the wide air, into a fairy-land of piping satyrs and nymphs with the faces of fair-haired girls he passed in the streets of Eastchester. As the swing reached its highest point, Arcady really lay just over the brow of a certain hill, where the brown road dwindled out of sight in a golden dot.[4]

Here one sees a strong poetic impulse at work, searching for images, and, in the description of Amory in the swing, almost finding one. The fineness of the sensibility can hardly be in question, but it is still not clear how best the sensibility can be used.

With characteristic self-awareness, Fitzgerald partly diagnoses the problem himself in the moonlight conversation between Amory and Tom D'Invilliers to which I have already referred:

2 Oscar Wilde, *The Picture of Dorian Gray, Works*, The Sunflower Edition, Vol. 2, New York, 1909, pp. 47—8.
3 Henry Dan Piper, *F. Scott Fitzgerald: a Critical Portrait*, London, 1965, p. 39.
4 *This Side of Paradise* BH3, p. 41.

54   *F. Scott Fitzgerald and the Art of Social Fiction*

... Amory declaimed 'The Ode to a Nightingale' to the bushes they passed.
'I'll never be a poet', said Amory as he finished. 'I'm not enough of a sensualist really; there are only a few things that I notice as primarily beautiful: women, spring evenings, music at night, the sea; I don't catch the subtle things like "silver-snarling trumpets". I may turn out an intellectual, but I'll never write anything but mediocre poetry.'[5]

Amory expresses a sense of the wide range of quality which is possible in the language of sensous romantic poetry. One can give added point to this feeling, in terms of Fitzgerald's own poetic preferences at the time, by juxtaposing passages from Keats and Rupert Brooke — the stanza from *The Eve of St Agnes* in which the phrase 'silver, snarling trumpets' actually occurs, and the closing lines of 'Kindliness':

> That ancient Beadsman heard the prelude soft;
> And so it chanc'd, for many a door was wide,
> From hurry to and fro. Soon, up aloft,
> The silver, snarling trumpets 'gan to chide:
> The level chambers, ready with their pride,
> Were glowing to receive a thousand guests:
> The carved angels, ever eager-eyed,
> Star'd, where upon their heads the cornice rests,
> With hair blown back, and wings put cross-wise on
> their breasts.

> That time when all is over, and
> Hand never flinches, brushing hand;
> And blood lies quiet, for all you're near;
> And it's but spoken words we hear,
> Where trumpets sang; when the mere skies
> Are stranger and nobler than your eyes;
> And flesh is flesh, was flame before;
> And infinite hungers leap no more
> In the chance swaying of your dress;
> And love has changed to kindliness.

Keat's language is distinguished from Brooke's by its dramatic precision: everything — the sounds, the visual detail, the sense of place and atmosphere — is defined with the same clarity. By comparison, Brooke's language is vague, insipid and unrealized: it is enough to place his colourless lines, 'And it's but spoken words we hear/Where trumpets sang', beside Keats's incomparable trumpet image. Through Amory, Fitzgerald makes his own conviction clear — that it is not worth trying to use this kind of poetic language unless one can do so with the precision of Keats. He recognizes, correctly, that his own gifts do not lie in this direction, and implicitly repudiates the second-rate alternative — of being the American Rupert Brooke. He had taken stock of his abilities to the extent of finding something he couldn't do, but he had still to find a genuinely creative use for his poetic sensibilities.

5   *Ibid.*, p. 90.

There is a hint of where the solution lay in the actual conversation between Amory and Tom. Besides romantic poetry, they talk about social life at Princeton. In the light of Fitzgerald's later achievements, it is clear that what he needed most was to find some way to bring these concerns together — to put his poetic sensibilites at the service of his developing social sense.

We see the beginnings of this process in a very early story, 'The Ice Palace', which appeared in May 1920, only a few weeks after the publication of *This Side of Paradise*. This is the first occasion on which Fitzgerald explores the possibilities of turning social fiction into a mode of poetry. The story deals with the brief, unsuccessful engagement of a Southern girl, Sally Carrol Happer, with a Middle Westerner, Harry Bellamy. They have inherited widely differing attitudes to life from the two regions they grew up in, and it is the conflict between these attitudes that causes the failure of their relationship. The plot is constructed out of two visits — one which Harry pays to Sally Carrol at her sleepy Georgia town during the fall; the other, when she travels north to his bustling Minnesota city at the season of winter carnival. The very considerable success of the story depends not on plot, however, but on the two images which convey Sally Carrol's sense of regional character and social contrast. The spirit of the South is evoked by the old cemetery to which the lovers stroll on the last afternoon of Harry's visit. There are mellow colourings; the crumbling monuments of a slowly vanishing age of romance and chivalry; an atmosphere of decrepitude and decay which is a form of quiet beauty rather than corruption; an easy-going acceptance of the compatibility of old nostalgias with present emotional needs — Sally Carrol is moved to tears by the associations of the place, but nevertheless waits impatiently to kiss Harry while three old women place flowers on Confederate graves.

Her sense of the frozen northland, when she returns Harry's visit, is given shape by the image of the ice palace. This is the centrepiece of the winter carnival, an immense construction built out of blocks of translucent ice, and embellished with every kind of Gothic decoration. Sally Carrol first sees it glowing luridly green through the murk of a snowstorm. It represents Harry's conception of the beautiful and the magnificent — a manifestation of that Middle Western taste for fantastic ostentation and display to which Gatsby gave expression in his parties. For Harry, it is also an expression of Middle Western energy, organizational skill and technical know-how — he is tiresomely knowledgeable about its dimensions and method of construction. Inside the main hall, they watch a torchlight parade of contingents from the region's social and country clubs: these revellers march and sing in crudely coloured costumes which have the rigidity of uniform rather than the carefree spontaneity of carnival dress. Sally Carrol is intimidated and chilled, and as the pageant proceeds, Fitzgerald uses the image of the ice palace to draw together her impressions of Middle Western life into a consistent view. She becomes aware of energies which are purely material, a raw vulgarity, a frigid puritanism, and a barbaric social ritual which is an expression not of freedom but conformity.

In this use of the Georgia cemetery and the ice palace as contrasted images of two dissimilar cultures, Fitzgerald anticipates an important element in the poetic pattern of *The Great Gatsby* — the way in which the valley of ashes is balanced against the glitter of East and West Egg.

Fitzgeralds's skills as a historian of manners are not merely anticipated by the early fiction — they are in may ways already present. There are many perceptive touches in *This Side of Paradise*, particularly where he writes about Middle Western adolescents, and about the 'jazz-nourished restlessness' of the immediate postwar period. The three consecutive sections 'Petting', 'Isabelle' and 'Babes in the Woods', which deal with the beginnings of Amory's affair with Isabelle Borgé, are probably the best sustained episode in the whole novel. The incident of the hotel scandal at Atlantic City, in which Amory finds himself unwillingly involved in an old Princeton friend's weekend liaison with a prostitute, is a good piece of writing on the whole. It catches the atmosphere of early Prohibition days — sleazy and exciting, amusing and sordid — in a way that looks forward to the New York scenes of *The Great Gatsby*. 'May Day', by far the best story of these early years, owes its success almost entirely to Fitzgerald's power to grasp a complex social mood, a moment of history. (It will be discussed in detail in the chapter on his short stories).

The opening of 'Bernice Bobs Her Hair', which, like 'The Ice Palace' appeared in May 1920, is an excellent example of how well, even at this date, Fitzgerald could bring to life the manners of a particular time and place. The scene is the Saturday night dance at a Middle Western country club. Fitzgerald describes it as if it were a theatrical performance, a device which enables him to establish the tone and mode of the story — those of a comedy of manners. The theatrical metaphor also enables him to divide both actors and spectators into groups, which he then uses to bring out the distinctions between classes and generations which are his main concern. In his description of the little crowd of spectators outside the club windows, he renders with admirable precision the simple and fairly fluid class structure of Middle Western society. Some of these — the golf caddies and chauffeurs — are definitely excluded, but there are others, kept out merely by their own diffidence, who might easily enter if they wished. Even more significant is the difference between generations, and here Fitzgerald is sensitive to the smallest vibrations of social change. Around the walls of the ballroom sit the mothers: they are the theatre balcony, and, as they watch the younger set amuse itself on the floor, they imagine that they understand the show. But they are not close enough to catch the expression on the actors' faces, 'the subtler byplay' of that 'shifting semi-cruel world of adolescence'. The note of instability and uncertainty does not characterize the relations between the generations alone: it is carried into the life of the younger set itself. The fine phrase, 'the shifting, semi-cruel world of adolescence', characterizes with exactly the right shade of emphasis the tentative love affairs and rivalries of Fitzgerald's flappers and parlour snakes.

The story goes on to show how Bernice, its heroine, is forced to emerge rather painfully from an unconscious acceptance of the views of her parents into the world of her contemporaries. She believes in the ideal of the 'womanly woman' — that her duty in life is to be serenely and beautifully passive, and that, provided she conducts herself with propriety and modest charm, she will be treated with the consideration and homage which are her due. When she visits her cousin Marjorie in a larger city where her family's position no longer supports her, she finds herself exposed to the realities of the social life of her generation. It is a situation in which a girl has to fight for attention and admiration in an atmosphere of immature but ruthless competition. Bernice, who is quite unprepared for such struggles, is neglected and treated with only half-concealed contempt. After a quarrel in which Bernice threatens to go home, Marjorie agrees to coach her into social success, but Bernice learns so quickly that her rise in popularity begins to undermine Marjorie's hitherto impregnable position. She sets a trap for Bernice, who doesn't have the cunning to avoid it, and is humiliated before her new circle of admirers. She is not destroyed or ruined by the experience but she is hardened by it: she came to the city wearing the thick luxuriant hair of the womanly woman; she goes home with the bobbed hair of the hard-boiled self-reliant woman of the 1920s.

'Bernice Bobs Her Hair' is marred by immaturities of style and a sentimental ending in which poetic justice triumphs over the probabilities of the situation, but it has enough good writing and true observation to be worth reading not only for its own sake but as an introduction to any discussion of the flapper. The sentimental education Bernice receives during her summer visit makes her a flapper, her cousin Marjorie is one already. What they both share by the end of the story is the outlook Rosalind expressed in *This Side of Paradise* — 'I'm bright, quite selfish, emotional when aroused, fond of admiration....' The large number of women characters in Fitzgerald's early work whose attitude to life could be defined in this way, merge to form a clear fictional type. In discussing this type, one is concerned both with specifically literary matters and with the history of popular taste. From the former point of view, Fitzgerald's creation of the flapper was an aspect of his work as historian of manners — he was turning elements in the social life of his time into the materials of his art. But because his early work appeared at the time it did, he found himself not only reflecting a change in manners, but helping to promote it. For a short period between 1920 and 1922, he became the kind of popular artist who, as well as being widely read, is accepted as an authority on current styles of behaviour. His portrayal of the flapper contributed more than anything else to this situation.

As a fictional character the flapper comes at the end of a long line of development. American novelists had been aware of the situation of the young American woman for at least seventy years before Fitzgerald began to interest himself in it. Hawthorne's Zenobia, the heroine of *The Blithedale Romance*, is the first character of any importance to show the combination of traits we are concerned with. She is young, beautiful, and rich; she is independent, adventurous, and masterful. She refuses to accept the submissive role traditionally assigned to women — she competes with men on their own ground of practical action and intellectual achievement, while, at the same time, she has no hesitation in using her sexual attractiveness to captivate and dominate them.

Henry James's young women, Daisy Miller, Gertrude Wentworth, Isabel Archer and Milly Theale, are less intimidating and more innocent than Zenobia, but nevertheless resemble her in all essentials. They are girls in whom the charm, high spirits, confidence and self-assurance of youth have been given an almost completely free rein through financial independence and the relative absence of parental restraint. Both early and late in his career — in 'Daisy Miller' and *The American Scene* — James expressed his conviction that more was given to the American girl and less expected in return than of any similarly placed young person in recorded history.

Both Hawthorne and James were acutely aware of the dangers implicit in such freedom. They were most concerned with its tragic potentialities — with personal catastrophes like Zenobia's suicide, Daisy Miller's pathetic death, and the tragedy of Isabel Archer's wasted life. Edith Wharton, by the turn of the century, was more aware of the possibilities of corruption. The only demands made upon the young American woman of James's generation were that she should be chaste and, in a not very exacting sense, a lady. By Edith Wharton's day, these requirements were growing slack, while the boldness with which a girl could use her freedom for her own ends became steadily more marked. With Mrs Wharton's two most interesting women characters, Lily Bart and Undine Spragg, (from *The House of Mirth* and *The Custom of the Country* respectively) we are at a fascinating point of transition. Lily remains uncorrupted though she is surrounded by examples of how far a young woman can go if she is ruthless and unprincipled enough. By contrast Undine Spragg's triumphant social career is the direct result of her refusal to be bound by any scruples.

In Scott Fitzgerald's portrayal of the flapper, we see the last stage in this process of development. The adolescent girls in his earliest fiction are still technically virtuous — this can be put down to the power which the residual puritanism of American life still had to inhibit sexual behaviour. (Perhaps it is truer to say that Fitzgerald's own very real puritanism made it almost impossible for him to portray a promiscuous woman as a sympathetic character.) The requirement that she should be a lady survived only in the sense that her outrageousness, to be socially acceptable, has to be carried off with a sense of style. Nancy Lamar, the heroine of 'The Jelly-Bean' (1920), gets away with the unladylike occupation of shooting craps because the panache and charm with which she does it silence criticism.

The earliest — and also one of the best — portrayals of the flapper in Fitzgerald's fiction is Helen Halycon. She appears in 'The Débutante', a sketch set out as a one-act play, which he published in the *Nassau Literary Magazine* at Princeton in 1917. He incorporated the piece, changing Helen's name to Rosalind, in *This Side of Paradise*, but in its later form it is grossly sentimentalized and almost ruined. The essence of the flapper is that she is hard and unsentimental — excitable but cold-blooded, captivating but ruthless, outrageous but calculating — and it is precisely this mixture of qualities Fitzgerald captures in Helen Halycon. In the process of telling her fiancé, John Cannel, why she is tired of him, she explains her attitude to men:

> HELEN — I want — Oh, I'll be frank for once. I like the feeling of going after them, I like the thrill when you meet them and notice that they've got black hair that's wavey, but awfully neat, or have dark lines under their eyes, and look charmingly dissipated, or have funny smiles, that come and go and leave you wondering whether they smiled at all. Then I like the way they begin to follow you with their eyes. They're interested. Good! Then I begin to place him. Try to get his type, find what he likes; right then the romance begins to lessen for me and increase for him. Then come a few long talks.... Then, John here's the worst of it. There's a point when everything changes... sometimes it's a kiss and sometimes it's a long before anything like that. Now if it's a kiss, it can do one of three things.... It can make him get tired of you; but a clever girl can avoid this. It's only the young ones and the heroines of magazine epigrams that are kissed and deserted. Then there's the second possibility. It can make you tired of him. This is usual. He immediately thinks of nothing but being alone with the girl, and she, rather touchy about the whole thing, gets snappy, and he's first love sick, then discouraged, and finally lost.... Then the third state is where the kiss really means something, where the girl lets go of herself and the man is in deadly earnest.
> JOHN — Then they're engaged?
> HELEN — Exactly.
> JOHN — Weren't we?
> HELEN — (*Emphatically*) No, we distinctly were not. I knew what I was doing every blessed second, John Cannel.[6]

In its hard limited clarity of line, this is a good piece of writing, but the range of manners and the psychology portrayed will not support the creation of major fiction. By the time he wrote *This Side of Paradise* and the stories he published between 1920 and 1922, Fitzgerald had become aware of the much deeper and more complex feelings present in relationships between mature men and women. However, the fictional type of the flapper had imposed itself so insistently upon his imagination that he was not able to respond fully to the implications of his own widening experience. This accounts at least in part for some of his poorest writing — for the extravagant silliness of 'The Offshore Pirate' (1920) or the equally extravagant

6 'The Débutante', *The Apprentice Fiction of F. Scott Fitzgerald, 1909—1917*, edited by John Kuehl, New Brunswick, NJ, 1965, pp. 98—9.

sentimentality of 'The Popular Girl' (1922). In some of the best of the early stories he is caught between contradictory attitudes which he cannot satisfactorily resolve. He oscillates between the cool detached style of narration he uses so well in creating Helen Halycon, and abrupt descents into sentimentality.

The portrayal of Nancy Lamar in 'The Jelly-Bean' shows this uncertainty very clearly. For much of the story, Fitzgerald secures for her the kind of attention a theatre audience might give to an attractive *comédienne* — an attitude in which amusement, titillation and a certain wariness play equal parts. One is entertained by her unconventional behaviour and her wild pranks — running off all the gasoline from a parked car in order to clean chewing-gum off her shoe; shooting craps for big stakes; getting married before a country justice of the peace as the last act of a Prohibition spree. At the same time, Fitzgerald's coolly dispassionate tone forces one to observe with what cynical dexterity she always manages to involve a male accomplice in her escapades. Nor does he minimize her outrageous rudeness, selfishness, and disregard for other people's feelings. It is therefore somewhat disconcerting to find her arrival at a country club dance described in some of Fitzgerald's weakest prose. He writes of her dress ('a costume of a hundred cool corners') as if he were turning out advertising copy, and the way in which he evokes the Jelly-bean's reactions, as the latter watches her talking and laughing with her partner, is equally unsatisfactory. The Jelly-bean — '... experienced the quick pang of a weird new kind of pain. Some ray had passed between the pair, a shaft of beauty from that sun that had warmed him a moment since. The Jelly-bean felt suddenly like a weed in a shadow.'[7] Even if one were disposed to discount the banal sentimental language in which this passage is written, one would have to reckon with the confusion it precipitates in one's view of Nancy Lamar. The tone of the story is predominantly that of light ironic comedy; there is no place in it for these hints of deep and subtle feelings.

The most complete confusion of this kind occurs in Fitzgerald's presentation of Gloria Patch in *The Beautiful and Damned*, where he is absolutely unable to bring her supposed charm and her very evident bitchiness into any comprehensible relation.

In *The Great Gatsby* and *Tender is the Night*, he learned to create women who were compellingly attractive and desirable, and at the same time trivial and destructive, but in order to do so he had to discard the flapper altogether. One cannot understand Daisy Buchanan and Jordan Baker by trying to relate them to the flappers of the early fiction; to attempt any such relation where Nicole and Baby Warren, Rosemary Hoyt and Mary North are concerned would be totally absurd. In these novels, the flapper appears merely as a background — to provide some of the chatter and restless movement at Gatsby's parties. She is presented most successfully in situa-

7   'The Jelly-Bean', BH5, pp. 204—5.

tions of social comedy — in the intrigues and rivalries of 'Bernice Bobs Her Hair'; in the tumultuous farce of Emily Castleton's wedding (in 'Majesty'); or in the adventurous figure of Nancy Lamar. The only exception appears to me to be 'The Last of the Belles', a relatively late story which is discussed in the next chapter.

The creation of the flapper was undoubtedly the most important single factor in Fitzgerald's early success, and helps to sharpen one's awareness of its paradoxical nature. When the popularity of a work of literature is accompanied by outstanding artistic merit — as it is in the Falstaff plays, the Waverley novels, or *Pickwick Papers* — it is easy to account for. In Fitzgerald's case, the relation between good writing and public acclaim is almost purely fortuitous, and any account of the reception of his early work belongs as much to the history of popular taste as to the history of literature. The section 'Petting' from *This Side of Paradise* is a good instance of the kind of writing which excited his contemporaries; it also points to almost all the elements in the American cultural scene which account for his success —

> Amory saw girls doing things that even in his memory would have been impossible: eating three-o'clock, after-dance suppers in impossible cafés, talking of every side of life with an air half of earnestness, half of mockery, yet with an air of furtive excitement that Amory considered stood for a real moral let-down. But he never realized how widespread it was until he saw the cities between New York and Chicago as one vast juvenile intrigue.
>
> Afternoon at the Plaza, with winter twilight hovering outside and faint drums downstairs... they strut and fret in the lobby, taking another cocktail, scrupulously attired and waiting. Then the swinging doors revolve and three bundles of fur mince in. The theatre comes afterward; then a table at the Midnight Frolic — of course, mother will be along there, but she will only serve to make things more secretive and brilliant as she sits in solitary state at the deserted table and thinks such entertainments as this are not half so bad as they are painted, only rather wearying. But the P.D. [Popular Daughter] is in love again... it was odd, wasn't it? — that though there was so much room left in the taxi the P.D. and the boy from Williams were somehow crowded out and had to go in a separate car. Odd! Didn't you notice how flushed the P.D. was when she arrived just seven minutes late? But the P.D. 'gets away with it'.
>
> The 'belle' had become the 'flirt', the 'flirt' had become the 'baby vamp'. The 'belle' had five or six callers every afternoon. If the P.D., by some strange accident has two, it is made pretty uncomfortable for the one who hasn't a date with her. The 'belle' was surrounded by a dozen men in the intermissions between dances. Try to find the P.D. between dances, just try to find her.[8]

Apart from a few uncomfortable modulations towards the coy and the merely chatty, this is a good piece of writing, full of wit and high spirits. *This Side of Paradise* did not gain its large and enthusiastic readership primarily through these qualities, however. In the process of drawing on his own

8 *This Side of Paradise*, BH3, pp. 65—6.

youthful experience, Fitzgerald told his contemporaries what they wanted to hear about themselves and the age they lived in. His customary sensitivity to the atmosphere of a particular historical moment was an essential element in this success, but the question of timing is still more important. All Fitzgerald's best writing as historian of manners is retrospective: *Gatsby*, published in 1925, recalls the summer of 1922; *Tender is the Night*, in 1934, looks back to the Riviera of 1926; 'Echoes of the Jazz Age' and 'My Lost City' analyse the 1920s from the vantage point of the next decade. But for a short time at the beginning of his career, Fitzgerald anticipated social change. He was not a revolutionary or a prophet: if he had been, he would have been persecuted or ignored. He achieved instead the kind of popularity which depends upon a writer's being fractionally ahead of his times: he was able to dramatize — to bring to the level of consciousness — ideas and feelings which were already current. He took half-conscious assumptions and unacknowledged patterns of behaviour and made them seem exciting, amusing, only slightly naughty, almost a new orthodoxy.

In the long run, an episode like 'Petting' was likely to reassure American readers, rather than disturb them deeply. It tells them that the choices which many of them appeared to be making in 1920 were the right ones. It shows a society turning away from strenuous ideals in favour of the pursuit of pleasure. It presented the new social freedom of women and the relatively relaxed attitude to sex which accompanied it as perfectly natural and normal. It initiates the cult of youth which, with successive transformations, has dominated American culture ever since. A highly significant feature is the image of New York which emerges here as elsewhere in Fitzgerald's early writings. As Henry Dan Piper has pointed out[9] Fitzgerald saw New York as a tourist: to him, it was the city of tall white buildings, of hotels, restaurants, and theatres, for which Times Square is the focal point. Earlier writers had not seen New York in this way. For Edith Wharton, it was a city of complex — mainly sordid — social and financial struggles, balanced between Wall Street and Fifth Avenue. For Stephen Crane and Theodore Dreiser, it was a brutal city — a place of crime, of poverty, of suffering, of ugliness. They missed what Fitzgerald saw because, paradoxically, they knew the city better than he, and dismissed as superficial the aspect which he regarded as all-important. Nevertheless, it is his picture — perpetuated and enlarged by literature, the cinema, advertising and television — which has held the popular imagination ever since. (It is interesting to note that the other major writer of the period who saw New York in this way, Hart Crane, was also an outsider from the Middle West.)

The tone of the passage I have quoted is quite as important as its content. It is mildly shocking (bearing in mind the received ideas of 1920) without being really subversive. It implies that although some people will be outraged by what it portrays, the enlightened modern reader will be too

9   Piper, *op.cit.*, pp. 72—6.

sophisticated and well informed to belong to so bigoted a minority. Frederick Lewis Allen quotes a vivid example of the attacks then being made upon the behaviour of young people from the *Catholic Telegraph* of Cincinnati;

> The music is sensuous, the embracing of partners — the female only half-dressed — is absolutely indecent; and the motions — they are such as may not be described, with any respect for propriety, in a family newspaper. Suffice it to say that there are certain houses appropriate for such dances, but those houses have been closed by law.[10]

In the atmosphere of the Jazz Age, Fitzgerald was bound to gain in popularity when criticism came from such a quarter and was expressed with such barbarity of language. In any case, there was nothing fundamentally disturbing in what he said. He believed that life — especially social life — could be intensely enjoyable; at the same time he was temperamentally a conservative, with a deep affection for the American past and with no wish to destroy the moral tradition at the heart of the culture. For a brief period it was possible for him not only to maintain this delicate balance in his own mind, but to see it reflected in the life around him. But as the decade advanced, his view of its activities became more sombre. The pleasure-seeking impulse, which had seemed so innocently exciting in *This Side of Paradise*, acquired the character of a destructive force. As he continued to observe his contemporaries, he found it necessary to devise new images for their pleasures — the equivocal atmosphere of Gatsby's parties, or even the squalor and brutality of Tom Buchanan's affair with Myrtle Wilson.

At this point Fitzgerald began to lose his original public, and with his second great novel, *Tender is the Night*, he lost them altogether. His early triumph, in this sense, proved to be a liability. Even as late as 'The Crack-up', he found it difficult to relinquish the belief that it was possible to attain popular success through artistic achievement. He never fully grasped the extent to which the reception given to *This Side of Paradise* depended upon accidents of cultural history. As a result, during the period 1924-34, when his self-confidence should have been greatest, his creative energies were often undermined by frustration and self-doubt. He gained little solid satisfaction from the work he knew to be artistically great, and he despised — often quite unreasonably — the work which was commercially succesful. The final irony of his case is that since his death, *The Great Gatsby* and *Tender is the Night* — more than any novel by Hemingway or Faulkner — have emerged as the true popular classics of modern American literature.

In *This Side of Paradise* and the short stories of 1920, there are unmistakable

---

10 Frederick Lewis Allen, *Only Yesterday: an Informal History of the Nineteen-Twenties*, New York and Evanston, 1957, p. 90.

signs that Fitzgerald was beginning to find his true bent as a novelist. By contrast, *The Beautiful and Damned* (1922) can be seen only as an unfortunate aberration. It is an extremely bad novel by any standard, but what makes it especially disturbing is that it seems to cancel out all the gains Fitzgerald had made so far. It carried him clean out of the path that appeared to be leading directly to the creative climax of 1924-26.

It deals with the gradual deterioration of Anthony and Gloria Patch as the remorseless pressures of life strip them of their youth, beauty and vitality. (This is to ignore the innumerable confusions of motivation and causation which complicate the work in so uninteresting a way.) The novel's subject matter provides the most obvious clue to its failure — Fitzgerald was experimenting with a mode of fiction entirely alien to him. He was led to do this largely through the influence of H. L. Mencken, who deeply affected many aspects of his thinking between 1920 and 1922. Mencken reviewed *This Side of Paradise* favourably, and was the first editor (outside Princeton) to accept Fitzgerald's stories for publication. For a short time, Fitzgerald felt that his own status as a new novelist was bound up with the journalistic campaign Mencken was conducting on behalf of American naturalistic fiction. He read such novels as Theodore Dreiser's *Sister Carrie* and Frank Norris's *Vandover and the Brute* enthusiastically, but when he tried to imitate them in *The Beautiful and Damned,* the consequences were disastrous.

Naturalistic tragedy was completely destructive of Fitzgerald's own particular talents. It made nonsense of his own gift for writing social comedy, and prevented him from developing his poetic impulse. A mechanistic view of life might leave Dreiser room for compassion and human concern, but it crippled Fitzgerald's fastidious and discriminating sense of human relationships. Above all, the doctrine of the meaninglessness of life was a denial of everything he really believed in, and frustrated what was perhaps his truest impulse — his sense of wonder at the inexhaustible possibilities of existence.

The extent to which *The Beautiful and Damned* falsified Fitzgerald's outlook on life as well as deflecting him from the true course of his artistic development can be seen most clearly in the notorious symposium scene. This is designed to give the story a philosophical centre — to enable Fitzgerald to make an authoritative statement on the meaninglessness of life. The drunken Socrates at this intellectual feast is Maury Noble, a character based on George Jean Nathan. (Nathan was co-editor with Mencken of *The Smart Set,* and the two men were frequent visitors to the Fitzgeralds' house.) The scene reaches its lowest point where Maury expresses his opinions on race and history:

...it seemed to me that there was no ultimate goal for man. Man was beginning a grotesque and bewildered fight with nature — nature that by the divine and magnificent accident had brought us to where we could fly in her face. She had invented ways to rid the race of the inferior and thus give the remainder strength to fill her higher — or, let us say, her more amusing — though still unconscious and accidental intentions. And, actuated by the highest gifts of the enlightenment, we were seeking to circumvent her. In this republic I saw the black beginning to mingle with the white — in Europe there was taking place an economic catastrophe to save three or four diseased and wretchedly governed races from the one mastery that might organize them for material prosperity.

We produce a Christ who can raise up the leper — and presently the breed of the leper is the salt of the earth. If anyone can find any lesson in that, let him stand forth.[11]

The symposium scene is bad in obvious ways: it is shallow and ignorant; worse, through its self-conceited tone, it implicitly lays claim to qualities of wit and intelligence which plainly aren't there. In his mature fiction, Fitzgerald is the wittiest American writer since Henry James, and possesses an exquisite comic sense, but he had great trouble in finding his true vein. He quickly recognized that the manner he had attempted in *The Beautiful and Damned* did not suit him, and set about eliminating it from his fiction as thoroughly as possible. In a letter of 1 February 1925, he told Ernest Boyd with satisfaction that no trace of this kind of writing had found its way into *The Great Gatsby*: 'All my harsh smartness has been kept ruthlessly out of it — it's the greatest weakness in my work distracting and disfiguring it even when it calls up an isolated sardonic laugh. I don't think that has a touch left.'[12]

Part of his difficulty — certainly what he has in mind here — was caused by the influence of Mencken. Fitzgerald's comic sense is always aroused by the particular character, the specific situation — Meyer Wolfsheim; Tom Buchanan on civilization or the sanctity of marriage; Myrtle Wilson buying a dog; Royall Dumphry and Mr Campion; Baby Warren and the American Consul in Rome. Mencken on the other hand works through general satire, and is fascinated by American types. In one of his finest essays, 'The American Novel' (*Prejudices*, Second Series), he recommends to the would-be writer of fiction a number of subjects, all of which are type-figures: the Washington politician, the lawyer, the journalist, and the American puritan or wowser. A short extract from his portrait of the last of these will give a sense of his best manner:

What a novel is in him! Indeed, what a shelf of novels! For he has as many forms as there are varieties of human delusion. Sometimes he is a tin-pot evangelist, sweating to transform Oklahoma City or Altoona Pa., into the New Jerusalem. Sometimes he is a hireling of the Anti-Saloon League, sworn to Law Enforcement. Sometimes he is a strict Sabbatarian, bawling for the police whenever he detects his neighbour washing bottles or varnishing the Ford on Sunday morning. Again, he is a vice-crusader, chasing the scarlet lady with fierce Christian shouts....

Since the earliest days, as everyone knows, American jurisprudence has been

11 *The Beautiful and Damned*, BH4, pp. 227—8.
12 *Letters*, p. 478.

founded upon the axiom that it is the first duty of every citizen to police his neighbours, and especially those he envies, or otherwise dislikes. There is no such thing, in that grand and puissant nation, as privacy. The yokels out in Iowa, neglecting their horned cattle, have a right, it appears — nay, a sacred duty! — to peek into my ancestral castle in Baltimore, and tell me what I may and may not drink with my meals. An out-at-elbow Methodist parson in Boston sets himself up to decide what I may read. An obscure and unintelligent office-holder in Washington, inspired by God, determines what I may receive in the mails. I must not buy lottery tickets because it offends the moral sentiment of Kansas. I must keep Sunday as the Sabbath, which is in conflict with Genesis, because it is ordered by people who believe that Genesis can't be wrong.[13]

Mencken's power to generalize depends upon an intimate acquaintance with the political temper of America and the oddities of its provincial life. Since Fitzgerald largely lacked this knowledge, his satire never achieves the edge, the precision, of Mencken's. Maury Noble's harangue is a particularly gross failure, but a characteristic misfire which is even closer to Mencken's style of journalism, is the passage in *The Beautiful and Damned* which announces America's entry into the War:

In April war was declared with Germany. Wilson and his cabinet — a cabinet that in its lack of distinction was strangely reminiscent of the twelve apostles — let loose the carefully starved dogs of war, and the press began to whoop hysterically against the sinister morals, sinister philosophy, and sinister music produced by the Teutonic temperament. Those who fancied themselves particularly broad-minded made the exquisite distinction that it was only the German Government which aroused them to hysteria; the rest were worked up to a condition of retching indecency. Any song which contained the word 'mother' and the word 'kaiser' was assured of a tremendous success.[14]

The passage has an air of clumsy and unintelligent ventriloquism which has deeper causes than Fitzgerald's simple failure to capture the distinctive quality of another writer. In Mencken's wartime journalism, flamboyant irony had had a real function — the effect of an icy dash of sanity in a feverishly mad world. In Fitzgerald, however, the lack of timeliness, of conviction, and above all of relevance to the action of the novel, make it seem silly and rather offensive.

Before he read Mencken, Fitzgerald had considered Oscar Wilde the best model for witty and satiric writing. He admired the dialogue of Wilde's comedies extravagantly, and the speeches and table talk of Lord Henry Wotton in *The Picture of Dorian Gray* even more. When he was writing musical comedy scripts for the Triangle Club at Princeton, he immersed himself in Wilde's work in order to reproduce the latter's sparkling epigrammatic manner. But, given his own particular gifts, Wilde was as unsuitable an influence as Mencken. Where Wilde creates an effect of

13 Henry L. Mencken, 'The American Novel', *Prejudices, Second Series*, Cape's Traveller's Library, London, n.d., pp. 176—8.
14 *The Beautiful and Damned* BH4, p. 271.

effortless spontaneity and a tone which is impudently gay, Fitzgerald seems pretentious, laboured and rather snobbish. Most of the self-consciously witty writing in *This Side of Paradise* fails in this way, a particularly clear case being the description of Amory's mother at the beginning of the novel.

Fitzgerald's own kind of wit — and especially his ability to write good comic dialogue — appear in other ways. From the very first he had a wonderfully accurate ear for the inane chatter of his flappers and parlour snakes — the way Amory Blaine and Isabelle Borgé talk to each other, and the conversation of the young people in 'Bernice Bobs Her Hair'. At other times, he shows a talent for the grotesque — the almost Dickensian sense of comic vulgarity which led him to create Meyer Wolfsheim, Myrtle Wilson and Gatsby himself. Most of all, his comic sense is present in the delicately rendered tones of flat, hard, Middle Western voices — in Tom Buchanan expatiating on the rising tide of colour; Baby explaining to Dick Diver how the Warrens plan to buy a doctor for Nicole; and in the dry, uninflected, self-deprecating irony of Nick Carraway and Abe North.

Irony itself is a mode of writing Fitzgerald learned to use only with difficulty. Being ironical has little value unless it is a form of intellectual and moral control over experience. Fitzgerald's irony, in his inferior writings, frequently lacks this essential quality because it is merely a facet of his fascination with himself. The narcissism of heroes like Amory Blaine and Anthony Patch, the self-regarding complacency or self-pity of many of the autobiographical pieces, cancel out any virtue the irony might have.

> In 1913, when Anthony Patch was twenty-five, two years were already gone since irony, the Holy Ghost of this later day, had, theoretically at least, descended upon him. Irony was the final polish of the shoe, the ultimate dab of the clothes-brush, a sort of intellectual 'There!'....[15]

In *The Beautiful and Damned*, Fitzgerald's career had taken a false turning; in 'The Diamond as Big as the Ritz' (1922), he not only recovered all the ground he had lost, but in certain ways advanced beyond anything he had written in 1920. This is not to say that 'The Diamond' is a flawless work of art: Fitzgerald is often self-indulgent in his treatment of physical luxury, and sentimental in his handling of the relationship between John and Kismine. He is not completely in control of his material: the impulse towards harsh social criticism in the story is not always satisfyingly related to the element of romantic fascination. Nevertheless, he shows himself to be in possession of almost all the resources he needed to write *The Great Gatsby*.

His social interests are much wider than they had been before. In his portrayal of the Washington family, he moves away from the standpoint of the younger generation, so that the American rich no longer appear merely as wealthy undergraduates or flappers cocooned in luxury. In the fiction of 1920, he had been living in the present — the best story of that year, 'May

15 *Ibid.*, p. 11.

Day', evokes the atmosphere of a single day — but in 'The Diamond', he presents the historical evolution of a class. The money his young people spend so nonchalantly has its own story — the history of America in the Gilded Age. Fitzgerald traces it through his account of the Washington family's rise to fortune — a brilliant mingling of burlesque and melodrama.

It is a story of the West — Fitzgerald had recognized from the beginning that American wealth is a specifically Western phenomenon. Shortly after the Civil War, Culpepper Washington discovers and appropriates a diamond mountain in an unexplored corner of Montana. His exploit seems scarcely more fantastic than some of the actual episodes of lawless adventure and individual enterprise during this phase of the nation's westward expansion. Mining in many ways typifies the economic activity of the Gilded Age: ruthlessly and often wastefully exploitative, it is the ultimate expression of personal greed and of indifference to the idea of a civilization. It is seen in this way in Frank Norris's *The Octopus*, a novel which Fitzgerald had quite possibly read. Norris uses mining as an image for all the varied enterprises of Western capitalism: agriculture mines the soil, and the railroads in turn mine the whole economy. Forty-niner, wheat farmer, and railroad tycoon alike have only one notion of profit — the bonanza, the lucky strike.

Culpepper Washington represents the exploitative phase of American capitalism; his son Braddock belongs to the period of consolidation. He seals up the mine and concentrates his energies on safeguarding what he has. He is an expert in banking and investment, an evader of taxes, a corrupter of legislatures. In theory he dislikes violence, but in practice he finds himself compelled to maintain a private army and to murder those who threaten his security.

Fitzgerald sees the American rich not merely as heirs to an economic history, but as creators of a style. 'The Ice Palace' offers a tentative sketch of what that style might be, but 'The Diamond as Big as the Ritz' goes much farther in subtlety and range of suggestion. This is apparent in the description of Braddock Washington's château:

> Full in the light of the stars, an exquisite château rose from the borders of the lake, climbed in marble radiance half the height of an adjoining mountain, then melted in grace, in perfect symmetry, in translucent feminine languor, into the massed darkness of a forest of pine. The many towers, the slender tracery of the sloping parapets, the chiselled wonder of a thousand yellow windows with their oblongs and hectagons and triangles of golden light, the shattered softness of the intersecting planes of star-shine and blue shade, all trembled on John's spirit like a chord of music. On one of the towers, the tallest, the blackest at its base, an arrangement of exterior lights at the top made a sort of floating fairyland — and as John gazed up in warm enchantment the faint acciaccare sound of violins drifted down in a rococo harmony that was like nothing he had ever heard before. Then in a moment the car stopped before wide, high marble steps around which the night air was fragrant with a host of flowers. At the top of the steps two great doors

swung silently open and amber light flooded out upon the darkness, silhouetting the figure of an exquisite lady with black, high-piled hair, who held out her arms towards them.[16]

The château is an expression of that 'vast, vulgar, and meretricious beauty' which (as I suggested in chapter 2) is perhaps the one distinctive style American civilization has evolved. Fitzgerald's actual writing in this description leaves a good deal to be desired. It takes itself too seriously: it lacks the comic and satiric note which is needed to bring out the latent absurdity in such a conception of the sublime and beautiful. When this passage is read in its context, however — in the light thrown upon it by other details of the story — it is seen to be subtler than one had at first supposed. When Percy Washington, for instance, explains to John that it was designed, not by an architect, a landscape gardener or a poet, but by a 'moving-picture fella', everything becomes clear. The château is nothing more than a vast Hollywood set. Almost every detail of Fitzgerald's description calls attention to effects of lighting — he himself sees it as if he were a director or a cameraman. The figure of Mrs Washington in the lighted doorway is not that of an aristocratic *grande dame*, but rather of a film star posed for a big scene. She is not at all like Isabel Archer framed in a doorway of Osmond's palace in Rome; she is more like Gloria Swanson at the head of the stairs in the superb last sequence of *Sunset Boulevard*. The sense of the insubstantiality and impermanence which are inseparable from this equivocal kind of beauty is particularly apparent at the end of the story. The château and the diamond mountain itself disappear together in a blinding white flash and a black pall of smoke. So it is with the other expressions of the American style: the glitter and noise of the State Fair vanish overnight leaving only the empty prairie; the abandoned and unlighted movie-set lurks in a deserted canyon; the American city itself, seen through the eyes of Henry James's Europeans, is no more than a vast temporary encampment, an Arabian bazaar that might disappear without warning.

It is not simply Fitzgerald's social interests which have broadened in 'The Diamond as Big as the Ritz', however: his use of the château image shows how far his sense of the poetic possibilities of language has developed since the writing of his earliest fiction. The process of discovering that social fiction could be a mode of poetry — that for him, indeed, it was the only possible mode of poetry — was virtually complete. In addition, his sense of the various ways in which a story could take on a poetic dimension was freer and more flexible than ever before. In 'The Ice Palace', he simply juxtaposed two strongly contrasted images — the Southern graveyard and the ice palace itself. In 'The Diamond', there is a constant play of the imagination over the social detail of the story so as to bring out a concentrated richness of suggestion and meaning.

One sees this new power impressively at work in the final episode of

16 'The Diamond as Big as the Ritz', BH5, p. 48.

Braddock Washington's career. A squadron of planes has discovered his mountain retreat and silenced its defences. The aviators have landed and are about to capture the château. Braddock Washington, followed by two negro slaves bearing an enormous diamond, climbs the diamond mountain at dawn in order to put a proposition to God. He has successfully bribed governments in the past; now he proposes to bribe the Almighty:

> For a while his discourse took the form of reminding God of this gift or that which Divinity had deigned to accept from men — great churches if he would rescue cities from the plague, gifts of myrrh and gold, of human lives and beautiful women and captive armies, of children and queens, of beasts of the forest and field, sheep and goats, harvests and cities, whole conquered lands that had been offered up in lust and blood for His appeasal, buying a meed's worth of alleviation from the Divine wrath — and now he, Braddock Washington, Emperor of Diamonds, king and priest of the age of gold, arbiter of splendour and luxury, would offer up a treasure such as princes before him had never dreamed of, offer it up not in suppliance, but in pride.
>
> He would give to God, he continued, getting down to specifications, the greatest diamond in the world. This diamond would be cut with many more thousand facets than there were leaves on a tree, and yet the whole diamond would be shaped with the perfection of a stone no bigger than a fly. Many men would work upon it for many years. It would be set in a great dome of beaten gold, wonderfully equipped with gates of opal and crusted sapphire. In the middle would be hollowed out a chapel presided over by an altar of iridescent, decomposing, ever-changing radium which would burn out the eyes of any worshipper who lifted up his head from prayer.[17]

Fitzgerald's control over language here is beyond praise. The false rhetoric of Braddock Washington's address to God combines two idioms. The tone is a kind of exalted horse-trading, in which the magnitude of what is offered and demanded cannot conceal the essential vulgarity of purpose. The images are those of a confused fundamentalism: Braddock Washington is reproducing — unintelligently and inaccurately — the language of the more primitive parts of the Bible and of the tradition of popular preaching which draws upon them. In this gross marriage of business and religion, Fitzgerald parodies the dominant form of cant in the America of the 1920s. But Braddock Washington is very far from being merely one of those provincial Rotarians or boosters whom Sinclair Lewis mocked in *Babbitt,* and whose absurdities were lovingly catalogued by Mencken in *The American Mercury.* There is an incoherent vulgar magnificence of intention in him. His monstrous and barbaric conception of the shrine of gold, diamond and radium is an expression of tragic impotence as well as monumental folly. American civilization has never succeeded in producing forms which contain the spirit of permanence. When it attempts the commemorative, the grandiose, the eternal, it runs to extremes scarcely less grotesque than Braddock Washington's chapel — the gigantic heads of presidents carved

17   *Ibid.,* pp. 78—9.

from the side of a hill in North Dakota, or the six-hundred-foot stainless steel arch on the Mississippi at St Louis. As Marius Bewley puts it, this is 'a level at which the material and the spiritual have bcome inextricably confused.'[18]

In this scene — and in several other places in 'The Diamond as Big as the Ritz' — we see Fitzgerald in full possession of his fictional vocabulary. He is able to create images; to capture subtle inflections of tone and meaning; to blend and mimic patterns of American speech; to balance and control conflicting attitudes to his material; to evoke with sympathy and to satirize. There was little more he needed to learn in order to write *The Great Gatsby* and the major stories of 1924-26.

There was a considerable delay before he was ready to embark on this period of intense creative activity. He wasted more than a year on *The Vegetable*, a play which flopped on its first night, and was never revived. But this diversion did not endanger his talent, as writing *The Beautiful and Damned* had done. In fact, 1922-24 seems, in retrospect, one of the most important periods of Fitzgerald's career — a period in which he took stock of his abilities; responded most fruitfully to Edmund Wilson's critical influence; read more widely and more discriminatingly than ever before; and developed a sense of his true place in the American literary tradition.

18   Marius Bewley, *The Eccentric Design*, London, 1959, p. 265.

4

Fitzgerald's short stories — the shape of a career

Scott Fitzgerald has never received his due as a writer of short stories. His tales have been relegated to a minor position: they are too often discussed as if they mattered only as aids to the understanding of his major novels. It is symptomatic of this situation that some fifty of them remained uncollected for four decades after the author's death. And yet Fitzgerald deserves the same respect as the undisputed masters of the genre among his American contemporaries — Sherwood Anderson, Hemingway and Faulkner.

Fitzgerald himself is partly to blame for this unsatisfactory position, since his more flamboyant statements about his own work — the ones which are most often remembered and quoted — veer between extremes of boastfulness and self-depreciation. In a prefatory note to *Tales of the Jazz Age*, he claims that 'The Camel's Back' was written in a single day in order to earn the money for a platinum and diamond wristwatch that Zelda wanted.[1] At other times he disparaged his own stories in the most violent terms: 'the more I get for my trash', he said in a letter of 1925, 'the less I can bring myself to write it'; and in a painfully embarassing letter to Hemingway at the end of the decade, he wrote that 'the *Post* now pays the old whore $4000 a screw. But that's because she's mastered the 40 positions — in her youth one was enough.'[2] Critics have been all too ready to take Fitzgerald's own unfavourable verdict at its face value without looking into the reasons that underlie it. A writer does not have to enjoy what he is doing in order to produce good work; nor are the explanations he gives for his discontent necessarily accurate or complete. While it is true that Fitzgerald often wrote badly under the pressure of time and money, he nevertheless created some of his finest short fiction under the same unfavourable conditions, and even the poorest of his magazine stories frequently contain unforgettable flashes of social and psychological insight, striking images, touches of wit, or a vivid sense of place and period. (A case in point is 'Majesty', which I have already discussed in some detail in chapter 2.) There is, in fact, no simple correlation between Fitzgerald's commercial writing and his bad writing; while the notion that he deliberately prostituted his talent to the magazines is totally absurd.

1 *Tales of the Jazz Age*, London 1923, pp. vii—viii.
2 *Letters*, pp. 195 and 307 respectively.

Nothing could be more futile than to attempt a detailed refutation of these misconceptions — to argue with them seriously is to concede that they have at least the status of half-truths. In any case, they are harmful not so much because they are false, but because they force the discussion of Fitzgerald's stories on to the ground of failure, whereas the essential thing is to base one's argument upon the fact of his success. For this reason, I shall not spend any time cataloguing the weaknesses of his poorer stories, but concentrate all my attention upon those tales which ought to have a secure place alongside the best short fiction of the twentieth century. Given this framework of analysis, his dislike of short-story writing instead of being an obstruction to the understanding of his work becomes potentially illuminating: it provides a deeper insight than any other aspect of his career into the difficulties he experienced because of his complex attitude to his role as an author; and it helps to draw attention to the exacting nature of his conception of short-story form.

Fitzgerald's ideas about the function of the artist, as we have already seen, are divided by a central conflict: on the one hand he believes that the artist is a heroic figure, and the values of art supreme; and, on the other, that writing is a middle-class vocation which involves the author in a network of responsibilities and obligations to other people. It is this latter view, with its implied standards of professionalism and hard work, which he invokes whenever he discusses his short stories seriously. In a letter of 1930, he spoke of his work for the *Saturday Evening Post* as 'honest' and 'not any spot on me'.[3] When the Hollywood producer Joseph Mankiewicz hastily rewrote his script for *Three Comrades*, he protested not in the name of high art but of his professional experience as a story writer: 'To say I'm disillusioned is putting it mildly. For nineteen years, with two years out for sickness, I've written best-selling entertainment, and my dialogue is supposedly right up at the top.'[4] As Fitzgerald's exchange with Mankiewicz indicates, a professional writer can only please himself up to a point: much of his work is inevitably a matter of adjustment to the wishes of others, a series of compromises, with all the frustrations and annoyances such a situation implies. Hollywood, indeed, seems to have crystallized in Fitzgerald's mind conflicts which go back to the beginning of his career — which arise quite as much from his struggles to write stories for the magazines as from his experience of the film industry. He presents the problem most vividly in a short scene from *The Last Tycoon*. Once again, it is a clash between a writer and a producer which brings the issues to the surface. George Boxley, a writer who has just been recruited by the studio, complains to Monroe Stahr that he cannot do satisfying creative work under mass-production conditions. Stahr rebukes him sharply:

3 *Ibid.*, p. 395.
4 *Ibid.*, p. 563.

'That's the condition,' said Stahr. 'There's always some lousy condition, We're making a life of Rubens — suppose I asked you to do portraits of rich dopes like Bill Brady and me and Gary Cooper and Marcus when you wanted to paint Jesus Christ! Wouldn't you feel you had a condition? Our condition is that we have to take people's own favourite folklore and dress it up and give it back to them.'[5]

In this scene the debate is settled conclusively in Stahr's favour, but it was never resolved in Fitzgerald's own mind. He was always uncertain whether he was a disciple of the religion of art, or whether he was one of those destined to produce art under 'conditions'. His uncertainty was deepest, his sense of inner conflict most acute, when he was writing short stories.

The same pattern of contradictory impulses is implicit in many of the stories themselves. They often conform very closely to Monroe Stahr's demand that the writer should 'take people's own favourite folklore and dress it up and give it back to them.' At the same time, they frequently give evidence of a kind of distinction which an artist can only achieve by pursuing the truth of his own visions. 'The Bowl' (1928) shows the effect of these tensions in a very marked degree. It is in many ways a good story, carefully plotted and unfalteringly well written, and yet no one anxious for Fitzgerald's reputation would place it unhesitatingly in the canon of his best work. It is built around two climactic moments in the life of a Princeton football player, Dolly Harlan: twice during his career, Princeton have to play the vital game of the season at the Yale Bowl, and on each occasion he saves them from defeat by a brilliant last-minute breakthrough. In essence, this is a piece of pure *Boys' Own* banality, and Fitzgerald had actually written such a story, 'Reade, Substitute Right Half', for his school magazine as far back as 1910. There is a further, equally predictable element in Dolly's situation: between the two encounters with Yale, he becomes engaged to a rich society girl, Vienna Thorne, who tries to make him give up football because her brother had been killed in a prep-school game. At first Dolly acquiesces, but honour recalls him to the Princeton squad just in time: he loses Vienna, but is more than compensated by the recovery of his manhood.

'The Bowl' is skilfully constructed so as to make the most of these well-worn materials, but at times it gives intimations of something far more subtle and original — a penetrating insight into the nature of achievement and popular success. One of the ironies of Dolly's football career is that his fluctuating status as a star player has little to do with his actual performances on the field. In his first game against Yale, he plays consistently well, and creates the opening that enables Princeton to win, but it is the man who makes the touchdown who becomes the hero of the newspaper headlines. In the second game two years later, he plays badly throughout, and scores the decisive point by a mere fluke, but nevertheless finds himself a national celebrity. Fitzgerald's narrator is led to reflect on the arbitrary quality of fame — the way in which popular success seems an accident of publicity

5   *The Last Tycoon* BH1, p. 426.

rather than a true reflection of events: 'all achievement was a placing of emphasis — a moulding of the confusion of life into form.'[6]

It is reasonable to think of 'The Bowl' as one of those pieces of 'best-selling entertainment' to which Fitzgerald referred in his letter to Joseph Mankiewicz. Its scope is limited since, however perfectly it functions on its own terms, it represents nothing more than a commercially proven formula brought to a high finish. But, as we have seen, it sometimes possesses a sharpness of insight and a precision of language which go far beyond anything that is strictly necessary for its commercial success. This is the point at which a work conceived in the first place as entertainment begins to approach the condition of art. 'The Bowl' does not quite pass through this invisible barrier, since Fitzgerald does not take its finer possibilities very far: in particular, it is marred by an absurdly sentimental ending, in which Dolly's shallow fiancée is replaced by a beautiful film star who appreciates his true worth. In this respect, the story resembles such forms of entertainment as the television police drama which, at the very moment when it seems about to say something interesting about crime or the nature of violence, retreats to the safer ground of some stock situation — an exciting car-chase or stylish gunfight. What differentiates good entertainment from art, in fact, is not that the former is necessarily trivial or meretricious, but that it deliberately refrains from following up the full implications of its material. For a professional writer who is also an artist, this is an irritating — often an agonizing — business, and it is easy to see why Fitzgerald, by the mid-1920s, had come to dislike writing short stories intensely. A less obvious, though far more important fact is that some of his finest tales — including 'The Last of the Belles', 'The Rough Crossing', 'Babylon Revisited', and 'Crazy Sunday' — emerged from the same unrewarding struggle. Furthermore, while such work may have given Fitzgerald himself little pleasure, it can often possess a unique kind of strength for the reader. The line which separates art from good entertainment is provisional, not absolute, a matter very frequently of degree, not of kind: 'people's own favourite folklore' may manifest itself as pure wish-fulfilment, but it may also represent those archetypal experiences which are the most powerful imaginative language of the human race.

Fitzgerald came to identify his professional worries not merely with the practical business of writing for the magazines, but with the form of the short story itself. This is particularly clear in a most interesting letter which he wrote to his literary agent Harold Ober during the summer of his crack-up: in the process of explaining why he cannot go on producing copy for the *Saturday Evening Post*, he defines the nature of his own conception of the short story as an art-form. It is the only occasion, as far as I know, on which he made a serious and considered statement to this effect.

> There is no use of me trying to rush things. Even in years like '24, '28, '29, '30, all devoted to short stories, I could not turn out more than 8-9 top-price stories a year.

6 'The Bowl' BH5, p. 374.

> It simply is impossible — all my stories are conceived like novels, require a special
> emotion, a special experience — so that my readers, if such there be, know that
> each time it'll be something new, not in form but in substance.[7]

It is impossible to imagine a more exacting view of the nature of the *genre*, or
one which involves a greater expenditure of resources in proportion to what
is actually created. As Fitzgerald points out, the strain of producing such
stories becomes absolutely intolerable when they have to be written on
demand and at regular intervals. His letter proves more conclusively than
any other single piece of evidence that his professional difficulties arose not
from approaching the short story cynically or irresponsibly, but from setting
himself standards of achievement he could not possibly realize.

Fitzgerald's views also had the effect of cutting him off from the two main
conventions of short fiction current at the time. They clearly ran counter to
the opinion of modernist writers and critics, who saw the short story, in the
main, as a sketch or episode in the manner of Chekhov or Joyce. Although
Fitzgerald wrote stories of this kind with considerable success after 1936, it
was not a method which really suited him, since it effectively prevented him
from making use of many of his most characteristic gifts. He found the more
traditional mode of the tightly plotted story equally uncongenial. He did not
have the facility for turning out the sort of machine-made product with
which O. Henry had set his mark on the American market; nor could he find
in this type of story the creative possibilities which Maupassant had
discovered and used. The carefully calculated, symmetrical plot of 'Boule de
Suif' is not a mere piece of engineering: in Maupassant's hands it is supple
and alive — a way of saying penetrating things about class and morality,
about greed, fear, lust and generosity.

Although Fitzgerald often attempted this kind of story, he was never successful with it, and eventually came to regard it as tiresome and artificial.
There is a sharp and witty paragraph in 'Afternoon of an Author' (1936), in
which he describes how the author of the title gets the idea for such a piece,
riding downtown on the bus:

> On the college football field men were working with rollers and a title occurred to
> him: 'Turf-keeper' or 'The Grass Grows', something about a man working on
> turf for years and bringing up his son to go to college and play football there. Then
> the son dying in youth and the man's going to work in the cemetery and putting
> turf over his son instead of under his feet. It would be the kind of piece that is often
> placed in anthologies, but not this sort of thing — it was sheer swollen antithesis
> as formalized as a popular magazine and easier to write. Many people, however,
> would consider it excellent because it was melancholy, had digging in it and was
> simple to understand.[8]

In this sense, Fitzgerald's best tales have no plots at all; and it is here that we
see the full significance of his claim that 'all my stories are conceived like

7 *As Ever, Scott Fitz-: Letters Between F. Scott Fitzgerald and his Literary Agent Harold Ober,
1919-1940*, edited by Matthew J. Bruccoli, London, 1973, p. 221.
8 'Afternoon of an Author', BH3, p. 377.

novels, require a special emotion, a special experience.' The structure of any one of these is a matter of subtle connections and transitions, something too complex to be discussed adequately through any notion of plot. They differ from *The Great Gatsby* and *Tender is the Night* only in scale, not in kind. The works of short fiction he is known to have admired most correspond very closely to this pattern: Edith Wharton's *Ethan Frome* and Conrad's 'Youth', which he discovered at the very beginning of his professional career; and James's 'Daisy Miller' and Mann's *Death in Venice*, which he read with enthusiasm in his later years. 'Daisy Miller', in particular, seems to me the perfect example of the mode of short fiction to which Fitzgerald, in his best moments, aspired. The living sequence of episodes which carries its heroine from her first charming appearance on the shores of Lake Geneva to her pathetic death in Rome is not a plot: it is a complex of emotions and observations; it is in the fullest sense the story of a life. Of all Fitzgerald's tales, it is 'The Rich Boy' which most completely realizes his exacting sense of the possibilities of the genre, but even in a good commercial story like 'The Bowl', we find the same density of texture, a similar multiplicity of characters and episodes, and an extended time scale. It is surely no accident that three of his finest short stories, 'May Day', 'Absolution' and 'One Trip Abroad', were fashioned out of material originally intended for inclusion in novels.[9]

Quite apart from their intrinsic merit, however, there is another reason for paying special attention to Fitzgerald's stories: it is only through them that we can gain a full sense of the shape of his career. His novels do not provide this, even though it was in the longer form that he did his finest work: *The Great Gatsby* and *Tender is the Night* stand almost a decade apart, like isolated monuments; *The Side of Paradise* and *The Beautiful and Damned* are merely apprentice fiction; *The Last Tycoon* only a brilliant fragment. But Fitzgerald wrote good short stories at every period of his working life, from 1920 to 1940. By this continual labour, he learned everything he knew about the writing of fiction: his two great novels represent the application of what he learned, not the process of learning. The pressure to keep up a constant flow of copy to the magazines forced him to experiment, to try out new ideas — both productive and unproductive. As a result, he came to understand the nature and limits of his own talent more precisely than any other American novelist of this century — to understand what his real strengths were, and also to recognize what he could not do and would be wise to avoid. This accounts very largely for the impression conveyed by his best work, of creative powers finely judged and confidently applied.

In 'Echoes of the Jazz Age' (1931), Fitzgerald names May Day, 1919, as the

---

9 'May Day' seems to have been adapted from the opening sections of a novel Fitzgerald began in 1920 and then abandoned (see Henry Dan Piper, *F. Scott Fitzgerald: a Critical Portrait*, pp. 69-70); 'Absolution' was the opening to the first version of *Gatsby*; 'One Trip Abroad' was put together from a discarded early version of *Tender is the Night*.

day on which the Jazz Age actually began, and in his story 'May Day' (1920), he attempts, with an extraordinarily sure instinct for the shape of things to come, to evoke the atmosphere of the postwar era. The story is made up of the interwoven actions and feelings of several groups of characters, in New York, between early morning on 1 May 1919, and early the following morning. The last of the returning soldiers from France still wander about the streets, but already a new hedonism, a new sense of irresponsibility, is beginning to assert itself. The spring weather, the glittering Fifth Avenue shops, the sense that money is being made and spent profusely, encourage people to grasp at immediate satisfactions. Gordon Sterrett, who has come to the Biltmore to borrow money from his rich friend Philip Dean, gazes enviously at the latter's piles of silk shirts and expensive woollen socks. Private Rose and Private Key peep out with incredulous delight, from their obscure hiding-place at Delmonico's, at the array of bottles in the bar. Edith Bradin breathes in with ecstasy the sensuous 'odour of a fashionable dance.' There seems no barrier, either, to the gratification of more sinister impulses. It is a day of public disorders and private violence: mobs beat up radical orators and wreck socialist offices; Gordon shoots himself in a cheap hotel room; and Edith, responding to the general hysteria, denounces Private Rose as the man who broke her brother's leg. The characters have the freedom to do what they like, but they have no way of knowing what the consequences of their actions will be. At one o'clock, in the middle of the dance, Edith suddenly decides that it would be fun to visit her brother, whose socialist newspaper office is only a few blocks away. This harmless fancy projects her in a few minutes from the rich and pampered atmosphere at Delmonico's to the horrors of the riot, where she is forced to witness her brother's injury and the death of Private Key.

Edith's adventure leads us directly to Fitzgerald's central perception about May Day, 1919, and the period which it inaugurated: that it was a time of social chaos. Nothing, it seemed, was more arbitrary than the distribution of happiness and misery. For the rich and fortunate, it was to be a wonderful decade: Philip Dean and Peter Himmel, as they drink champagne for breakfast, feel dimly that they are in at the beginning of 'a memorable party, something that they would remember always.' But for the weak and the failures, it was an age without compassion. Dean is exasperated by Gordon's request for a loan, and still more by his miserable demeanour. A single short conversation is enough to convince Edith that she must dismantle the structure of romantic feelings she has built around Gordon since before the War: 'Love is fragile — she was thinking — but perhaps the pieces are saved, the things that hovered on lips, that might have been said. The new love words, the tenderness learned, are treasured up for the next lover.'[10] Neither Edith nor Dean are especially callous — certainly not the former — nor is Gordon especially deserving of pity: what is significant

10   'May Day', BH5, p. 168.

is their disposition to turn quickly aside from anything that threatens to spoil the party.

'May Day' not only conveys the atmosphere of a historical moment with incomparable vividness: it is also a triumph of artistic form. In order to write it, Fitzgerald had to find a way of representing social chaos which would, nevertheless, avoid condemning his story to a similar formlessness. He began with a device common to much naturalistic fiction — that of taking a single day in the life of a city — but went on to discover a far more subtle and creative structural principle: that the rhythms of city life could be made to function as the rhythms of his story. The various groups of characters are drawn together and flung apart again as these rhythms exert their influence. During the daylight hours, they are mostly apart, occupying themselves with their own private concerns: Philip Dean shopping and gossipping; Gordon worrying about money; Edith at the hairdresser's; the soldiers searching hopefully for liquor and entertainment. Then, during the climactic pleasure-seeking hours between ten and one, they are all brought together in the dance at Delmonico's, which is for that night the city's great revel, and therefore a centre of magnetic attraction. In the secret time between one and four, they disperse again, and then reassemble at Child's, Fifty-ninth Street, to refresh their tired bodies and jaded nerves with coffee and scrambled eggs. By this time, however, Private Key is dead, and Edith too is absent, presumably looking after her brother. The process of disintegration continues through the dead hours of early morning: Gordon moves towards suicide; Edith returns, distraught and exhausted, to the Biltmore; Private Rose is arrested. Only Mr In and Mr Out manage to keep the party going.

One of Fitzgerald's greatest gifts as a social novelist is this sensitivity to the rise and fall of nervous energy by day and night, which produces the rhythms of social life. His success in 'May Day' depends not merely on moving his characters through the right places and activities at the right times, but on a deep understanding of moods and atmospheres. A long night's revel, in particular, develops a subtly shifting pattern of sensations — anticipation, excitement, fatigue and depression. In order to give this pattern its full value, he had to master many contrasting modes of social comedy: the frothy absurdity of Edith's conversation with her dancing partners; the slapstick adventures of the two soldiers; and the bacchanalian fantasy of Mr In and Mr Out. This comedy has, in turn, to be balanced against other elements — unhappiness, strain, hysteria and despair — before the full complexity of the story can emerge. This is the artistry which enabled Fitzgerald much later in his career, to evoke the atmosphere of Gatsby's parties and Dick Diver's Riviera days.

In 'Basil and Cleopatra' (1929), Fitzgerald speaks of his hero, Basil Duke Lee, in these terms: 'Like most Americans, he was seldom able really to grasp the moment, to say: "This, for me, is the great equation by which everything else will be measured; this is the golden time." [11] In Fitzgerald's view, Americans, characteristically, attach more importance to dreams than to grasped experiences: their inner lives may be rich and colourful, even when their outer circumstances are conventional, drab or sordid. Their youth is filled with dreams of an 'orgastic' future (the word he uses on the closing page of *Gatsby*). Later, they become victims of nostalgia, and their lost youth, which slipped by in mere anticipation, now seems to them the period when they truly lived. Finally, with middle age, comes disillusionment: the inner life of dreams loses its power, and they find themselves alone in the emptiness of a purely material universe. The whole pattern, foreshortened in time though not in emotional fullness, is explored in *Gatsby*, but aspects of it form the basis for many of Fitzgerald's stories, particularly in the 1920s. I should like to discuss three of the best of these in some detail: 'Absolution', which deals with the period of youth; 'The Last of the Belles', which examines the phase of nostalgia; and 'Three Hours Between Planes', which presents the terminal stage of disillusionment.

'Absolution' (1924) is a story about the origin of dreams. It has a Middle Western setting, though of a very different kind from those in 'Bernice Bobs her Hair' and 'The Ice Palace'. Its two principal characters, Rudolph Miller and Father Schwartz, are remote from the wealthy and comparatively sophisticated life of the country clubs and the big cities — they live in a lost Dakota prairie town. The habit of dreaming is born out of the circumstances of their lives. After the brief exciting drama of frontier life, the town stagnates in an atmosphere of perpetual anticlimax. Theoretically, this is still a land of opportunity, but in fact the inhabitants are condemned to lives of isolation, monotony and inaction. Only dreams can fill the vast vacant spaces of their boredom. The brutal violence of the Middle Western climate, and the meagre but garish sensations of prairie life, ensure that their dreams take on a sensuous if not a directly sexual character. Father Schwartz, in the long emptiness of summer afternoons, is tormented by the harsh blaze of the wheatfields and the laughter of yellow-haired Scandinavian girls; while in the evenings, he is assaulted by the bright lights and cheap perfumes of the drugstore.

By giving Father Schwartz's dreams a social, indeed a historical origin, Fitzgerald overcomes one of the main difficulties inherent in his theme. A story which deals with a man's hidden imaginative life is capable almost of vanishing through the sheer tenuousness and vagueness of its material. This had already happened in the case of a slightly earlier piece, 'Winter Dreams' (1922), where the hero has no tangible human existence at all. Such a story needs ballast in the form of precise social observation and intense poetic images. These elements, which are clear enough in Fitzgerald's portrayal of Father Schwartz, are still more apparent in his treatment of Rudolph Miller.

11 'Basil and Cleopatra', *Afternoon of an Author*, edited by Arthur Mizener, London, 1958, p. 82.

Rudolph's dreams are given an added dimension by the fact that he is eleven years old and on the brink of adolescence. He has been avoiding confession for a month because he is ashamed to tell Father Schwartz about his 'impure thoughts'; and yet these thoughts have become the most exciting part of his imaginative life. He manages to convey the external facts to the priest — how he lingered to eavesdrop on a pair of lovers in a barn — but he cannot tell him 'how his pulse had bumped in his wrist, how a strange, romantic excitement had possessed him when those curious things had been said.' Adolescence, as Fitzgerald sees it, intensifies and complicates a child's imaginative life, driving his thoughts inwards as he attempts to make sense of the turmoil of his feelings. Rudolph is torn between new, half-understood, romantic emotions and old idealisms. For a moment he relives the incident in the barn with intense vividness, but immediately rejects it, and tries to fix his mind on thoughts more suitable to the confessional. In this state of confusion, he is taken off balance by the priest's next question, and claims virtuously that he never tells lies. By the time he realizes his error, it is too late to retract: he has told a lie in confession and is in danger of making a sacrilegious communion at mass the following day. He devises an ingenious plan to avoid this latter contingency, but it fails. The supernatural world, symbolized in the ritual of the Church, has not yet lost its terrors for him, and he is convinced that God will strike him dead at the very moment when the priest places the host in his mouth.

But when he goes to Father Schwartz the same afternoon, to ask for absolution from his mortal sin, his feelings are unexpectedly placed in a new light; and, by the end of the interview, he is led to believe that 'there was something ineffably gorgeous somewhere that had nothing to do with God.' Father Schwartz's behaviour is disconcerting to say the least. Having dismissed Rudolph's spiritual problems with a comically brusque scrap of pastoral theology, he begins to talk about that other forbidden world which so fascinates them both. The lonely, half-crazy, old man struggles incoherently to put into words thoughts he has never dared to acknowledge before. He speaks of people for whom things 'go glimmering', and of a great light in Paris bigger than a star; but it is in the Middle West itself that he eventually finds the image he is groping for:

> 'Did you ever see an amusement park? ... It's a thing like a fair, only much more glittering. Go to one at night and stand a little way off from it in a dark place — under dark trees. You'll see a big wheel made of lights turning in the air, and a long slide shooting boats down into the water. A band playing somewhere, and a smell of peanuts — and everything will twinkle. But it won't remind you of anything, you see. It will all just hang out there in the night like a coloured balloon — like a big yellow lantern on a pole.'[12]

I have already discussed the importance of the fairground as an image of American civilization in an earlier chapter. In 'Absolution', this image is the

---

12 'Absolution', BH5, pp. 278—9.

poetic and dramatic climax of the story: it draws Rudolph and Father Schwartz together in a new secret community of feeling; and it turns their dreams into something more than mere personal fantasies — into expressions of the American consciousness. For Rudolph in particular, it becomes a symbol of the future, hovering before him, leading him away from old allegiances towards the lure of a more expansive life.

'Absolution', a fairly early story, deals , appropriately, with the origin of dreams, but, by the late 1920s, Fitzgerald was becoming more interested in nostalgia as a fictional subject. Of the group of stories which reflect this concern, 'The Last of the Belles' (1929) is very much the best. Superficially, it seems a mere reworking of some of his most familiar romantic properties — the War, the wayward aristocractic Southern girl, and the Northern suitor whom she rejects. In fact, however, he brings a more complex attitude, and a greater subtlety of narrative method to these materials than anywhere else except in *Gatsby*.

The design of 'The Last of the Belles' is like a woven fabric, with threads which go this way and that. The long threads of the warp are provided by its extended development in time. It tells the story of a beautiful Southern girl, Ailie Calhoun — how she is gradually transformed from a Southern belle of the old-fashioned type into a flapper of the later Jazz Age. At the same time, it conveys a sense of the more general changes in American manners which have formed the background to her career. More important still, it is the history of one man's dreams, of the narrator's growing nostalgia for the lost romance of his youth. The cross threads of the woof are woven into the story by the action of the narrator's own voice — his ironic and yet absorbed commentary upon all the changing elements of the situation.

He first meets Ailie at the beginning of the War, when he is posted to an army camp near the town where she lives. Prewar conventions have not yet begun to crumble, and she seems to him to represent 'the Southern type in all its purity':

> She had the adroitness sugar-coated with sweet, voluble simplicity, the suggested background of devoted fathers, brothers and admirers stretching back to the South's heroic age, the unfailing coolness acquired in the endless struggle with the heat. There were notes in her voice that ordered slaves around, that withered up Yankee captains, and then soft, wheedling notes that mingled in unfamiliar loveliness with the night.[13]

She is vain, selfish and callous: when Canby, a young flying officer whose love she has rejected, crashes his plane, she sees the event mainly as an exciting tribute to herself. On the other hand, she has a degree of physical beauty and aristocratic style which makes her irresistibly attractive even to those who are fully conscious of her faults.

Her firm sense of her position, her power and her aims (reflected in the care with which she chooses her beaux) implies a great social stability. As the

13   'The Last of the Belles', BH5, p. 472.

War proceeds, however, she begins to lose this inner certainty: the new conditions have produced a mixing of the classes in which she is no longer sure of her bearings. This is apparent in her affair with Earl Schoen. She is deeply attracted by his physical strength and grace, but she finds it impossible to place him socially. She laughingly complains that he behaves like a street-car conductor, but the uniform he wears makes him an officer and gentleman — even an admissible suitor perhaps. After the War, when she sees him in civilian clothes, she is able to place him all too well, and her inherited attitudes reassert themselves. But, by now, these standards have little meaning, and when the narrator visits Ailie six years later, he finds that she has become a creature of the Jazz Age, rivalling the younger set in her reckless, febrile gaiety. The South, too, has changed: it has lost its traditional courtesy and charm; and the manners of the dancers have become rougher and cruder. In this social chaos, Ailie is even more confused than she was during the War; and the marriage she is contemplating is, even by her own account, a desperate stab in the dark.

Towards the end of the 'The Last of the Belles', it becomes clear that Ailie's story has not been told simply in sequential narrative: rather, it has crystallized slowly in the narrator's mind, and the actual process of remembering has been quite as important as the events remembered. The narrator recalls how, when he first went to the South, he still believed in the romance of youth and war. In both he was disappointed — he did not find love, and he was never sent on combat duty overseas — and yet, with the passage of time, the South and Ailie herself have come to seem the most significant elements in his experience of life. He is brought back, long after the War, by the force of his nostalgia, in the delusory hope of recapturing the essence of feelings he merely imagines he once had. When he revisits the camp, which now holds so many memories for him, he finds that it has vanished beneath cottonfields and underbrush: none of the old landmarks remain, and he stumbles about, 'looking for my youth in a clapboard or a strip of roofing or a rusty tomato can.' He discovers, too, that the Ailie he meets is not the Ailie he remembers: even so, he proposes to her halfheartedly, but she, not surprisingly, turns him down.

The narrator is saved from sentimental fatuity by his ironic self-awareness: he sees clearly that, in his infatuation with Ailie, genuine romance and tawdry illusion are inextricably mingled. Nevertheless, he achieves a fine balance in his feelings towards her: he is prepared to love her in spite of her defects — indeed, he realizes that he finds her defects an integral part of her charm. He regards with amused regret the very quirk of character which leads her to reject him. Throughout their acquaintance, he is puzzled by her insistence that her admirers should be 'sincere': it intrigues him that she should value a quality which she herself so evidently lacks, but at last he grasps what she means. In spite of her air of being an 'instinctive thoroughbred', she too has an accurate sense of her own deficiencies, and cannot believe that any man who sees them can really love her. This is why she only feels safe with men like Canby and Earl Schoen, who are 'incapable of passing judgements on the ostensibly aristocratic heart.' The complexity of attitude which makes the narrator interesting to us, is the very trait which renders him forever untrustworthy to her.

Fitzgerald returned interestingly to these themes in a very late story, 'Three Hours Between Planes' (posthumously published in 1941). It deals with that moment in a man's life when he loses his dreams, when he is forced to pass from nostalgia into disillusionment. Donald Plant, finding that he has to break his journey in a Middle Western city where he once lived, decides on impulse to visit a childhood sweetheart he hasn't seen for twenty years. At first their reunion is a great success — indeed they seem about to fall in love all over again. But, as they exchange reminiscences, they are slightly disconcerted to find that they always disagree about what actually happened. Nancy unearths an old photograph album in order to prove to Donald that they were both present on an occasion he cannot recall. Then the truth suddenly emerges: the great emotion they think they have recaptured is an absurd illusion resting on a grotesque confusion of identity. Because of a chance similarity of names, Nancy has imagined for a moment that Donald is somebody else. In reality, she had always detested him when they were children, and now, as all her old feelings return, she shows him the door with an icy expression of dislike and contempt. The story concludes with a touch of the bleak wisdom that enters Fitzgerald's work only after his crack-up. As Donald's plane carries him away from this ludicrous and painful adventure, he reflects on the folly of trying to recapture the past, and the futility of retaining illusions which an ageing man must learn to do without.

Between 1920 and 1924, Fitzgerald lived almost continuously in New York or within commuting distance of it, and during this period the nature of his understanding of city life changed profoundly: in 'May Day' he had shown the insight of the brilliant outsider, but by the time he wrote 'The Rich Boy' in 1926, he possessed the deepened awareness of the settled resident. None of the characters in the earlier story actually belong to New York, and they experience only those sensations which are accessible to the casual visitor or the tourist. But Anson Hunter, the hero of 'The Rich Boy', is an entrenched member of the city's upper class, and his life is an expression of its underlying structure, not its glittering surface. There are many elements in the complex fabric of his existence: the wealthy and conservative family background; the fashionable weddings and unobtrusive, aloof dinner parties; the impeccable and prosperous Wall Street investment firm; the Yale Club and the Fifth Avenue Episcopalian church; the love affairs with girls of his own class, and the discreetly managed adventures in the Broadway *demi-monde* of chorus girls and prostitutes.

This is still substantially the world of *The House of Mirth* and *The Custom of the Country*: Anson Hunter, just like the Trenors, Dorsets and Van

Degens of Edith Wharton's novels, owes his wealth, position and manners to the Gilded Age. Fitzgerald's narrative style, too, is remarkably close to Mrs Wharton's — indeed this seems to me a case where one can reasonably speak of a direct influence upon his work. As a rule, the most distinctive quality in his writing is the constant delicate play of atmospheric and poetic suggestion, but what impresses one particularly in 'The Rich Boy' is the sustained pressure of a fine moral intelligence. The tone is dispassionate, sober, analytical; it does not rise to high points of climactic intensity or wit, and so, unlike most of Fitzgerald's writing, it is not especially quotable. Nevertheless, it is possible to suggest some of its power even in a comparatively short passage:

> He [Anson Hunter] was twenty-seven now, a little heavy without being definitely stout, and with a manner older than his years. Old people and young people liked him and trusted him, and mothers felt safe when their daughters were in his charge, for he had a way, when he came into a room, of putting himself on a footing with the oldest and most conservative people there. 'You and I', he seemed to say, 'we're solid. We understand.'
> He had an instinctive and rather charitable knowledge of the weaknesses of men and women, and, like a priest, it made him the more concerned for the maintenance of outward forms. It was typical of him that every Sunday morning he taught in a fashionable Episcopal Sunday school — even though a cold shower and a quick change into a cut-away coat were all that separated him from the wild night before.[14]

Fitzgerald maintains this tone, with its carefully judged inflections of irony and sympathetic insight, throughout the story — a degree of artistic control which is unique in his short fiction.

The character of Anson Hunter is Fitzgerald's one unquestioned success in portraying the sophisticated Eastern rich. As a possible American aristocrat, Anson is a failure, but his inadequacies lurk beneath the surface of an apparently flawless good form. In this respect, it is interesting to contrast him with rich Middle Westerners like Tom Buchanan and Baby Warren: he could never be guilty of their crude and frequent lapses — Tom's outbreaks of uncouth violence, Baby's rudeness and her tantrums. Even his coarseness is of a subtler kind than Tom's. Tom's affair with Myrtle Wilson is merely sordid — it represents the breakdown of a style. Anson's gentlemanly dissipations, on the other hand — the ritualized college drunkenness he keeps up with his Yale Club friends, and his adventures with 'the gallant chorus girls' — are the expression of a style; he knows how to choose women of a certain class for a party, how much to spend on them, and how to get rid of them.

The essence of his failure lies still deeper, however, in that complex area where the psychology of an individual and the manners of a class become alternative expressions of the same situation. Fitzgerald believed that people

14 'The Rich Boy', BH5, p. 300.

who possess enormous wealth, particularly wealth acquired in an earlier generation, constitute a distinct psychological and moral type:

> Let me tell you about the very rich. They are different from you and me. They possess and enjoy early, and it does something to them, makes them soft where we are hard, and cynical where we are trustful. ... They think, deep in their hearts, that they are better than we are because we had to discover the compensations and refuges of life for ourselves.[15]

This inbred sense of superiority does not make Anson in any simple sense arrogant or snobbish: it is, rather, the basis of his cynicism and his indifference. Life has given him so much already, that he cannot believe that any of the remaining prizes are worth a serious effort. As a boy, he would not compete or struggle with his fellows: if they did not concede the precedence which was his due, he retreated into his family, whose huge house, immense wealth and assured social position gave him a sense of impregnable solidity.

This trait of character does not show its full effects until he falls in love with Paula Legendre. She returns his love, and nothing stands in the way of their marriage except his fatal sense of superiority, his unwillingness to exert himself even for her. It distresses her that he gets drunk and passes out when he is supposed to be escorting her to a formal dinner party: he apologizes handsomely the next day, but he does not see that, if he wants her, he will have to take her susceptibilities into account. More seriously, his habitual attitude makes him insensitive to the deeper emotional and sexual rhythms of her nature. When they meet again in Florida after the War, she is still desperately in love with him, but his egotism blinds him to the fact that he must respond to this high point in her emotions or risk losing her for good.

Only a direct challenge to his sense of pre-eminence has the power to stimulate him into energetic action, and when this happens, extremely unattractive sides of his character are revealed. Some time after Paula's marriage to another man, he becomes involved in a flirtation with Dolly Karger, a girl whom he despises both for her lightness of character and because of her family's recent emergence from obscurity. He soon becomes tired of her, and is about to end the affair, when she attempts by an ineffectual manoeuvre to force him to commit himself. His attitude suddenly changes: she has presumed to take the lead in their relationship, and so he feels he owes it to himself to teach her a lesson. He leads her to the point where she agrees to go to bed with him, and then, having established his dominance, throws her over. He behaves with equal brutality when he forces his Aunt Edna, whose infidelities have begun to threaten the family name, to give up her lover.

As the postwar decade proceeds, however, Anson finds himself increasingly alone with his own sense of superiority, and his story broadens into a further chapter in Fitzgerald's history of the Jazz Age. His class, the

15 *Ibid.*, p. 286.

pseudo-aristocracy of the Gilded Age, are being rapidly engulfed in the on-ward rush of new conditions. When his father dies, Anson is disconcerted to find that the family isn't even particularly rich by current standards; and he is dismayed when his younger sisters insist on selling up the baronial country estate in Connecticut, which they regard as an irrelevance and a bore. His Yale Club cronies get married and disappear one by one, either to live abroad, or to settle into the new and unassuming sytle of domesticity which, even for the rich, has replaced the portentous splendours to which Anson is accustomed. One hot Saturday afternoon in New York, he finds himself a stranger and alone, in the city which once belonged, by dynastic right, to the Hunters and a handful of other leading families. As he gazes up at the windows of one of his clubs, he catches sight of a solitary old man, staring vacantly into the street. It is a portent of the future, an image of the isolation and neglect which await a man whose habits of thought and feeling no longer have any relation to the society he lives in.

But, although Anson's feelings of superiority are not supported by any external social reality, they are still psychologically necessary to him. At the end of the story, he leaves New York, the city which has forgotten him and his family, for a vacation in Europe. As soon as he boards the liner, he begins a flirtation with the most attractive girl on the ship, and it becomes clear that the admiration of women is his one remaining resource; only by making them respond to him and love him can he sustain a little of his accustomed sense of himself.

Anson Hunter's life in New York ends with his departure for Europe. Countless well-to-do Americans were to make the same journey by the end of the 1920s, as Paris and the Riviera, rather than New York, became the setting for the most extravagant manifestations of the Jazz Age. In Fitz-gerald's fiction, this shift is reflected not only in *Tender is the Night*, but in an important group of short stories. They are international stories, though not of the kind one usually associates with that term in American literature, and, in order to define their unique character, it is necessary to say a little about Fitzgerald's contacts with Europe.

From 1924 until the early 1930s, he lived abroad for long periods, but by comparison with other distinguished American expatriates — Henry James, Edith Wharton, Ezra Pound, T. S. Eliot and Ernest Hemingway — it is apparent that Europe itself mattered little to him. He summed up his first visit in 1921 in the phrase, 'God damn the continent of Europe'[16], and his subsequent expressions of opinion, while less explosive, were scarcely more appreciative. He did not see Europe as a distinctive culture to which he carried his American consciousness as something separate and foreign. Unlike Henry James's Lambert Strether or Isabel Archer, the characters in his stories are rarely exposed to the delights and pitfalls of life in an

16   *Letters*, p. 326.

unfamiliar civilization. Fitzgerald's European experience was merely an extension of his American experience, just as Paris and the Riviera were extensions of New York. In France, prices were lower, the climate was more agreeable, and there was a welcome freedom from Prohibition, but beyond this his sense of difference does not seem to function very clearly. On both sides of the Atlantic, his drinking habits were the same, and he went to similar parties with similar — often the same — people. He met no Europeans socially, and he spent his time in places where Americans clustered together. He gives an amusing sketch of his prejudices in 'How to Live on Practically Nothing a Year' (1924), but this essay as a whole is an unwitting record of how little he got out of Europe.

As a result, the characters in his international stories are not so much Americans in Europe as Americans overseas. But, although he does not concern himself with European manners, his observation of his fellow-countrymen is as acute as ever. His own experience showed him that it was possible to realize a unique kind of happiness and freedom in the new setting. He believed, for a time at any rate, that his friends Gerald and Sara Murphy had achieved a perfectly harmonious existence in their beautiful villa at Antibes: their wealth, their taste, their charm, and the ritual of their social life seemed to him an embodiment of the aristocratic ideal he had always cherished in imagination. Some of the aura of the Murphys' success found its way into *Tender is the Night*, but in the short stories Fitzgerald was much more aware of the destructive aspects of expatriate experience. He drew a savage portrait of 'the cosmopolitan rich' years afterwards, in a letter to his daughter:

> I have seen the whole racket, and if there is any more disastrous road than that from Park Avenue to the Rue de la Paix and back again, I don't know it.
>   They are homeless people, ashamed of being American, unable to master the culture of another country; ashamed, usually, of their husbands, wives, grandparents, and unable to bring up descendants of whom they could be proud, even if they had the nerve to bear them, ashamed of each other yet leaning on each other's weakness, a menace to the social order in which they live ....[17]

These are the people, in the main, who inhabit the fictional world of Fitzgerald's international stories.

For almost all of them, the dubious adventure of life overseas begins with a departure by ocean liner from New York, and Fitzgerald's first important expatriate story, 'The Rough Crossing' (1929), opens with a magnificent evocation of a night sailing from one of the Hudson River piers: 'The past, the continent is behind you; the future is that glowing mouth in the side of the ship; this dim turbulent alley is too confusedly the present.'[18] An uncertain destiny, both exciting and menacing, awaits the travellers, and it soon becomes clear that Fitzgerald is presenting the ship as a microcosm of

17   *Ibid.*, p. 102.
18   'The Rough Crossing' BH5, p. 426.

the Jazz Age. The passengers are a particularly pure sample of the cosmopolitan rich: for a whole week they are cut off from all other influences,
whether European or American; and as the voyage proceeds, the characteristic elements in their way of life are concentrated and intensified. Even
people who are unlike them to begin with, find it difficult to withstand their
influence. Adrian and Eva Smith, the attractive, successful and happily
married couple who are the story's main characters, believe that they can
enjoy the expatriate adventure on their own terms. They decide to share
everything, and to isolate themselves as far as possible from their fellow-pas-
sengers, but the pressures of shipboard life (and, by implication, those of the
Jazz Age) are soon too much for them. Their rather old-fashioned good
manners and reserve are no protection against the indiscriminate social
mixing, and they are rapidly drawn into a non-stop drunken party. In this
atmosphere, they forget all their resolutions, and their apparently stable
relationship begins to break down: Adrian becomes infatuated with the
beautiful Betsy D'Amido, and Eva, only partly out of revenge, encourages
the attentions of a fatuous young man called Butterworth. Their activities
are given an especially feverish quality by the knowledge that, on the fourth
day out of New York, they are due to sail into a hurricane. Like the *Titanic* a
generation earlier, Fitzgerald's ship becomes an image of an arrogant and
doomed civilization.

The gala dinner, the traditional festive climax to a transatlantic voyage,
takes place as the liner moves into the zone of the storm. Almost everyone is
prostrated by seasickness, but a few drunken survivors, including Adrian,
gather in the dining room: sardonically overhung by lanterns and streamers,
they attempt to eat and drink, while the ship groans and plunges, wine is
spilled and crockery hurled this way and that. Afterwards they even try to
dance, 'shuffling and galloping here and there in a crazy fandango.' The
disorder caused by the storm is barely distinguishable from the chaos of their
lives. When Adrian returns to his cabin, Eva is missing: he eventually finds
her wandering about the boat deck in a state of distraction and hysteria, and
they are almost swept overboard before he manages to take her below. After
the shock of this near disaster, they are reconciled, and in the boat-train
speeding towards Paris, they are inclined to look back on the voyage as a
mere nightmare — something that never really happened. But for the
reader, their marriage now seems a somewhat precarious affair, and their
renewed determination that, in Paris, they will see no one, and live only for
each other, has a hollow ring.

The situation of a marriage in danger provides the main dramatic interest
in 'The Rough Crossing', and impaired or broken marriages are an
important element in all of Fitzgerald's best international stories. 'One Trip
Abroad' (1930) traces the gradual deterioration of Nelson and Nicole
Kelly's relationship during a period of four years' travel overseas. Fitzgerald
put the story together from a discarded early version of *Tender is the Night*,
and in both works, his sense of place is always made to serve a dramatic

purpose or to strengthen his moral and social analysis — he is never merely picturesque or anecdotal. The distinctive atmosphere of each new place the Kellys visit is used to mark a significant stage in their decline. They first appear in the romantic and exotic setting of North Africa at a point when the experience of travel is still as fresh and new as their marriage. By the time they reach Sorrento, however, they are already a little bored and discontented: they feel in need of occupation, and begin to dabble in the arts — Nelson paints a little, and Nicole takes singing lessons. But they cannot escape the dreariness of hotel life in a winter resort, and one evening a casual impulse of Nelson's projects them into an absurd but ugly dispute with the mouldering English residents who regard the place as their own. Feeling that they are not, after all, everything to each other — that they need other people to amuse them — they drift to Monte Carlo and Paris. Here they are drawn into a rowdy and dissipated expatriate life, in which drunkenness, quarrels, infidelities and violence become part of the texture of their everyday existence. Finally they drag themselves to a Swiss health resort, where they lie inertly with other wreckage from the Jazz Age adventure overseas: they have reached the terminal stage of their trip abroad.

As in all Fitzgerald's best short stories, the form of 'One Trip Abroad' is a particularly felicitous expression of the underlying structural necessities of its subject. Its episodes succeed each other like a series of moral tableaux — a kind of Jazz Age *Rake's Progress* — and within the broad canvas of each picture, there are striking vignettes, the excellent satirical sketches of minor expatriate types. Count Chiki Sarolai, the exiled Austrian nobleman who sponges on rich Americans in Paris, is a well observed case of the aristocratic confidence man. Better still are Mr and Mrs Liddell Miles, a pair of professional cosmopolitans, who turn even their ignorance and boredom into a pretext for feeling superior to their fellow travellers.

The expatriate life portrayed in 'The Rough Crossing' and 'One Trip Abroad' came to an end with singular abruptness: within a year of the Wall Street Crash of 1929, the swarms of Americans with their millions of dollars had vanished from the European scene. The opening pages of 'Babylon Revisited' (1931) are an evocation of the silence and emptiness in the Ritz bar, which had been filled only a year or so earlier with a shouting drunken crowd. When Charlie Wales asks the barman for news of old friends, the latter responds with a litany of ghosts — the names of men who have lost their health, their reason or their money. Later that same evening, he wanders through the city like a man in a state of shock, recognizing everything he sees and yet not feeling a part of it. He looks in at a Montmartre night club which had been one of his favourite haunts back in the 1920s. It is as quiet as the grave, but at his appearance, it explodes into a grotesque semblance of gaiety: the band starts to play; a couple of employees masquerading as patrons leap to their feet and begin to dance; and the manager rushes up to assure him that the evening crowd is about to arrive. In this macabre image of the unfamiliarity of the familiar, Fitzgerald conveys the first shock of the Depression more effectively than any other American writer.

Charlie has not come to Paris, however, to renew old associations, but to regain custody of his nine-year-old daughter Honoria. Like the friends for whom he enquires at the Ritz bar, he lost his money in the Crash, and destroyed his health and his marriage in the final madness of the Boom. His wife died after a period of dissipation and bitter estrangement, and the care of their child passed to the dead woman's sister Marion. But now Charlie believes he has recovered sufficiently to look after Honoria himself: he has learnt to control his drinking and is physically fit once more; and he is working and making enough money to support them comfortably. He knows it will be difficult to persuade Marion — a vindictive and envious woman — to let the child go, but he is confident that if he accepts her recriminations patiently and convinces her of his newly acquired steadiness of character, he will ultimately be successful. Fitzgerald describes with tenderness and delicacy the scenes in which Charlie tentatively re-establishes contact with Honoria — buying her toys and taking her to the circus, creating once again an atmosphere of love between them. Even Marion grudgingly admits that Charlie has earned his right to his child, and he is about to take her away, when he is unexpectedly thwarted by two unwelcome survivors from his past. Duncan Shaeffer, an old drinking companion, and Lorraine Quarles a faded blonde with whom he had flirted in former days, turn up drunk at a crucial stage in his negotiations with Marion. She decides that he is not, after all, a reformed character, and withdraws her consent; and Charlie, with bitter chagrin, realizes that he has lost Honoria just when he thought he was sure of her.

In many ways, as this account indicates, 'Babylon Revisited' is a simple story, and its strength lies in its simplicity. Like a lyric poem or a folksong, it deals directly with deep and powerful emotions: a father's love for his daughter, the ugliness of family quarrels, the disturbing way in which ghosts may return from a seemingly buried past. In one important respect, however, the story is extremely subtle — in its treatment of the psychology of disaster and the nature of recovery. For Charlie, the suddenness of the Depression has produced a sense of dislocation, a feeling that he is living in two worlds at once: he is committed to the idea of recovery and to the new way of life he has painstakingly created, but he still clings half-consciously to many of the mental habits which he formed during the Boom. It is this division in his mind which accounts for his odd inconsistencies of behaviour: in the Ritz bar he makes a parade of his new drinking habits, and yet he takes a taxi through the *quartier de l'Opéra* in order to recapture the atmosphere of festive Paris evenings. He catches himself telling Marion of all people how wonderful it was to be a rich American in Paris in the days before the Crash; and even the inopportune arrival of Duncan and Lorraine at her apartment is not entirely accidental. He does not really want to meet them under any circumstances, and as soon as he sees them he knows they represent everything he is trying to forget, and yet, in obedience to old habit, he left Marion's address with the Ritz barman so that they could get in touch with him. As he reflects on these trifling but fatal mistakes, he is forced to realize that recovery is not as simple a matter as he had thought: it is one thing to get back his health and his money; it is quite another to regain wholeness of being. Charlie's personal experience is a distillation of the social history of the age: during the period of economic chaos which followed the stock market collapse, President Hoover became notorious for his facile promise that recovery was 'just around the corner'; but Fitzgerald understood, with his usual fine instinct for the spirit of the age, that the Depression was going to last a long time.

Fitzgerald sometimes returns in a very late story to a theme more characteristic of an earlier period in his work ('Three Hours Between Planes' is a case we have considered already); and 'News of Paris — Fifteen Years Ago', a piece he left unfinished at his death, may be regarded as a sort of postscript to the international stories of 1929-31. It is a reminiscence of expatriate life marked by that clarity and detachment of vision which come only with the passage of time. (From this point of view though not in most other ways, it resembles the sketches in Hemingway's *A Moveable Feast*.) Fitzgerald uses the perspective of time to create a sense of diminishment: there is no hint of the 'touch of disaster' which is so important an element in stories like 'Babylon Revisited'; his Americans in Paris now seem to him mere ridiculous marionettes in a comedy of intrigue. The main character in the story is Henry Haven Dell, a self-regarding lady-killer whose adventures have the formalized absurdity of situations in comic opera or bedroom farce. He says a last goodbye to his mistress as they walk together to a fashionable wedding; flirts with the bride who is an old flame of his; engages in some elegantly casual love-making with a guest at the reception — an affair which begins in a taxi before lunch, and ends in an art gallery before tea; and finally visits his ward, a French war orphan who, he piously hopes, will not finish by marrying some dissipated American. 'News of Paris — Fifteen Years Ago' is not only very funny in itself, but makes a penetrating comment on the quality of expatriate life: as Fitzgerald's romantic involvement lessens with the passage of time, he is able, like a classical moralist, to uncover the element of fatuity latent in all vice.

Most of the stories I have discussed so far deal with members of the leisure class, but during the 1930s Fitzgerald became increasingly concerned with people whose lives must be measured in terms of professional dedication or creative achievement. This is apparent in his novels — Dick Diver is a doctor and Monroe Stahr a film producer — and is also reflected in some of his stories. In these, the main characters are usually artists or entertainers, and the principal theme often arises from Fitzgerald's sense of the dual nature of the artist — a topic with which we are already familiar. This line of development coincides with a significant shift of emphasis in his attitude to the creative imagination. From one point of view, this faculty may be regarded as a common possession — Rudolph Miller and the narrator of 'The Last of the Belles' are representative, not exceptional, in their capacity to experience dream and nostalgia — but from another, it is a special gift. In the artist, imagination is heightened and concentrated so that it becomes a uniquely dynamic and creative force, and it is this latter aspect which interests Fitzgerald in his later fiction.

'Crazy Sunday' (1932) is a bold and successful attempt to bring all these concerns together within the limits of a single story. The action takes place in Hollywood, a setting which enables Fitzgerald to present the artist-entertainer both as as hardworking professional and as a Promethean figure creating images for a whole civilization. These alternative possibilities are linked through the agency of Joel Coles, a young script-writer who is trying to find his feet in the film industry. He himself is not the main character in the story, however: he merely acts as the *ficelle* by which we are led to a better understanding of Miles Calman, the director for whom he works. Nevertheless, Joel is at the centre of the first episode, a Sunday afternoon cocktail party given by the Calmans. Fitzgerald uses this scene to bring out the nature of a professional community: for the members of such a group, social life becomes, very largely, an expression of their feelings of solidarity and exclusiveness. Joel has not been invited to an important Hollywood party before, and he feels that his presence at the Calmans' house signifies formal admission to the film community. Warmed by a few drinks, he decides incautiously that he would like to entertain them, to draw them together around him, and, incidentally, to show off for Miles's wife Stella with whom he is beginning to fall in love. He does an impersonation of a gross and philistine producer developing a story idea, but his act is a disastrous flop. Nobody laughs, and, at the end, the Great Lover of the screen shouts 'Boo, boo!', voicing openly what the silence of the others implies: 'the resentment of the professional towards the amateur, of the community towards the stranger, the thumbs-down of the clan.'[19] Joel is brought up sharply against the fact that the sense of professional solidarity is not a blurred and sentimental feeling of togetherness, but an expression of mutual respect. He is at the party because the community has begun to respect his work as a script-writer, work it cannot do without; but for him to presume to entertain the best actors, comedians and singers in the industry is implicitly to treat their work with contempt.

Next day, Joel tries to retrieve the effects of his blunder through an approach to Stella, but from this point onwards, his private anxieties drop into the background. He becomes merely the point of view from which Stella is observed, and she in turn is important only as a way of suggesting the scale of Miles Calman's genius. She has just discovered that Miles is

19 'Crazy Sunday', BH6, p. 299.

having an affair with her best friend, and under the strain of this situation, the extent of her dependence upon him is made fully apparent. It is not simply the normal emotional reliance of a wife upon her husband: she is Miles's creation, and their marriage is a re-enactment of the Pygmalion myth. The sequence of events is the same in both cases. Pygmalion has a vision of beauty which first finds expression in a work of art — the ivory statue of a woman; then, with the aid of Aphrodite, he brings her to life and becomes her husband.

Similarly Miles begins by making Stella into a film star, and then, falling in love with his own creation, makes her a woman too, and marries her. As Joel reflects at the end of the story, 'Everything he touched he did something magical to...he even brought this little gamine alive and made her a sort of masterpiece.'[20] Miles has breathed qualities into Stella which she herself does not possess; he has given her a new identity which she cannot sustain without his support; and so, when their marriage begins to break up, she feels that she is losing not merely her husband but herself.

The full nature of her predicament, however, only becomes clear in the events surrounding Miles's death. A week after their first quarrel, he flies east to see a football game, knowing that she and Joel may become lovers while he is away. He is still jealously posessive in his attitude to Stella, and during his absence he bombards her with telegrams in order to keep himself constantly in her thoughts. She has no intention of betraying him, however, since she still hopes to get him back. Joel is about to leave her for the night, when a final telegram arrives telling her that Miles has been killed in a plane crash. Suddenly her behaviour towards Joel changes: instead of keeping him at a distance, she begs him to stay the night, to make love to her. At first he is bewildered and appalled, but gradually he begins to realize what is going on in Stellas's mind. Ever since her marriage, her existence, both as woman and actress, has consisted entirely of roles devised for her by Miles: for this weekend, he had cast her as the unfaithful wife, and she now believes that if she plays out this part to its conclusion, she will be deferring the full realization of his death: 'In her dark groping Stella was trying to keep Miles alive by sustaining a situation in which he had figured — as if Miles's mind could not die so long as the possibilities that had worried him still existed.'[21] That Miles should have elicited this extraordinary last performance from her is a final tribute to his creative genius.

In *The Last Tycoon*, Fitzgerald portrays the public face of Hollywood, its cultural and historical significance and its economic power, but in 'Crazy Sunday', he explores its inner psychology. From this point of view, Miles Calman's relationship with Stella resembles a domestic tragedy at a Renaissance court. *Othello* is a tale of love and jealousy, and yet it is filled with echoes of statecraft and war; in the same way Miles's story conveys

20   *Ibid.*, p. 313.
21   *Ibid.*, p. 312.

obliquely a sense of the subtler mechanisms of the film industry.

Fitzgerald's best stories between 1920 and 1932 convey an overall impression of consistency rather than change. There are shifts of emphasis in his choice of subject matter, but few fundamental departures from the concerns already apparent in 'May Day' and 'Absolution'. From this point of view, his international stories are not so much an innovation as a variation within the pattern of his understanding of the Jazz Age. Similarly, his attitude to the form of the short story remains substantially the same, even though he made enormous advances (particularly in the earliest years of his professional career) in his mastery of fictional technique. But after 1932 the nature of his short fiction changed radically. For several years he had little time or energy to spare for writing for the magazines: during 1932-34, he was completing *Tender is the Night*, and throughout 1935 he was immobilized by his crack-up. As he explained to Harold Ober, in a letter from which I have already quoted, he no longer had the capacity to produce those stories 'conceived like novels' which had been the mainstay of his professional career and the ground of his artistic achievement. Besides, as the result of changes in public taste and editorial policy, the *Saturday Evening Post* was no longer prepared to publish him as it had formerly done. When he resumed an active working life in 1937, it was in the entirely new context of Hollywood: film scripts took the place once occupied by magazine fiction, with the consequence that the writing of short stories took up less of his attention during these last years than at any other period of his life. Nevertheless, the best of his late stories are not only excellent in themselves, but are a remarkable tribute to his professionalism — his ability to make the most of the working conditions available to him.

The most strikingly novel characteristic of these tales is how short they are — often no more than five or six pages. In the main, this was undoubtedly a response to the new commercial pressures we have been considering, and in particular to the fact that, after 1936, the main outlet for Fitzgerald's work was *Esquire*, whose editor preferred short pieces, and in any case paid such small fees that there was no incentive to write at length. These *Esquire* stories, however, are far from being mere truncated versions of Fitzgerald's earlier tales. They represent a fundamentally new approach on his part to the problem of short-story form, in which he was led to adopt a position very close to that of the modernist writers and critics. Like them, he now appeared to prefer the form of the sketch or episode, as practised by Chekhov and Joyce, Sherwood Anderson and Hemingway. This type of story is compressed and oblique; it relies on poetic evocation or outright symbolism, it eliminates authorial intervention and dispenses with fictional narrators; its rhetorical mode implies an attitude of complete objectivity. Joyce's 'Clay', Anderson's 'Hands', and Hemingway's 'Hills Like White Elephants' are particularly clear examples. A number of Fitzgerald's most successful late stories conform to this pattern.

In subject matter, the contrast with his earlier fiction is less clear-cut: as we have seen already, stories like 'Three Hours Between Planes' and 'News of Paris — Fifteen Years Ago' carry forward old preoccupations into the new form. Nevertheless, there is one important development which it is impossible not to associate with his crack-up — a group of tales which deal with personal disaster and unhappiness, alcoholism, mental illness, psychological trauma, broken marriages, the sense of failure, and the increasing loneliness and declining vitality of middle age.

'Afternoon of an Author' (1936) the best of all these stories, gives an almost unbearably painful sense of the author's exhaustion, discouragement and loneliness after some unspecified illness or breakdown. For weeks he has been confined to his apartment, but now, at last, he is tempted out by the fine spring weather into making a short excursion to the barbershop. As he rides downtown on the bus, and carefully negotiates the busy streets, his impressions are vivid but distressing. The sights and sounds of the external world do not stimulate his imagination, but only serve to turn his thoughts inward, reminding him of his own essential emptiness and weakness. He is tormented by images of vitality and youth — a pair of lovers glimpsed as they sit unselfconsciously on the pediment of a statue; the strains of a dance band from the hotel cocktail lounge; men preparing a college football ground for the next season's games. He catches himself behaving like an old man — waiting for the traffic lights to change at every crossing, and holding tightly to all the handrails as he gets off the bus. Above all, he finds that his capacity to function as an author is now in doubt: new ideas do not come to him, old ideas have lost their significance; he is, as he informs himself with sardonic weariness, in need of re-afforestation. Because of the dry, ironic impersonality and wit of its narrative style, this sketch does not have a trace of the self-pity and exhibitionism which frequently disfigure the crack-up essays.

In 'Afternoon of an Author' (and other similar late stories), the extent to which Fitzgerald's attention is directed towards the inner, psychological condition of his characters has an interesting effect upon his treatment of the outer social reality which surrounds them. Here it is convenient to make use of an image from the story itself: as the author rides downtown, the overhanging branches of trees brush against the windows of the bus, and, in the same way, random impressions of the city flicker across his mind in vivid but unstable succession. In his shaky mental state, the disintegration within seems matched by fragmentation without. The real significance and value of this new way of looking at social life, however, is that it represents much more than simply the reflection of a sick mind. It corresponds very closely with Fitzgerald's conviction that the solid fabric of American wealth and American manners which he had made imaginatively his own, had collapsed in the Crash of 1929 leaving only shattered memories behind. He makes this view explicit in 'My Lost City' and 'Babylon Revisited', and his late stories — 'The Lost Decade', 'Financing Finnegan', 'Afternoon of an

Author' itself — are filled with the reverberations of a vanished era. The new impressionistic technique which he began to develop in the last named of these, was admirably suited to the exploration of the unstable consciousness and shifting social reality of recent American conditions, and it is not surprising to find that postwar American novelists (most notably John Updike) have learnt much from it.

There are several other excellent late stories — for example, 'I Didn't Get Over' (1936), 'An Alcoholic Case' (1937), and 'The Lost Decade' (1939) — which I could have discussed in the same way as 'Afternoon of an Author'; but there is one, 'Financing Finnegan' (1938), which has a special interest. It reflects obliquely on those personal problems in the life of an author which became pressing for Fitzgerald after his crack-up, but its main concern brings us back full circle to the point where we began — to a renewed awareness of Fitzgerald's conflicting ideas about the artist's role. Finnegan himself, the hero of the story, is pre-eminently the artist as conqueror: half wayward genius and half confidence-man, he rises superior to the conventions of professional reliability, financial probity and sexual morality, but does undeniably produce on occasion work which is incomparably fine. He never appears in person, but his mysterious doings, magnified by hearsay, are relayed to us through the conversations of his agent and publisher, who have invested so much in him in the form of loans and advances, that they have come to regard him with a mixture of infatuation and dread. The whole situation is described, with ironic disapproval, by a narrator who is in every way Finnegan's antithesis, a sober hard-working professional writer who possesses all the good qualities that Finnegan lacks, and is at the same time without a trace of the latter's genuine distinction. By pushing these alternative possibilities to the extreme, Fitzgerald is able to create a story which is at once a brilliant farce in the manner of 'News of Paris — Fifteen Years Ago', and something more — a uniquely clearsighted view of the disturbing cross currents always present in his conception of art.

Indeed from several points of view, 'Financing Finnegan' is a good story with which to conclude a discussion of Fitzgerald's short fiction. Like so many of the other tales we have considered, it shows his consummate skill at blending the social with the individual: Finnegan's obscure difficulties are set against the wider context of the Depression, and the problematic nature of recovery acquires a double sense. Above all, this story gives evidence of the strong element of continuity in Fitzgerald's development, his ability to keep returning to certain themes with a fresh awareness of their potentialities; and at the same time his adaptability, the way in which he could always respond creatively to new conditions both in his professional work and in the social life around him.

5

The Great Gatsby

The power of a great novel often depends, more than anything else, upon the firmness and suitability of its underlying structure. 'On this hard fine floor', Henry James wrote in his Preface to *The Awkward Age*, 'the element of execution feels it may more or less confidently *dance.*' A novelist cannot hope to compensate by mere 'treatment' for 'the loose foundation or the vague scheme.' He can best avoid this kind of weakness by making his work express as far as possible the necessities of dramatic form: 'The dramatist has verily to *build*, is committed to architecture, to construction at any cost; to driving in deep his vertical supports and laying across and firmly fixing his horizontal, his resting pieces.'[1] If a novel is to have this secure basis, it should be written, like a play, in scenes; and each scene should have a definite shape and a precise location — those qualities we associate with theatrical performance.

The most striking formal characteristic of *The Great Gatsby* is its scenic construction, and Scott Fitzgerald himself, as we have seen, spoke of it as a 'dramatic' novel. In this respect, it shows extraordinarily close affinities with the theory and practice of James's later fiction. James's vivid account of the little diagram he drew in order to explain the structure of *The Awkward Age* to his publisher, corresponds exactly with what we find in *Gatsby*:

> I drew on a sheet of paper ... the neat figure of a circle consisting of a number of small rounds disposed at equal distance about a central object. The central object was my situation, my subject in itself, to which the thing would owe its title, and the small rounds represented so many distinct lamps, as I liked to call them, the function of each of which would be to light with all due intensity one of its aspects ... Each of my 'lamps' would be the light of a single 'social occasion' in the history and intercourse of the characters concerned, and would bring out to the full the latent colour of the scene in question and cause it to illuminate, to the last drop, its bearing on my theme. I revelled in this notion of the Occasion as a thing by itself, really and completely a scenic thing ...[2]

The 'central object' of *The Great Gatsby* is clearly Gatsby himself, and the chapters of the novel are in the main a series of dramatic scenes, each illumi-

---

1 Henry James, *The Art of the Novel*, edited by R. P. Blackmur, New York, 1934, p. 109.
2 *Ibid.*, p. 110.

spect of his character and situation. The scenes are invari-
ons'; often they are parties, in that special sense which is so
itzgerald's understanding of the 1920s. Chapter I is built
r party at the Buchanans' at which Nick Carraway
le charm and the inner corruption of Daisy and of the
the woman and the class which Gatsby has made the
ms. Chapter II presents the 'foul dust' that floats in the
s. It opens with a poetic and atmospheric evocation of the
ut its main source of energy is once again dramatic — the
ion-style party in Myrtle Wilson's apartment. In Chapter
ne of Gatsby's own parties for the first time, and begins to
equivocal nature of the latter's creative powers — his
he beautiful with the vulgar, the magical with the absurd.
tions like an act in two scenes, each revealing a contrasted
's identity: the lunch in New York, at which Nick meets
m and has a glimpse of Gatsby's under-world connections;
ing which Jordan Baker tells him the story of Gatsby's
with Daisy. The dramatic focus of Chapter V is the tea party
when Gatsby and Daisy are reunited; and in Chapter VI
second party at Gatsby's, at which Daisy herself is present.
Chapter VII, like Chapter IV, is an act in two scenes: the lunch party at the
Buchanans' where Tom realizes for the first time that Daisy and Gatsby are
lovers; and the abortive cocktail party at the Plaza Hotel in New York, where
Tom not only ends the affair, but succeeds in destroying Gatsby's 'platonic
conception' of himself. Only in the last two chapters does Fitzgerald largely
abandon the dramatic method, and, even here, some of the most vivid
moments depend on effects which are scenic in character — Mr Gatz's
arrival at Gatsby's house, Nick's second meeting with Meyer Wolfsheim in
New York, and Gatsby's funeral.

Nick Carraway is a key element in the success of this scheme, indeed he is
no less vital to the structure of *The Great Gatsby* than to its tone and
meaning. He is both stage manager and chorus, re-creating situations in all
their actuality, and at the same time commenting upon them. Sometimes he
even devises the action — contrives the circumstances by which the actors
are brought together on the stage: it is he who arranges the reunion of Gatsby
and Daisy. Nick has a further value from the structural point of view:
through him, Fitzgerald is able to maintain a kind of flexibility which James
considered impossible in the dramatic mode of fiction. James believed that,
in order to benefit fully from the firmness of dramatic construction, the
novelist was compelled to relinquish the privilege of 'going behind' the
action so as to analyse and comment upon it.[3] But, thanks to Nick Carraway,
Fitzgerald has the best of both worlds: he moves from the dramatic
concentration of 'the scenic thing' to the rich texture of narrative without the

3 *Ibid.*, pp. 110—11.

smallest effect of incoherence or inconsistency.

This principle of construction affects every aspect of Fitzgerald's artistry: in particular, the language of *The Great Gatsby* often rises at moments of intensity to the level of dramatic poetry; and the element of social comedy, which gives the novel its predominant tone and colouring, always finds expression through specifically theatrical effects of action and spectacle. The structure of a dramatic novel, however, is not an end in itself: each scene, to use James's metaphor, is a lamp illuminating a central object, and it is this object which must remain the reader's primary concern. For this reason, a scene-by-scene analysis is by no means the best way to approach *The Great Gatsby*, and a thematic treatment is far more likely to bring out the true nature of Gatsby himself. I shall therefore discuss his situation and character from three points of view: the external social reality — the way of life of the American rich — by which he has been deluded and betrayed; the texture of his inner imaginative life, which becomes, in Fitzgerald's hands, an image of the romantic sensibility and its maladies; and his dramatic identity — his essentially comic nature.

The evolution of Gatsby's dream is the history of his involvement with a social class, the American rich. The turbulent imaginings of his adolescence first take shape in the scheme of self-advancement which he draws up in imitation of Benjamin Franklin and Horatio Alger. At this time, he has a plan to make himself rich, but no clear mental picture of what wealth and success would be like. This gap is partially filled when Dan Cody's yacht anchors off the Lake Superior shore, and Gatsby meets Cody himself. At once Cody, the Western tycoon, who is spending his money in the flamboyant style of the Gilded Age, becomes Gatsby's image of the wealthy and successful man. He changes his name from Jimmy Gatz to Jay Gatsby in an attempt to embrace this new conception in all its aspects. Cody's swagger is the basis of his own social style, and, like the former, he sees the acquisition of wealth as essentially an activity of the frontier — if not the actual geographical and historical frontier, then the no-man's-land between business and criminality.

As well as an image of himself, however, Gatsby needs an image of something beyond him to which he can aspire, and this final stage in his imaginative development is completed when he meets Daisy during the War and becomes her lover. When he kissed her for the first time, he 'wed forever his ineffable vision to her perishable flesh': from that moment, she was the substance of his dream, and 'the incarnation was complete'. In his eyes, she is intensely desirable both as a woman and as the symbol of a way of life:

> Gatsby was overwhelmingly aware of the youth and mystery which wealth imprisons and preserves, of the freshness of many clothes, and of Daisy, gleaming like silver, safe and proud above the hot struggles of the poor.[4]

4 *The Great Gatsby*, BH1, p. 243.

Daisy's charm involves a subtle fusion of two powerful sources of attraction, sex and money: one might say that, in her, money becomes sexually desirable. This quality is concentrated in her voice, the one facet of her beauty which can never fall short of Gatsby's dream. As Nick Carraway reflects, when he leaves them alone together for the first time after their five year separation, 'I think that voice held him most, with its fluctuating, feverish warmth, because it couldn't be over-dreamed — that voice was a deathless song.'[5] Nick's tone surrounds the metaphor of song with an aura of high romance, but it is Gatsby himself who uncovers the secret of those elusive cadences, when he remarks with impressive simplicity that 'her voice is full of money.' Many American novelists, including Henry James, Edith Wharton and Theodore Dreiser, were well aware that a beautiful woman may contain within herself all the beguiling characteristics of a social class, but no one apart from Fitzgerald has ever found so felicitous an image for the interior music of wealth.

Gatsby is incapable of seeing the American rich in any other way, but Fitzgerald, through Nick Carraway, makes us equally aware of their short-comings from the very beginning of the novel. His introductory portraits of Daisy and Tom Buchanan are sketched in with delicate irony. Nick is half dazzled by their wealth, and yet knows that their lives are pervaded by an atmosphere of rootlessness and futility. Since their marriage, they have 'drifted here and there unrestfully wherever people played polo and were rich together' — a year in France, a season or two on Chicago's North Shore, and now a summer on Long Island. Tom's discontent seems an expression, in part, of his permanent immaturity. He had been a great football star at Yale, 'a national figure in a way, one of those men who reach such an acute limited excellence at twenty-one that everything afterwards savours of anti-climax.' Nick suspects that he will 'drift on forever seeking, a little wistfully, for the dramatic turbulence of some irrecoverable football game.'[6]

These weaknesses are serious enough, but worse is to follow, and when Nick accepts Daisy's invitation to dinner he quickly learns the full extent of the Buchanans' corruption. Their failure is presented as the failure of a civilization, of a way of life. Nick Carraway imagines that he will find among the sophisticated Eastern rich, the high point of American civilization. The expanse of the Buchanans' lawns, the graciousness of their house, the formality of dinner, the poised, confident social tone give all the outward signs that a high civilization has been achieved. Nick contrasts the occasion with parties in the Middle West, where people hurry from one phase of the evening to the next in a state of 'continually disappointed anticipation' or in 'sheer nervous dread of the moment itself'. 'Your make me feel uncivilized,' he says to Daisy, 'can't you talk about crops or something.' At once he is ludicrously disillusioned by Tom, who is provoked by Nick's remark into an

5 *Ibid.*, p. 201.
6 *Ibid.*, p. 129.

incoherent account of a book he has just read which 'proves' that 'civilization — oh, science and art, and all that' is threatened by the rise of the
coloured races. To our sense of the restlessness and futility of their lives is
now added an element of brutality and arrogance. A telephone-call from
Tom's mistress, and a tense whispered quarrel with Daisy offstage on which
Jordan Baker eavesdrops shamelessly, conclude the scene. The rottenness of
these people is conveyed with a fine sense of comedy.

Nick's disappointment has already been prefigured poetically in his first
glimpse of the Buchanan household:

> A breeze blew through the room, blew curtains in at one end and out the other like
> pale flags, twisting them up toward the frosted wedding-cake of the ceiling, and
> then rippled over the wine-coloured rug, making a shadow on it as wind does on
> the sea.
>   The only completely stationary object in the room was an enormous couch on
> which two young women were buoyed up as though upon an anchored balloon.
> They were both in white, and their dresses were rippling and fluttering as if they
> had just been blown back in after a short flight around the house.[7]

The house, the draperies, the young women themselves, seem positively
airborne upon Nick's romantic sense of expectation, until Tom enters:
'Then there was a boom as Tom Buchanan shut the rear windows and the
caught wind died out about the room, and the curtains, and the rugs and the
two young women ballooned slowly to the floor.'[8] Tom brings everything
quite literally down to earth. There is no more impressive instance of how
much Fitzgerald's fiction gains from his sense of the specifically poetic
possibilities of the novel. And, as I have already suggested in chapter 2, we
are dealing here with dramatic poetry, not the large abstractions of symbol
and myth. In a way which is both subtler and more flexible, the local effects
of language are finely adapted to the immediate demands of the scene, the
moment.

The element of physical brutality in Tom Buchanan's character is insisted
upon from the beginning. An arrogant stare; a manner which is both
supercilious and aggressive; 'a great pack of muscle shifting when his
shoulder moved under his thin coat' these are the details of his appearance
which catch our attention. His brutality is constantly breaking through the
veneer of his surface gentility, just as the movements of his 'cruel body'
show under the 'effeminate swank' of his riding clothes. At that first dinner
Daisy displays a finger he has bruised in some domestic tussle; he breaks
Myrtle Wilson's nose with a singularly efficient application of force; and he
takes a vindictive pleasure at the end in setting Wilson on Gatsby.

Tom's style of physical dominance, his capacity for exerting leverage, are
not expressions merely of his individual strength but of the power of a class.
Fitzgerald does not make the mistake of imagining that because the rich are

7   *Ibid.*, p. 131.
8   *Ibid.*

corrupt, they must necessarily be weak. That fallacy was to be a part of the sentimentality of the 1930s — as we see in *The Grapes of Wrath,* where the rich appear as impotent scared little men hiding behind barbed wire and hired guns. Tom Buchanan is a far truer representative: he draws on the sense of self-assurance his money and position give him as directly as he draws upon his bank account. The consciousness that, in contrast to himself, Gatsby is 'Mr Nobody from nowhere', gives him a decisive psychological advantage in their struggle over Daisy.

The rich have subtler styles of dominance than the brute power of Tom's money or of his pampered athletic body. One of these appears in the behaviour of Jordan Baker when Nick first sees her stretched out at full length on the sofa in the Buchanans' drawing room. She takes no apparent notice of his entrance, but maintains a pose of complete self-absorption as if she were balancing some object on her chin. Far from resenting her discourtesy, Nick feels almost obliged to apologize for having interrupted her. After he and Daisy have chatted for a few moments, Daisy introduces Jordan to him:

> ... Miss Baker's lips fluttered, she nodded at me almost imperceptibly, and then tipped her head back again — the object she was balancing had obviously tottered a little and given her something of a fright. Again a sort of apology arose to my lips. Almost any exhibition of complete self-sufficiency draws a stunned tribute from me.[9]

This was the quality Fitzgerald had been trying to isolate in the character of Dick Humbird in *This Side of Paradise.* By the time he wrote *The Great Gatsby,* he had learnt enough about the novel of manners to be able to make such subtle notations with complete success. In terms of dramatic conflict, these are the forces which defeat Gatsby, although clearly there are self-destructive potentialities in his own romanticism.

By the end of his first dinner party at the Buchanans', Nick Carraway is already disillusioned with the American rich. He is forced unwillingly to observe the violent contrast between their opportunities — what is implied by the gracious surface of their existence — and the seamy under-side which is its reality. In the Buchanans — and in Nick's reactions to them — we see once more how completely the American upper class has failed to become an aristocracy. Nick's disappointment is so sudden and complete that the episode has an effect of comic anticlimax. The chapter ends, however, not with his small disappointment but with Gatsby's first appearance. Gatsby is still totally committed to his dream: he stretches out his arms in a great yearning gesture, across the dark waters of the bay towards the green light at the end of Daisy's dock. He never discovers how he has been betrayed by the class he has idealized, and, for him, the failure of the rich has disastrous consequences.

9 *Ibid.,* pp. 131–2.

Gatsby's unique quality is his capacity to dream —

> ... some heightened sensitivity to the promises of life, as if he were related to one of those intricate machines that register earthquakes ten thousand miles away ... an extraordinary gift for hope, a romantic readiness such as I have not found in any other person and which it is not likely I shall ever find again.[10]

His tragedy lies in the impact of reality upon his dreams: neither the circumstances of his own life, nor the pseudo-aristocratic style of the American rich to which he aspires, offer him anything 'commensurate with his capacity for wonder'. Most of the ironies of his situation arise from the balancing of illusion against reality. The clearest, though by no means the most important of the ways by which Fitzgerald gives poetic substance to this duality is that of creating two settings with strongly contrasted atmospheres. The glittering palaces on Long Island Sound are set against the ash-heaps on the outskirts of New York. Gatsby's dreams are concentrated upon the former; the sordid realities which shatter his illusions and destroy his life lurk among the latter. Among the ashes, in or near Wilson's garage, Tom's rottenness and Daisy's cowardice are fully revealed; while Wilson himself, the ash-grey phantom gliding on Gatsby's track, is a singularly appropriate instrument for murder — there is after all nothing more dangerous than the hatred of the mean-spirited.

The ironic relation between illusion and reality in Gatsby's situation is conveyed most interestingly, however, by the actual language of the novel. Fitzgerald takes some of his own most vicious forms of writing — his journalistic chatter, his false rhetoric, and the cheap style of his poorest magazine fiction — and turns them into something which is artistically satisfying. It is a strange process of transmutation, by which styles that seem fitted only for crude and vulgar sentiments are, paradoxically, made to carry subtle shades of meaning and emotion. The bad writing produced with uncritical facility in the inferior pieces is here employed with conscious and elaborate artistry. An obvious and highly successful example is the list of 'the names of those who came to Gatsby's house that summer' at the beginning of Chapter IV. This is, among other things, a parody of the style of the gossip columns — of the cheap journalistic tone Fitzgerald could slip into all too easily himself. But it is more than a parody, or a mere compilation of those funny names which are a consequence of the diverse origins of Americans. It is a poetic composition (critics have often pointed to a similarity with T. S. Eliot's use of proper names in *Gerontion*) which gives expression to the social chaos of the Jazz Age. The names and scraps of rumour are interwoven to show how people are being hurried indiscriminately together in the frenetic pursuit of money and pleasure — the wealthy, the criminal, the disreputable, the pretentious, the showy and the frivolous, the rootless and the abandoned — even the respectable. The whiff of

10 *Ibid.*, p. 126.

violence is in the air, and the presence of disaster is never far away. This is the foul dust that floated in the wake of Gatsby's dreams — the motley crowd that flock to the glittering and lavish entertainments he conceives at West Egg.

Fitzgerald takes this kind of writing farthest in his treatment of Gatsby's love for Daisy. Gatsby's taste in language is as flashy and overblown as his taste in cars or clothes: when he talks about his feelings to Nick Carraway, the words he uses retain echoes from many cheap and vulgar styles. Fitzgerald is able to catch these inflections in Gatsby's voice, and yet give to the paltry phrases vibrations they never had before. In order to see how this happens, it is necessary to quote an example of Fitzgerald's own worst writing, before turning to some passages from *The Great Gatsby*. For this purpose I have chosen the opening of 'Love in the Night', a story which was published only a few weeks before *Gatsby* itself:

> The words thrilled Val. They had come into his mind sometime during the fresh gold April afternoon and he kept repeating them to himself over and over: 'Love in the night: love in the night'. He tried them in three languages — Russian, French and English — and decided that they were best in English. In each language they meant a different sort of love and a different sort of night — the English night seemed the warmest and softest with the thinnest and most crystalline sprinkling of stars. The English love seemed the most fragile and romantic — a white dress and a dim face above it and eyes that were pools of light.[11]

In the conversations with Nick in which Gatsby talks about Daisy, the same kind of writing is used:

> ... he had never been in such a beautiful house before. But what gave it an air of breathless intensity was that Daisy lived there. ... There was a ripe mystery about it, a hint of bedrooms upstairs more beautiful and cool than other bedrooms, of gay and radiant activities taking place through its corridors, and of romances that were not musty and laid away already in lavender, but fresh and breathing and redolent of this year's shining motor-cars and of dances whose flowers were scarcely withered ... .[12]

In the first passage, Fitzgerald is tastelessly and embarassingly self-indulgent; in the second the validity of his rhetoric is incontestable. It is the same style but it is now being used consciously and with controlling irony. Gatsby's feelings for Daisy, the moment he tries to define them, become the banal stereotypes of romantic magazine fiction, and so it is fitting that the language he uses should be vitiated by worn-out images and sentimental clichés. Fitzgerald indeed states this quite explicitly in the scene in which Gatsby drives Nick Carraway to New York, and tells him the story of his life. Gatsby recounts the autobiography he would like to have had — the

---

11 'Love in the Night', *Bits of Paradise*, edited by Matthew J. Bruccoli, London, 1973, p. 66.
12 *Gatsby*, BH1, p. 242.

wealthy family in the Middle West; the Oxford education; the grand tour —

> 'After that I lived like a young rajah in all the capitals of Europe — Paris, Venice, Rome — collecting jewels, chiefly rubies, hunting big game, painting a little, things for myself only, and trying to forget something very sad that had happened to me long ago.'
> With an effort I managed to restrain my incredulous laughter. The very phrases were worn so threadbare that they evoked no image except that of a turbaned 'character' leaking sawdust at every pore as he pursued a tiger through the Bois de Boulogne.[13]

The tale concludes with the amazing heroism of Gatsby's war service: 'Every Allied government gave me a decoration — even Montenegro, little Montenegro down on the Adriatic Sea.' 'It was', Nick comments, 'like skimming hastily through a dozen magazines.'

Nick has just dismissed him as an extravagant impostor, a liar on the grand scale, when there is an astonishing volte-face: Gatsby produces the Montenegrin medal and a photograph of himself with a cricket bat (superb authenticating touch!) at Oxford. Nick veers to the other exteme — 'Then it was all true': he pictures Gatsby, surrounded by tiger skins, in a palace on the Grand Canal, gazing into a chest of rubies to find relief from the 'gnawings of his broken heart.'

It is not 'all true', of course, nor is it all imposture: it is a question of language, a question of images. From one point of view, it is of the essence of Gatsby's greatness that he can make these threadbare phrases and magazine stereotypes the vehicle for his stupendous capacity for wonder and imaginative response, in the same way as much of Fitzgerald's greatness in this novel lies in his ability to transmute a bad style into great art. From another angle, however, it is Gatsby's tragedy that the purest element of truth in his life-story should be conveyed in the most false and sentimental of his words: 'trying to forget something very sad that had happened to me long ago.' The fusion of wonder and vulgarity is caught with superlative tact again and again in the novel.

We find an illuminating parallel to Gatsby's case in the greatest of all novels about the romantic sensibility — *Madame Bovary*. It is interesting to note that *Madame Bovary* had been much in Fitzgerald's mind during the period when he was writing *The Great Gatsby*. In an article which was syndicated to a number of newspapers, he listed what he considered to be the ten greatest novels ever written, and among these *Nostromo*, *Vanity Fair*, and *Madame Bovary* were singled out for special emphasis.[14] When he wrote to Maxwell Perkins about last minute revisions he was making to the text of *Gatsby*, he warned him that the proof 'will be one of the most expensive affairs since *Madame Bovary*'.[15] Flaubert's heroine shows the same capacity

13   *Ibid.*, p. 176.
14   Arthur Mizener, *The Far Side of Paradise*, Boston, 1951, p. 336.
15   *Letters*, p. 172.

for wonder, the same restriction to banal images, and the same failure to find speech that can match the intensity of her feelings, as Gatsby does. This is particularly apparent in Flaubert's account of her affair with Rodolphe, a jaded middle-aged *roué*:

> 'I love you so much,' she burst out. 'So much I can't live without you! I long for you sometimes till my heart almost breaks with jealousy! I say to myself, Where is he now? Talking to other women, perhaps. They smile at him, he comes — Ah, no! no! Tell me there's none you care for! There are women more beautiful than I, but none that can love as I can. I am your slave, your concubine. You are my king, my idol — you are good, handsome, intelligent, strong!'
> He had listened to so many speeches of this kind that they no longer made any impression on him. Emma was like any other mistress; and the charm of novelty, gradually slipping away like a garment, laid bare the eternal monotony of passion, whose forms and phrases are for ever the same. Any difference of feeling underlying a similarity in the words escaped the notice of that man of much experience. Because wanton or mercenary lips had murmured like phrases in his ear, he had but scant belief in the sincerity of these. High-flown language concealing tepid affection must be discounted, thought he: as though the full heart may not sometimes overflow in the emptiest metaphors, since no one can ever give the exact measure of his needs, his thoughts, or his sorrows, and human speech is like a cracked kettle on which we strum out tunes to make a bear dance, when we would move the stars to pity.[16]

Emma Bovary is condemned to express herself in the enfeebled phrases of early nineteenth-century sentimental fiction, just as Gatsby uses the debased coinage of the magazines. In their predicament, both Fitzgerald and Flaubert show an awareness not only of the problems of the romantic sensibility, but, more specifically, of the agonies of the romantic artist — a sense that the artist himself is foredoomed to defeat whenever he tries to put his inexpressible visions into words. It has always been recognized that *The Great Gatsby* gives a wonderfully intimate picture of American manners in the 1920s, and that it is a profound exploration of the nature of American civilization, but no one has fully grasped the extent to which it is the great modern novel of romantic experience. In the entire history of the novel, only Flaubert has gone as deeply into the dangers and despairs of romanticism, and only Stendhal has seen as much of the comedy.

Gatsby himself is not an artist, however — unless one regards his parties as in some sense works of art — and he is certainly not aware that the language he uses is vulgar and ridiculous. For him, the most destructive aspect of romantic experience lies in a somewhat different direction: he finds that attaining a desired object brings a sense of loss rather than fulfilment. Once his dream loses its general and ideal quality and becomes localized within the confines of actuality, his life seems emptier and poorer. On the afternoon when Daisy first visits his house, they pause at a window to look

---

16 Gustave Flaubert, *Madame Bovary*, translated by Alan Russell, Harmondsworth, 1950, p. 203.

out across the waters of the Sound, and Gatsby tells her that, but for the rain and mist which obscure the view, they would be able to see the end of her dock where the green light burns every night. Daisy takes his words as a movement of tenderness, and puts her arm through his, but Gatsby is far away — lost in what he has just said. His sense that the green light is no longer the central image in a great dream but only a green light at the end of a dock, is momentarily stronger than his response to Daisy herself touching him with her hand: 'His count of enchanted objects had diminished by one.'

This feeling is made still more explicit in the conversation in which Gatsby tells Nick how he first kissed Daisy. Gatsby has made a decisive choice — from this point onwards all his capacity for wonder is concentrated upon her. Even if she were far more remarkable than she is, she could not possibly measure up to such fabulous expectations, and the affair must inevitably end in some personal disaster for Gatsby. It is only because of their five-year separation that the catastrophe is delayed for so long — in Daisy's absence, Gatsby is able to dream and idealize once more without having to subject his visions to the test of actuality. Once he is reunited with her, ruin comes almost immediately: Her personal weaknesses and the inadequacies of the way of life she represents only serve to aggravate the self-destructive tendencies of Gatsby's own romanticism. This passage also raises once again, in a most interesting way, the question of language and the romantic sensibility. Nick Carraway, in the paragraph which follows it, comments explicitly on the way Gatsby talks, and on the difficulties he himself experiences in finding words for what Gatsby is trying to say:

Through all he said, even through his appalling sentimentality, I was reminded of something — an elusive rhythm, a fragment of lost words that I had heard somewhere a long time ago. For a moment a phrase tried to take shape in my mouth and my lips parted like a dumb man's, as though there was more struggling upon them than a wisp of startled air. But they made no sound, and what I had almost remembered was incommunicable forever.[17]

The sober precision of Nick's account of his own difficulties with language makes a marvellous contrast with the turgid unrestraint, the 'appalling sentimentality', of the images which evoke Gatsby's first kiss. This seems to me to be the clearest evidence in the novel that the ironic use of bad writing in *The Great Gatsby* is the result of conscious artistry on Fitzgerald's part.

Gatsby's ruin is accomplished in a single afternoon, in the stifling hotel room in New York where he and Tom struggle for possession of Daisy, with Nick and Jordan as unwilling bystanders. The ease of Tom's victory shows the extent to which Gatsby's identity is an insubstantial fabric of illusions. There is no occasion on which Tom appears to greater disadvantage: his homilies on the sanctity of family life are as absurd as they are hypocritical; his manner towards Gatsby is crassly snobbish, towards Daisy disgustingly

17 *Gatsby*, BH1, p. 213.

maudlin. He does not have the least conception of what exists between Gatsby and Daisy, nor the smallest understanding of the former's complex inner life, and yet he blunders, as unerringly as if he knew exactly what he was doing, into the area where Gatsby is most vulnerable. Through his crude accusations, he presents Gatsby, as if in a distorting mirror, with a picture of himself which is unfamiliar and yet horribly real. Tom forces him to realize that he does not necessarily appear to others in the forms which he assumes in his own magnificent conception of himself: to settled respectable people, perhaps even to a 'nice girl' like Daisy, he is simply a vulgar *arriviste*, a bootlegger, a cheap swindler, the associate of crooks and gambling operators like Meyer Wolfsheim. Gatsby cannot survive this attack, clumsy as it is. The identity he has constructed for himself out of dreams and illusions, banal images and sentimental clichés, is so fragile that it disintegrates at a touch: ' "Jay Gatsby" had broken up like glass against Tom's hard malice, and the long secret extravaganza was played out.'[18]

After this, his dream of Daisy too begins to recede: while he watches her bedroom window all night from the grounds of her house, she seems to be moving steadily away from him; and when she fails to telephone him the next day, he is at last compelled to relinquish 'the old warm world' which he has inhabited for so long. In these final moments of his life, he is forced to contemplate 'a new world, material without being real', a world in which the loss of his dream changes the very quality of his perceptions. The common objects which surround him — sky, leaves, grass and flowers — come to seem unfamiliar, frightening, grotesque.

The core of Gatsby's tragedy is not only that he lived by dreams, but that the woman and the class and the way of life of which he dreamed — that life of the rich which the novel so ruthlessly exposes — fell so far short of the scope of his imagination. Daisy is a trivial, callous, cowardly woman who may dream a little herself but who will not let her dreams, or such unpleasant realities as running over Myrtle Wilson, disturb her comfort. That Gatsby should have dreamt of her, given his marvellous parties for her, is the special edge to his fate. Fitzgerald shows Gatsby watching over Daisy from the grounds of her house, on the night of the accident, imagining that she might still come to him, and that he is protecting her from her brutal husband. Meanwhile, Tom and Daisy are sitting comfortably in their kitchen over fried chicken and bottled ale, coming to a working arrangement for their future lives. There is a banal and shabby intimacy about their marriage, it is a realistic, if worthless, practical arrangement that suits their shallow personalities. Outside, in the night, stands Gatsby, the man of tremendous and unconquerable illusions, 'watching over nothing'.

By the close of the novel, Fitzgerald has completed his immensely difficult task of convincing us that Gatsby's capacity for illusion is poignant and heroic, in spite of the banality of his aspirations and the worthlessness of the

18 *Ibid.*, p. 242.

objects of his dreams. The poignancy is conveyed through one incident in particular — that of the car which drives up to Gatsby's house one night long after he is dead. 'Probably it was some final guest, who had been away at the ends of the earth and didn't know that the party was over.' The heroic quality is there in his vigil in the garden, in the scale of his entertainments, the determination behind his criminality.

In the closing paragraphs of the novel there is a sudden enlargement of the theme — a vision of America as the continent of lost innocence and lost illusions. The Dutch sailors who first came to Long Island had an unspoilt continent before them, something 'commensurate with their capacity for wonder'. Gatsby's greatness was to have retained a sense of wonder as deep as the sailors' on that first landfall. His tragedy was to have had, not a continent to wonder at, but only the green light at the end of Daisy's dock, and the triviality of Daisy herself. The evolution of such triviality was his particular tragedy, and the tragedy of America.

It is easier to discuss Gatsby's significance and the nature of his experience, as I have done so far, than to say what kind of fictional character he is. A number of early readers of the novel including Edith Wharton and H. L. Mencken, felt that as a character he virtually didn't exist. Most later critics have evaded the problem altogether by elevating him to the status of a mythic figure. Approached in this way he becomes a symbolic abstraction, the vehicle for a few school-book platitudes about American history, and the question of whether or not he is a tangible dramatic and human presence conveniently disappears. If one simply reads the novel, however, his dramatic and human presence obstinately and delightfully remains:

> Gatsby, his hands still in his pockets, was reclining against the mantelpiece in a strained counterfeit of perfect ease, even of boredom. His head leaned back so far that it rested against the face of a defunct mantelpiece clock, and from this position his distraught eyes stared down at Daisy, who was sitting, frightened but graceful, on the edge of a stiff chair.
> 'We've met before', muttered Gatsby. His eyes glanced momentarily at me, and his lips parted with an abortive attempt at a laugh. Luckily the clock took this moment to tilt dangerously at the pressure of his head, whereupon he turned and caught it with trembling fingers and set it back in place. Then he sat down, rigidly, his elbow on the arm of the sofa and his chin in his hand.
> 'I'm sorry about the clock', he said.
> My own face had now assumed a deep tropical burn. I couldn't muster up a single commonplace out of the thousand in my head.
> 'It's an old clock', I told them idiotically.
> I think we all believed for a moment that it had smashed in pieces on the floor.[19]

The reality of Gatsby's character here is, overwhelmingly, comic, and it is this comic Gatsby — not a shadowy abstraction — who dominates the novel.

19 *Ibid.*, pp. 192—3.

The only warrant for considering him as a mythic figure is given on the last page of the novel and, while it would be foolish to deny that the language of this passage is the language of myth, it should be remembered that what Nick Carraway says here is an afterthought, an aspect of Gatsby's case perceived only after he is dead. The living Gatsby who dominates one scene after another is a creature of comedy not myth — a literary relative not of Davy Crockett but Trimalchio.

The Great Gatsby itself is best regarded as a social comedy, but the phrase doesn't perhaps sufficiently convey the extent to which the comic is the vital creative element in Fitzgerald's achievement. The term social comedy, usually implies a mode of writing which is satirical and moral, and this is certainly true of his treatment of a number of characters and episodes — in particular of Tom Buchanan. But frequently his writing rises to a level of rich absurdity where comedy is not subordinated to a satirical or moral point, but is itself the point — the truly creative thing. Such a moment occurs in the episode in which Myrtle Wilson buys a dog:

> We backed up to grey old man who bore an absurd resemblance to John D. Rockefeller. In a basket swung from his neck cowered a dozen very recent puppies of an indeterminate breed.
>
> 'What kind are they?' asked Mrs Wilson eagerly, as he came to the taxi-window.
> 'All kinds. What kind do you want, lady?'
> 'I'd like to get one of those police dogs; I don't suppose you got that kind?'
> The man peered doubtfully into the basket, plunged in his hand and drew one up, wriggling, by the back of the neck.
> 'That's no police dog', said Tom.
> 'No, it's not exactly a police dog', said the man with disappointment in his voice. 'It's more of an Airedale'. He passed his hand over the brown washrag of a back. 'Look at that coat. Some coat. That's a dog that'll never bother you with catching cold.'
> 'I think it's cute', said Mrs Wilson enthusiastically. 'How much is it?'
> 'That dog?' He looked at it admiringly. 'That dog will cost you ten dollars'.
> The Airedale — undoubtedly there was an Airedale concerned in it somewhere, though its feet were startlingly white — changed hands and settled down into Mrs Wilson's lap, where she fondled the weatherproof coat with rapture.
> 'Is it a boy or a girl?' she asked delicately.
> 'That dog? That dog's a boy'.
> 'It's a bitch', said Tom decisively. 'Here's your money. Go and buy ten more dogs with it'.[20]

To say that this incident illustrates the false gentility of Myrtle Wilson or the crudeness of Tom Buchanan's desires would be true but inessential. What really matters is the irresistibly joyous and liberating sense of the ridiculous which Fitzgerald conveys — that quality in literature which we call, not loosely but precisely, Dickensian. As Grahame Smith admirably expresses it in his study of Dickens à propos of Mrs Gamp — 'we recognize

20 *Ibid.*, pp. 145–6.

that we are enclosed in a magic circle of pure comedy from which it is impossible to break out with explanations of satirical intent or didactic purpose'.[21] The whole ensuing scene of the party at Myrtle Wilson's apartment is conceived on the same level of pure comedy. Nick Carraway's two encounters with Meyer Wolfsheim have the same quality. Wolfsheim isn't in the novel to give us tangible proof of Gatsby's underworld connections — the cryptic telephone calls the latter occasionally receives are enough to do that. Wolfsheim's monstrous absurdity — his nostrils, his cuff buttons, his sentimentality and his philosophy of life — is an end in itself. It is significant that Edith Wharton considered him ('your wonderful Jew') the best thing in the novel.[22]

Fitzgerald's greatest success by far in this mode of comedy, however, is the character of Gatsby himself. It is the comic element in Gatsby which makes him seem credibly alive — which gives him an independent existence as a fictional character. We depend on Nick Carraway's testimony for much of what we believe about him. Without the benefit of Nick's wide privilege of interpretation, and the assurance of his sober integrity, we should not be able to guess at the stupendous imaginative life that lies beneath Gatsby's trivial aspirations. But we don't need Nick to tell us how funny Gatsby is — we see it for ourselves. Here, Nick no longer interprets and guarantees, he merely records — he might almost as well not be there. We should probably be less ready to take his word even for Gatsby's imagination, if Gatsby were less comic. His sole creative talent — it is one of which he is entirely unconscious — is his power to arouse wild incredulous laughter. His life has the aspect of a non-stop theatrical performance — an 'unbroken series of successful gestures' even his name, Jay Gatsby, is a farcical stunt. He does not provoke the superficial kind of laughter which is a mere brief contortion of the facial muscles; he appeals to a profound comic sense which makes life seem richer and fuller than it normally is. When one laughs at his car, his clothes, his parties, his manner, his autobiographical confidences, one is not merely amused, one is responding, through him, to the fertile, creative ludicrousness of life itself.

Gatsby's account of himself during the car ride to New York (from which I have already quoted) is one of the finest of such moments. The episode is too long to give in full, but a single detail — the way in which the car itself is described — will serve to bring out the nature of Fitzgerald's comic vision. Gatsby's car is a fantasy of colours, shapes and noises: its horn emits bursts of music; its 'labyrinth of wind-shields' mirrors a dozen suns; its monstrous length is swollen with 'triumphant hat-boxes and supper-boxes and tool-boxes'. It is clearly not so much a means of transport as a theatrical gesture, a fantastic expression of personality, as characteristic in its way as Falstaff's

---

21   Grahame Smith, *Dickens, Money, Society*, Berkeley and Cambridge, 1968, see chapter 1 throughout, and especially p. 5.
22   In a letter to Fitzgerald reprinted by Edmund Wilson in *The Crack-up*, New York, 1945, p. 309.

belly. (Falstaff, as Grahame Smith points out[23] is as essential as Dickens to any discussion of pure comedy.) There are certain striking similarities between the ways in which Gatsby and Falstaff function as comic characters. One of these becomes apparent in the scene from *Henry IV, Part 2*, in which Falstaff comments on the ludicrous contrast between his tiny page and his own monstrous bulk:

> The brain of this foolish-compounded clay, man, is not able to invent anything that intends to laughter more than I invent, or is invented on me; I am not only witty in myself, but the cause that wit is in other men. I do here walk before thee like a sow that hath overwhelmed all her litter but one.[24]

Gatsby is never consciously witty as Falstaff is — indeed he seems to be totally without a sense of humour — but he is certainly 'the cause that wit is in other men'. Both characters need only to exist in order to be comic.

The Falstaff parallel is illuminating in a further sense. It is usual to speak of the wreck of Gatsby's dreams as a tragedy — a statement of the case which appears to contradict the view that he is essentially a comic character. Gatsby, however, clearly isn't a tragic hero in any strict sense: if one calls his end a tragedy, one is simply giving the word the meaning it has in everyday speech — that of the sudden and shocking ruin of a human life. No inconsistency is involved if a comic character dies in this way. Falstaff is cruelly rejected by the king, and the manner of his death as narrated by Mistress Quickly is deeply moving, but these circumstances do not alter his essentially comic nature. The emotions aroused by Gatsby's death, similarly, do not negate the effect of earlier scenes.

The most successful of Gatsby's theatrical gestures are his parties. At the simple level they are fun, an aspect of the novel's meaning which is as true and as important as Nick Carraway's moral disapproval of Gatsby's guests. We are reminded once again of what Henry James and Henry Adams were forced to concede, however reluctantly — that the charm, the success, of American life is in democratic manners, even in social chaos. The corresponding failure of the aristocratic experiment — the stuffy, boorish, hypocritical life of the Buchanans — is clear enough, and throws Gatsby's achievement into sharp relief. Daisy finds — and this is perhaps the sole basis of her love for Gatsby — that there are romantic possibilities in the disorderly riot of his world totally absent from her own. Even the dissipations he offers, or condones, at his house are frank, lively and diverting — very different from Tom Buchanan's crude and furtive relaxations.

Gatsby's parties, too, are virtually his only genuine acts of creation. His dream of Daisy and the way of life she represents, whatever imaginative intensity he puts into it, is an absurd and vulgar illusion. His 'platonic conception' of himself does not differ very significantly from the pattern of

23 Grahame Smith, *op.cit.*, pp. 1—3.
24 Shakespeare, *Henry IV, part 2*, I ii 5—11.

Dan Cody's career — the robber baron turned playboy. But his parties are triumphant expressions of that 'vast, vulgar and meretricious beauty' which, as we have already seen, is one of the most characteristic manifestations of American life. When Nick tells Gatsby that his house looks like the World's Fair, and reflects that his guests 'conducted themselves according to the rules of behaviour associated with an amusement park'; or when Tom Buchanan calls Gatsby's car a 'circus-wagon', the implications are clearly unfavourable. And yet, taken in relation to the parties themselves, these gibes help to direct our attention to something very different: 'There was music from my neighbour's house through the summer nights. In his blue gardens men and girls came and went like moths among the whisperings and the champagne and the stars.'

> The lights grow brighter as the earth lurches away from the sun, and now the orchestra is playing yellow cocktail music, and the opera of voices pitches a key higher. Laughter is easier minute by minute, spilled with prodigality, tipped out at a cheerful word. The groups change more swiftly, swell with new arrivals, dissolve and form in the same breath; already there are wanderers, confident girls who move here and there among the stouter and more stable, become for a sharp, joyous moment the centre of a group, and then, excited with triumph, glide on through the sea-change of faces and voices and colours under the constantly changing light.[25]

That Gatsby should have brought to life all this miraculous shimmering ephemeral beauty and excitement places him among the great artist-showmen of America — the architects who designed the World's Fairs and Expositions; the circus ring-masters, and the gifted mountebanks of the state and county fairs; the directors of Hollywood epics and musicals; and the scientists, astronauts and media men who, between them, turned the Apollo moon-shots into the best television entertainment ever made.

To these creative gifts, Gatsby adds the gift of comedy. His parties always seem about to bubble over into a burst of irresistible laughter. Even the mechanical housekeeping arrangements have a comic effect: the servants who toil 'with mops and scrubbing-brushes and hammers and garden-shears, repairing the ravages of the night before'; the caterers who, with tempting foods, yards of canvas, and hundreds of coloured lights, turn Gatsby's gardens into an enormous Christmas tree; the crates of oranges and lemons which arrive like expected guests from New York, have their juice extracted, and leave his back door in a 'pyramid of pulpless halves.' When, a little later in the evening, Nick Carraway speaks of 'the premature moon, produced like the supper, no doubt, out of a caterer's basket', the whole scene seems to hover between the magical and the absurd. A similar effect is obtained at the beginning of Orson Welles's *Citizen Kane*, in the newsreel which describes Xanadu — not Kubla Khan's pleasure-dome but Kane's monstrous Florida estate. A particularly felicitous touch is the reference to

25 *Gatsby*, BH1, pp. 155–6.

Kane's collection of animals — 'a specimen of every animal, bird and reptile in the world — the largest private zoo since Noah's Ark.'

As Nick's evocation of the atmosphere of Gatsby's parties gradually modulates into his account of the first one he actually attended, the comic element becomes more explicit. At the beginning, it is like a ripple of suppressed laughter half-heard in the general concert of sounds, but soon, like the mounting hilarity of the guests themselves, it becomes unmistakably the dominant note. It is at this phase of the evening that Nick and Jordan find the owl-eyed man admiring Gatsby's library. Then the rhythm of the party changes again — from hilarity to comic uproar: a drunken soprano performs with tears of black mascara streaming down her face, and, in the riotous finale, the owl-eyed man reappears — as the uncomprehending passenger of a car which has lost one of its wheels. The presiding genius at this scene of comic revelry is Gatsby: he surveys his departing guests from the steps of his house, his hand raised, amid the din of motor-horns in a formal gesture of farewell.

It is in this respect that he most resembles Trimalchio, a character who was very much in Fitzgerald's mind while he was writing *The Great Gatsby*. When Gatsby abruptly stops giving his parties, Nick remarks that 'his career as Trimalchio was over'; and at one stage Fitzgerald actually considered *Trimalchio* and *Trimalchio in West Egg* as possible titles for the novel.[26] Trimalchio's banquet, the longest episode in the *Satyricon* of Petronius, is one of the great comic scenes of classical literature, and has certain obvious resemblances with Gatsby's parties. Both are set in times of wealth and decadence (Petronius himself is usually — though not certainly — identified with that Petronius Arbiter described by Tacitus, who presided over the revels at the court of Nero). The guests in each case are a motley collection of adventurers and entertainers, while the two hosts are *nouveaux riches* with the uncertain taste common to that position. In both entertainments the life and virtue are comic, and both reach their dramatic climaxes in scenes of comic disorder. Gatsby's pose — aloof, dignified, ceremonial almost — is in ludicrous contrast with the turmoil of farcical misunderstandings and caterwauling motor-horns in his drive. The *débâcle* of Trimalchio's banquet has the same relation to the whole, and contains similar comic incongruities. In order to parade his wealth and liberality, he has his will brought in and read aloud. As his slaves and guests weep drunkenly, he is inspired by the thought that they can pretend the occasion is his funeral wake. He lies down on a couch as if he were the corpse, libations are poured out, and a brass band is summoned to play suitable music. But the leading performer gives such a piercing blast on his instrument that the whole neighbourhood is awakened. The fire brigade is aroused, and the guests flee in terror as the firemen rush in with their axes and buckets of water.

26 Matthew J. Bruccoli, *Apparatus for F. Scott Fitzgerald's 'The Great Gatsby'*, Columbia, S.C., 1974, p. 6 and fn.

While it is almost certain that Fitzgerald learned something from Petronius about the dramatic organization of such scenes — about the mounting rhythms that run through huge entertainments — his comic sense is entirely his own. In Trimalchio's banquet there is no trace of that magical lightness and beauty which hover over Gatsby's parties — indeed, the tasteless display, the revolting food, the boring songs and recitations, and the fatuous practical jokes are only redeemed by the comic vitality of Trimalchio himself. Petronius's comedy is excellent, but it is straight-forwardly Rabelaisian, neither very subtle nor very varied. One cannot but feel that Fitzgerald's comic sense is, by contrast, finer and more inventive. Gatsby's nature contains both grossness and delicacy; his oblique relation to his guests allows of many ironies which are outside Petronius's range; and his parties display an incomparable variety of mood and atmosphere. *The Great Gatsby* is the only work in which Fitzgerald realized the full potentialities of his comic genius, but in this one novel he equalled the masters of world literature.

Fitzgerald's vision of life in *The Great Gatsby* is a complex one: he appreciates the comic vitality of Gatsby and the grandiose scope of his romantic imagination; at the same time, there is an equally important element of moral rigour in the novel, which is most apparent in Fitzgerald's attitude to the American rich. The relation these conflicting elements have to each other has some similarities with the complex meaning of Falstaff's position in the *Henry IV* plays: the mere fact of Falstaff's existence is a creative and liberating force, and yet one cannot deny the baseness of most of what he does. As both Shakespeare and Fitzgerald recognize, these two perceptions do not cancel each other out, nor is there any convenient formula that will resolve them. Each artist seems to say in effect, life is like that — that is a part of its complexity. That this sense of complexity is so successfully conveyed in *The Great Gatsby* is due almost entirely to the figure of Nick Carraway.

Nick combines the role of stern moral critic with that of fascinated and disinterested spectator of life. Fitzgerald is careful to define these attitudes at the beginning of the novel in such a way that this double vision can be seen as a plausible expression of a single unified character. The way in which Nick describes his ancestry — light and almost flippant as it is — suggests that the explanation may lie there. According to family tradition, the Carraways are descended from the Dukes of Buccleuch, but in reality their story begins with Nick's great-uncle, who came West in 1859, sent a substitute to the Civil War, and started the wholesale hardware business which is still the basis of their fortunes. The sense of divided loyalties is clear — to a romantic, pseudo-aristocratic ideal on the one hand, and to the standards of a sober, practical, commercial respectability on the other. It is wholly characteristic of Fitzgerald that this conflict of allegiances should be presented partly in terms of social class. Only through an aristocratic conception of man can the largest human possibilities be realized, but middle-class life is the only source of moral integrity and of stability in personal relationships.

Fitzgerald makes the same distinction in somewhat different terms in the first words of the novel. Nick Carraway recalls how his father, in a somewhat enigmatic manner, had once reminded him that 'a sense of the fundamental decencies is parcelled out unequally at birth' — a superior moral sense is one of the many advantages a man inherits from being born into a good family. The awareness of this privilege has made Nick tolerant when he encounters lower moral standards in others, and his tolerance has, in turn, made him the recipient of many strange confidences. But there are times when his impulse towards tolerance and receptivity is met by an equally strong principle of moral restraint: 'When I came back from the East last autumn I felt that I wanted the world to be in uniform and at a sort of moral attention for ever.' Only Gatsby is exempt from Nick's recoil into disapproval — 'Gatsby, who represented everything for which I have an unaffected scorn.'[27] This passage is the key to Nick's position as narrator: it explains why he is able gradually to recognize Gatsby's extraordinary qualities. It also accounts for his prompt reaction to the Buchanans — why it is that his initial fascination with their way of life turns to disgust in a single evening: 'To a certain temperament the situation might have seemed intriguing — my own instinct was to telephone immediately for the police'. Most interestingly of all, perhaps, Nick's self-analysis tells us why, having recognized the Buchanans' rottenness so early, he puts up with them socially for so long.

Nick's moral stand, the point at which the limits of his tolerance are reached, involves, we notice, a return from the East to the Middle Western city where his family lives. Almost at the end of the novel he remarks, 'this has been a story of the West, after all' and at least part of the significance of these words is the bearing they have upon his complex moral position. The Middle West is home, the place to return to after dubious, if exciting, adventures in the East, a place where the sober, provincial, domestic virtues continue to maintain an unquestioned authority. Like the contrast in class values, this difference in regional cultures adds a further element of interest to Nick's responses.

It would be a mistake to see Nick simply as a narrator, however: he is a definite and important character. One of his functions is as Gatsby's shadow, a man who would have the same dreams as Gatsby if he could. Like Gatsby, he is a Middle Western boy who finds, after the upheaval of the War, that, 'Instead of being the warm centre of the world, the Middle West now seemed the ragged edge of the universe'. He comes East to make a quick fortune in the bond business and to become a part of a more sophisticated way of life. The fact that he can neither dream, nor live out the implications of his dreams, as Gatsby does, makes him a useful foil to Gatsby: by the

27 *Gatsby*, BH1, pp. 125–6.

measure of his ordinariness, we appreciate Gatsby's greatness all the more. Nick, too, pays his own modest tribute, at many points in the novel, to Daisy's charm, adding the necessary touch of credibility to Gatsby's dreams. His own half-hearted romance with Jordan Baker — a girl who, like Daisy, is careless, dishonest and 'a rotten driver' — again reminds one by contrast of the stupendous scale of Gatsby's love. The only decisive step Nick ever takes towards Jordan, in fact, is on the afternoon when she tells him what she knows of Gatsby's affair with Daisy five years before in Louisville. Moved momentarily by the story of another man's love, he kisses her.

It would be absurd to attempt to sum up Fitzgerald's achievement in *The Great Gatsby* in a single concluding phrase; all one can do is to try, as I have done, to show some of the sources of its greatness. However, there is one general comment that is in place: the novel is remarkable for the extent to which it succeeds in combining imaginative power and vitality with faultless artistry. The depth and range of its analysis of American civilization, the intensity with which it evokes the life of the romantic sensibility, and the wonderful comic vision that led to the creation of its hero, are balanced and controlled by a miraculously precise attention to detail — a poet's sense of the possibilities of language. *The Great Gatsby*, in achieving this particular kind of success, is not only unique among American novels of the twentieth century, but an undoubted masterpiece of world literature.

6
Tender is the Night

When D. W. Harding reviewed *Tender is the Night* for *Scrutiny* in 1934,[1] he used the word 'harrowing' to characterize its precise emotional tone. In the process of Dick Diver's deterioration, we feel the presence of unbearable pain, which is not relieved by any tragic catharsis. Although Harding in most ways failed to do justice to the novel's complexity and maturity, in this one respect he responded to it more sensitively than any other of Fitzgerald's critics. The harrowing quality of *Tender is the Night* is remarkably consistent: it is concentrated in the figure of Dick Diver, but it is diffused through many other characters and incidents. There are almost infinite variations in the level of intensity, there are even apparent remissions, but it is never entirely absent.

There is, to begin with, a great deal of violence in *Tender is the Night*. For the Divers and their friends, violence isn't confined to rare moments of personal conflict — it is part of the texture of everyday life. When Dick and Nicole go to the Gare St Lazare to see Abe North off to America, they become the casual witnesses of a murder. As the boat train is about to leave, an American woman takes a revolver out of her handbag and shoots her departing lover. 'Then, as if nothing had happened, the lives of the Divers and their friends flowed out into the street.' The 'echoes of violence' which reverberate behind them are part of a hideous normality — like the condition of men at war. This is made explicit in a fragment of conversation between two porters, who discuss the shooting while the Divers wait for a taxi outside the station: '*Assez de sang pour se croire à la guerre.*' Echoes of violence and the actuality of violence are a constant element in the atmosphere and structure of the novel. Even when the violence is farcical — in the duel between Tommy Barban and Albert McKisco, for instance, or in the scene where Gausse, the hotel proprietor, kicks Lady Caroline Sibly-Biers's bottom — it is a disturbing element. Often it is brutalizing and sordid, as it is in Dick's Roman brawl, or when Rosemary finds the body of the murdered negro, Peterson, casually dumped on her

1 D. W. Harding, 'Mechanisms of Misery', reprinted in Alfred Kazin, *F. Scott Fitzgerald: the Man and his Work*, New York and Cleveland, 1951, p. 100. (First appeared in *Scrutiny*, Cambridge, 1934.)

bed. Sometimes it is unspeakably horrible — the news of how Abe North was beaten to death in a New York speakeasy, which Dick hears being callously talked over in a Munich beer-cellar; and, above all, Devereux Warren's rape of his own daughter. The historical reverberations of the Great War, as in the porters' conversation, are a constant undertone to the lives of the individual characters. There is frequently, too, a sense of psychological violence, most obviously in the periodic outbreaks of Nicole's insanity, but most deeply in Dick's inner conflicts and the shocks inflicted on his sensibilities.

It is at this point that the echoes of violence are blended with other, no less disturbing, vibrations — the self-disgust, despair and mental anguish which so many of the characters feel. Fitzgerald's treatment of these states of feeling is at the farthest possible remove from the sort of *nostalgie de la boue* which is so tiresome a feature of, say, the existentialist novel. On the contrary, the surface of *Tender is the Night* is urbane, polished, often beautifully serene: the horrors Fitzgerald's people experience are those which lurk beneath the most civilized and reassuring forms of existence. They are 'nice people', as Mary North explains to Dick in their last conversation — all they want is 'to have a good time'. And, if they are not having a good time in Paris or on the Riviera, they are in clinics and sanatoriums in Switzerland, being looked after in the best modern way. We are given many glimpses of the sorts of lives these latter may be supposed to lead, but one in particular stands out for the quality of unspectacular misery it conveys. Dick goes to the clinic one rainy night expecting to meet Nicole:

> His eyes followed a beret, not wet with waiting like Nicole's beret, but covering a skull recently operated on. Beneath it human eyes appeared, found him and came over:
> 'Bonjour, Docteur.'
> 'Bonjour, Monsieur.'
> 'Il fait beau temps.'
> 'Oui, merveilleux.'
> 'Vous êtes ici maintenant?'
> 'Non, pour la journée seulement.'
> 'Ah, bon. Alors — au revoir, Monsieur.'
> Glad at having survived another contact, the wretch in the beret moved away.[2]

The many moments of nostalgic beauty and gaiety do not contradict the effect of such episodes as this, but throw them into even sharper relief. The description of Gausse's beach with which the novel begins, acquires its full significance only in later scenes. Fitzgerald never lets us experience again that first moment of glowing, shimmering tranquility — that flow of light and colour which is both sensuous and airy, serene and trembling with life. Next time we see it the freshness has gone: our vision is complicated by Rosemary's already suspect romanticism, by the tarnished lives of Mrs

Abrams, the McKiscos and their circle, and by the Divers' obscure secret. When Dick visits it for the last time and bestows on it his ironic papal blessing, it is as raucous as Coney Island.

An even more interesting example is the way in which Fitzgerald rounds off his account of the all-night party in Paris which Dick organizes in honour of Rosemary's birthday. It is already daylight, and they begin to laugh because the people in the streets have the delusion it is next morning, while they are certain it is still the night before. All at once, a strange object comes into view, a huge chestnut tree in full bloom strapped to a truck and moving slowly towards the Champs Élysées. As it jolts along, it seems to Rosemary to be, like herself, 'simply shaking with laughter.' The loveliness of the tree, because of its startling arrival on the scene, has a bizarre surreal character. Although it is part of the freshness of the morning, it suggests a quality of vision overstimulated by alcohol and fatigue. The laughter of the tree, like the laughter of Rosemary and her friends, has a slightly hysterical quality. As Fitzgerald himself had said a little earlier in analysing the dissipations of American and English expatriates in Paris: 'everything they did had a purely nervous inspiration.' The passage also anticipates the end of Book One, where we are allowed at last to witness one of Nicole's breakdowns into raging hysteria.

There are many varieties of suffering and tension in *Tender is the Night*, but all of them are subordinated in some degree to the case of Dick Diver — to the horror of watching a man who once possessed intellectual brilliance, moral integrity and charm, disintegrate slowly into an inert alcoholic wreck. Even Nicole, who is not gifted with sympathy or understanding, grasps something of what is going on inside him as she watches him sitting alone on the terrace of their Riviera house. She is about to leave him — she has already become Tommy Barban's mistress — but she contemplates with some compunction the ruins of what she is leaving behind:

> He was thinking, he was living a world completely his own and in the small motions of his face, the brow raised or lowered, the eyes narrowed or widened, the lips set and reset, the play of his hands, she saw him progress from phase to phase of his own story spinning out inside him, his own, not hers. Once he clenched his fists and leaned forwards, once it brought into his face an expression of torment and despair — when this passed its stamp lingered in his eyes.[3]

The most important thing to notice about Dick's deterioration is that it is not a simple process. The general failure to recognize this fact has had serious consequences for the reputation of *Tender is the Night*: it has been subjected to a great deal of adverse criticism — most of it singularly inept — and to almost as much half-hearted praise. Critics have uneasily admitted, or loudly complained, that the novel is confused — that Fitz-

3 *Ibid.*, p. 390.

gerald was never clear in his own mind what caused Dick Diver's decline; that in consequence he told the story in the wrong order, and that even when Malcolm Cowley[4] put it right for him after his death, it still didn't make sense. These critics usually proceed by selecting one of the possible explanations — that Dick is a victim of the rich, that his moral will is destroyed when he abandons his profession as a psychiatrist, that he exhausts himself emotionally by giving too much to other people — and then censure Fitzgerald for filling out the novel with false clues and irrelevant material. The conviction that it should be possible to isolate a single cause for so complex a change in personality, while it is intellectually absurd, faithfully reflects twentieth–century habits of thought. The rise of psychology and the social sciences has tended to give us a false sense of assurance in approaching human situations. Emboldened by spurious notions of scientific certainty, we are often led to claim for a single traumatic, environmental or historical factor the status of a complete explanation. The effect of these new sciences has been the contrary of what their greatest thinkers presumably intended: they have not refined our notions of human motivation but made them cruder. To be specific, they have created a climate of thought in which it is more difficult to read novels like *Tender is the Night* intelligently.

Fitzgerald, by not succumbing to the temptation to schematize and simplify, takes his place in the best traditions of the art of fiction. It would not have seemed strange to the masters of classic European realism, nor presumably to their readers, that the deterioration of a human character — of, say, Tolstoy's Anna Karenina, or Stendhal's Julien Sorel, or George Eliot's Walter Lydgate — is not something to be summed up in a single confident formula. These novelists recognized that a multiplicity of factors contribute to the ruin of a human life and, in addition, they saw something which is possibly even more important: that a part of the horror of such situations is that they contain an element of mystery — beyond a certain point they are inexplicable.

Fitzgerald's treatment of Dick Diver has precisely this quality. *Tender is the Night* is conceived on a scale which makes it possible for him to explore a human life in all its complexity and variety. It has an extraordinary richness and density of texture, so that the pattern of Dick Diver's inner life, the external facts of his career, the social pressures which bear down upon him, and the historical context within which he lives, are all given to us with minute and vivid particularity. At the same time, Fitzgerald conveys a sense of the mysterious, the unknowable, element in Dick's ruin — the things in him we can only guess at, as, like Nicole, we watch him sitting alone in his chair at the edge of the cliff. If the cumulative effect of the novel were not enough, Fitzgerald states the matter explicitly:

4   *Tender is the Night. A Romance by F. Scott Fitzgerald. With the Author's Final Revisions.* [sic]. Preface by Malcolm Cowley, New York, 1951.

He had lost himself — he could not tell the hour when, or the day or the week, the month or the year. Once he had cut through things, solving the most complicated equations as the simplest problems of his simplest patients. Between the time he found Nicole flowering under a stone on the Zurichsee and the moment of his meeting with Rosemary the spear had been blunted.[5]

Dick's moment of self-analysis is interesting not only as a comment upon the process of his deterioration: it also contains the principle which underlies the structure of *Tender is the Night*. If it is true that no single cause can be assigned to the break-up of a human personality, then it is also true that one cannot assign the deterioration to a particular moment in time — 'he could not tell the hour when, or the day or the week, the month or the year'. This rules out the possibility of a simple chronological narrative, which only makes sense in the case of a character like Hurstwood in Dreiser's *Sister Carrie*. Hurstwood is the victim of a very simple equation of forces which push him down a kind of staircase one step at a time. For Dick Diver there is no simple equation of forces — in that sense there is no staircase to descend. And so Fitzgerald did what the logic of his story demanded — he began in the middle, at a point where the complexities of Dick's case were at their greatest.

When Rosemary first meets Dick, he is outwardly at the height of his powers: he is physically healthy and attractive; he has an effortless charm and social dominance, which make him a wonderful host and deviser of civilized entertainments; his relationship with Nicole seems so close that people think of them as 'the Divers' rather than as separate persons; and he is confident that he can complete his ambitious scientific projects. At the same time, there are ominous symptoms of an inner sickness: the streak of cynicism and cruelty which appears in the way he plans the dinner-party at the Villa Diana; the cold-blooded sentimentality with which he begins to 'work over' Rosemary; a growing weariness in his attitude to his friends, which is particularly clear in his dealings with Abe North; and the constant strain of Nicole's illness. Until his emotional involvement with Rosemary brings these obscure maladies to the level of consciousness, Dick is completely unaware that the fabric of his personality has been gradually weakened over the years. When Collis Clay tells him that Rosemary once spent an afternoon with a man in a locked railway compartment, he is overwhelmed by an ugly crisis of sexual jealousy which sends him hurrying across Paris to loiter outside the film studio where she is working. His behaviour on this occasion forces him to realize that there is something seriously the matter with him, but it does not occur to him at this time that an irrevocable deterioration has already taken place. After the shock of Peterson's murder and Nicole's breakdown in the hotel, he acts as if he had been brought to his senses and resumes his responsibilities — his care for Nicole and his scientific work. He even engages in a period of clinical

5 *Tender is the Night*, BH2, p. 286.

practice, and it is only three years later, during the leave of absence which terminates in his disastrous visit to Rome, that he is forced to recognize that 'the spear had been blunted' before he met Rosemary.

In the process of Dick's deterioration, it should be clear that Rosemary is only a catalyst, not a cause. She does not, in herself, bring about any radical change in his personality. It is only that, under the influence of his sudden infatuation, the elements of his character, both positive and destructive, arrange themselves in a recognizable pattern. Book One of *Tender is the Night* gives us this moment of catalytic change — we watch the pattern appearing, like a precipitate in a chemical solution.

Book Two, to extend the chemical metaphor, tells us what is in the solution. It tells us about Dick's parentage, his education, his early ideals, his professional career, his social contacts, his relation to his times, his strengths, his weaknesses, his mistakes, the crucial decisions of his life, his marriage, his friends, his habits, his diversions. It does not attempt to isolate causes: instead, it sets out to immerse us in the complexity of an individual human being, to make us realize how much is involved in the disaster of a wasted life. Just as the precipitate is suspended in the solution, so Book One is enveloped by Book Two. The events of Book One occupy a period of about a fortnight in the summer of 1925; Book Two covers a period of eleven years, beginning with the 'heroic period' of Dick's psychiatric studies at Vienna in 1917, and ending with his drunken brawl in Rome in 1928. Until this last episode, his deterioration is not at all apparent to those around him, nor is it altogether clear to Dick himself: it is the period during which the fabric of his personality is crumbling within its shell — as he says to Rosemary at the very end, 'the manner remains intact long after the morale cracks'.

Book Three deals with the terminal phase during which even the manner no longer remains. The hidden forces which have been sapping him for years erupt visibly and dramatically, and what is left of his personality does not take long to break up.

Given the nature of Dick's decline, the structure of *Tender is the Night* is wholly admirable, but one would hardly get this impression from reading most of Fitzgerald's critics. The doubts which he himself expressed in his last years have undoubtedly contributed to the general confusion, and the publication in 1951 of the version which Malcolm Cowley put together from Fitzgerald's pencilled notes, has done incalculable harm. No one now attaches any importance whatever to Cowley's edition, and it is unnecessary to restate the case against it at length. One may merely note in passing that Fitzgerald had no doubts about his novel until after its commercial failure and his own crack-up. As Matthew J. Bruccoli has shown conclusively[6], Fitzgerald's notion of the structure of the novel remained absolutely unchanged from the moment he took up the Dick Diver subject in 1932

---

6   Matthew J. Bruccoli, *The Composition of 'Tender is the Night.' A Study of the Manuscripts*, Pittsburgh, 1963.

until the publication of the completed work in 1934. Fitzgerald himself, when he wrote to H. L. Mencken a few days after the novel appeared, insisted several times that it had been written 'to a definite plan', [7], and that if he were to write it again, he would set about it in exactly the same way. A month later, writing to Gilbert Seldes, he complained that the reviewers had been 'entirely cuckoo'[8] in their discussions of the technique of *Tender is the Night*. With what one can only regard as prophetic insight, he cited Malcolm Cowley as being particularly at sea.

Although Cowley's edition no longer stands in the way, the misunderstandings of which it is a symptom remain, with the damaging consequence that the structure of *Tender is the Night*, instead of being seen as one of its chief glories, is treated with embarrassment. Even those who admire it tend to speak of it as 'a noble failure' or 'a flawed masterpiece'. An ingenious variation which is currently fashionable is to argue that *Tender is the Night* is all the better for being somewhat confused, and that *The Great Gatsby* suffers, by comparison, from being 'almost too perfect'.

Faced with such absurdities, it is necessary to present the case for the structure of *Tender is the Night* with some pertinacity. As well as providing the perfect form for the exploration of Dick Diver's decline, it enables Fitzgerald to draw upon the advantages of point-of-view narration in a most interesting way. In one of his working notes, he sketched out the following idea:

> To call him
>   I Dick
>   II Dr Diver
>   III Diver [9]

As Bruccoli points out, this scheme, in its literal form, was dropped, but it seems to me that the intention behind the scheme — to present each of the three books from a distinctive point of view — remains.

In Book One ('Dick'), we see the hero primarily as Rosemary sees him. It is important that we should first respond to him as a brilliant and magnetic figure, since otherwise the horror of his subsequent decline will be greatly diminished. Fitzgerald is able to convey this first impression far more convincingly through Rosemary's romantic immaturity and her readiness to fall in love, than he could through direct authorial narrative. Because of her relation to Dick, she is an admirable device, too, for the gradual uncovering of Dick's inner sickness, and the dark secret of his marriage. She is so close to him that she is bound, sooner or later, to gain some knowledge of his weaknesses. On the other hand, since she is not particularly intelligent, and since her love for Dick makes her adoring rather than analytical, she does not make her discoveries with undue haste — indeed a large part of the situation

---

7 *Letters*, p. 510.
8 *Ibid.*, p. 513.
9 Bruccoli, *op.cit.*, p. 85.

remains forever beyond her comprehension. (The letter she writes her mother after the *débâcle* in the hotel in Paris is a fair sample of Rosemary's limited capacity for understanding other people.) Because of this combination of qualities, Fitzgerald can use her to tell us a great deal about Dick, without compromising our sense of the complexity of the case — a more intellectual observer could not have been restrained from presenting us with a premature diagnosis.

Book Two ('Dr Diver') presents the situation not only from the hero's own point of view, but for the most part as he himself would like us to see it. His moral and personal identity is inseparable from his sense of vocation. The profession of medicine gives him an ideal of moral responsibility, a social position, a field for creative intellectual activity, and scope for honourable ambition. Even when he abandons clinical practice for several years, he considers it a professional decision and not a self-indulgence: Nicole is his patient as well as his wife, and it is right that she should benefit from travel and from the serene vitality of the Riviera climate. The work house, which he builds with his own money in a remote corner of the villa garden, is an indication of his determination not to give up scientific research.

It is in this section that Dick appears at his most admirable and sympathetic. We see him as he was in the 'heroic period' at the beginning of his career, not yet damaged by life, and with all his potentialities intact; and our concern for his subsequent errors and misfortunes is not qualified by any suspicion that perhaps it is only Rosemary who is moved by them. His innermost thoughts and feelings are always present to us, so that his intelligence and wit, his essential honesty, and his restless self-awareness become vital and appealing elements in our sense of his character.

This dimension is significantly absent from Book Three ('Diver'). As the brusque use of his surname suggests, the treatment of the hero is objective. It is as if the completeness of his collapse has removed him to a great distance. His sufferings and humiliations, while they are distressingly real, seem to be happening to a comparative stranger: we can only infer them from external signs like the expressions of his face during the aquaplane episode. The point of view from which we see him at this time is generally Nicole's. She is self-centred and rather deficient in her feeling for other people, and these traits in her character are now reinforced by the fact that she is consciously drawing away from Dick. She is suspended between two egotisms — the self-absorption of the mentally sick, and the selfishness of her class: to her, Dick is in part an old habit, in part an obstacle. It is this use of Nicole's point of view that enabled Fitzgerald to bring off the 'dying fall' effect at the end of the novel, of which he was so proud.[10] The last vague rumours of Dick's whereabouts come to us, appropriately, through her fading consciousness of him, as she becomes absorbed in her new life with Tommy Barban.

10   *Letters*, p. 310.

While it is important to emphasize the coherence and consistency of *Tender is the Night*, the quality which contributes most to its artistic greatness is its richness and fullness of detail. Fitzgerald himself spoke of it as being 'full and comprehensive' where *The Great Gatsby* was 'selective'[11]. Every part of this material has a bearing, however indirect, on the disintegration of Dick Diver. For convenience in analysis, it seems best to proceed, as far as possible, from the particular to the general: to begin with the pattern of Dick's inner life; then to examine his personal and social relationships; and finally to consider the historical character of the age in which he lives.

Whatever else may be wrong with him, Dick is not in the ordinary sense a weak man — in fact, he almost always gives an impression of unusual strength. When one considers the pressures on him, it is astonishing that he lasts for so long. Even at the end, he has the capacity to endure and to obliterate himself without fuss — he comes out of the final showdown with Tommy Barban rather well.

Dick's cast of mind, however, makes him dangerously vulnerable. His habitual attitudes and favourite assumptions provide a poor basis for deciding how to live. This note is sounded at the beginning of his career by his Rumanian friend, who warns him, 'That's going to be your trouble — judgement about yourself.' Dick's sense of the balance between his own capabilities and limitations is clouded by a naive and rather presumptuous kind of American optimism — a feeling that he can become a great psychiatrist or even a complete man simply by an act of will. More seriously, he has a profound belief in the value of romantic failure — a view of the human situation which, as I have shown in chapter 1, appealed to Fitzgerald from his earliest childhood. It must be said that Fitzgerald's attitude to this trait in Dick's character is highly equivocal: he does seem to imply that it is a reason for regarding the latter as a potentially heroic figure; on the other hand he is fully aware that there is something perverse in Dick's conviction that 'intactness' means 'incompleteness', and that, unless a man is 'a little damaged' by life, he remains forever unfulfilled. Dick's consequent tendency to take unnecessary risks, to match himself against impossible odds, certainly has much to do with his decision to marry Nicole. When he takes the case to his colleagues, Dr Dohmler and Franz Gregorovious, for their advice, the result is a foregone conclusion: Franz reminds him of what he knows already — that there is virtually no chance of building a happy marriage upon a mental patient's transference to her psychiatrist — while Dohmler doesn't find it necessary even to express an opinion on a question where the issues are so clear. Dick accepts their professional diagnosis, and at the same time ignores it: his love for Nicole is an overwhelming force, but, besides this, he is undoubtedly attracted by a situation in which defeat is almost inevitable. This is not merely the emotional basis for many of his most important choices: it is a conscious

11 *Ibid.*, p. 551.

theory which he expounds, on occasion, with doctrinaire intensity. When Nicole complains, *à propos* of Abe North's alcoholism, that 'so many smart men go to pieces nowadays', Dick takes her up sharply: 'Smart men play close to the line because they have to — some of them can't stand it, and so they quit.'[12]

The pattern of Dick's mental processes exposes him to dangers no less great. Although his intellectual training is in the sciences, the basis of his thought is largely intuitive and imaginative, and the quality of these insights depends almost entirely on his emotional state at the time. On the afternoon of the shooting at the Gare St Lazare, he is prostrated by a nervous fatigue which is accentuated by his unhappiness over Rosemary. As he sits on a café terrace with her and Nicole, he finds that he has lost contact with them, has no sense of what they are thinking and feeling, no idea of how he might help them or even talk to them. Exhaustion turns him in upon himself, and deprives him of 'the long ground-swell of imagination that he counted on for his judgements'.

He carries these habits of mind into his scientific and clinical work with consequences that are generally disastrous. He relies too much upon his emotions to be a dependable psychiatrist. At times he exhausts himself by becoming over-involved in his patients — in the woman artist suffering from nervous exzema, and most of all, of course, in Nicole. At other times he cannot interest himself in his cases, and he is quite unable to deal with repellent people like the Australian family who precipitate his final departure from the clinic. He altogether lacks the quality of sympathetic detachment which a doctor needs in order to maintain his balance and his professional effectiveness. William Carlos Williams defines this special kind of humanity with unique precision in poems like 'Complaint' and 'The Injury', which draw upon his own medical experience. In the latter, the doctor participates in a sick man's struggle for breath, and yet a part of his mind is disengaged, free to observe other kinds of breathing — the panting of a freight locomotive in the nearby railroad yards, and the effortless song of a whitethroat at dawn.

Through his marriage, Dick condemns himself to a process of exhaustion. He gives himself extravagantly, and he is exploited: 'there was a pleasingness about him that simply had to be used.' In his relations with Nicole, he commits himself to an impossible set of conflicting demands: to being her husband and her psychiatrist; to conducting her through a series of gracious expatriate adventures, and at the same time continuing with his own scientific work; to becoming a pensioner of the American rich, and maintaining his personal independence. As the roles of lover and psychiatrist become inextricably confused, his confidence in his own professional judgement is progressively undermined. He gives up using hypnosis as a method of treatment because Nicole once laughed at his attempts to hypnotize her. At times the compulsive force of her psychosis threatens to engulf him: in the scene where she has one of her mad fits at a fairground, we are told that 'he could not watch her disintegrations without participating in them.' As a result, the Divers' marriage is not a mutually re-creative relationship: Dick gets nothing in return for the enormous drain on his energies, and his affair with Rosemary is in part an acknowledgement of this fact.

When Dick gives way to Nicole's 'sweet bullying' and becomes her husband, he does not merely marry a psychological problem, however — he marries into a class. The American rich are the chief external agents of his destruction, and the series of compromises through which he gradually abandons his inherited values for their way of life is a major element in his moral decline. Fitzgerald had expressed similar attitudes in earlier novels and stories, but there is a significant change of emphasis in *Tender is the Night*. This change appears particularly in his altered sense of the social power of women in American upper-class life. Formerly, he had felt that men were ultimately responsible for creating and sustaining the social style of the wealthy: Dick Humbird, Braddock Washington, Tom Buchanan and Anson Hunter perpetuate the heavily patristic, pseudo-baronial ethos of the Gilded Age. Within this pattern, the flapper leads a sort of piratical existence: she can break hearts and wreak havoc on a considerable scale among men of her own generation, but her adventures could scarcely be said to shake society to its foundations. Josephine, in the group of five stories Fitzgerald wrote around 1930, achieves great triumphs through the exercise of her wits, her beauty, her audacity and her unscrupulousness, but her hands are never on the actual levers of social and economic power. In *Tender is the Night*, however, it is Nicole and Baby Warren who exercise control and set the social tone. Their father, Devereux Warren, is by comparison deplorably weak. His bullying hypocrisy and maudlin remorse disturb even Dr Dohmler's professional calm: Dohmler is impelled to exclaim 'Peasant!' as Warren leaves his consulting room. Even the wonderful way of life Dick devises on the Riviera and in Paris does not proceed from an inner conviction of his own: he creates it because his women demand it of him. He married Nicole in order to look after her — that at least is her view and Baby's — and a restful aristocratic style of living is good for her. Besides, as Baby lucidly explains to him on a number of occasions, Nicole has a great deal of money, and there is no reason why she should not live like other people in her class.

The secret of their power is that they, and women like them, have absolute control over one of the most important economic functions of their society — consumption and spending. Unlike the flapper, who is in the dependent position of a spoilt child with unlimited pocket money, they hold their wealth firmly in their own hands. Because they are somewhat older — Nicole is married, and Baby is a woman of a certain age — they are accorded a unique degree of financial independence. Henry Adams, a generation earlier, observed this situation in terms which are peculiarly apposite to my argument:

> He had seen artificial energy to the amount of twenty or five-and-twenty million steam horse-power created in America since 1840, and as much more economized, which had been socially turned over to the American woman, she being the chief object of social expenditure, and the household the only considerable object of American extravagance. According to scientific notions of inertia and force what ought to be the result?
>
> ... in America the result seemed evident and undisputed. The woman had been set free — volatilized like Clerk Maxwell's perfect gas; almost brought to the point of explosion, like steam. One had but to pass a week in Florida, or on any of a hundred huge ocean steamers, or walk through the Place Vendôme, or join a party of Cook's tourists to Jerusalem, to see that the woman had been set free, but these were ephemeral like clouds of butterflies in season, blown away and lost, while the reproductive sources lay hidden.[13]

The sense of the huge economic forces which have been placed in the hands of American women is vividly conveyed. Still more apparent is Adams's ironic view of the magnitude of their failure: he dismisses the way of life they have created in a series of brilliantly derisive phrases — 'volatilized like Clerk Maxwell's perfect gas', 'ephemeral like clouds of butterflies in season.' As for their freedom, it is merely the freedom of the Cook's tourist to wander expensively and aimlessly over the face of the earth.

These themes recur in one of the finest pieces of writing in *Tender is the Night*, the passage in which Fitzgerald describes Nicole and Rosemary shopping in Paris:

> Nicole bought from a great list that ran to two pages, and bought the things in the windows besides. Everything she liked that she couldn't possibly use herself, she bought as a present for a friend. She bought coloured beads, folding beach cushions, artificial flowers, honey, a guest bed, bags, scarfs, love-birds, miniatures for a doll's house, and three yards of some new cloth the colour of prawns. She bought a dozen bathing suits, a rubber alligator, a travelling chess set of gold and ivory, big linen handkerchiefs for Abe, two chamois leather jackets of kingfisher blue and burning bush from Hermes — bought all these things not at all like a high-class courtesan buying underwear and jewels, which were after all professional equipment and insurance — but with an entirely different point of view. Nicole was the product of much ingenuity and toil. For her sake trains began their run at Chicago and traversed the round belly of the continent to California; chicle factories fumed and link belts grew link by link in factories; men mixed toothpaste in vats and drew mouthwash out of copper hogsheads; girls canned tomatoes quickly in August or worked rudely at the Five-and-Tens on Christmas Eve; half-breed Indians toiled on Brazilian coffee plantations and dreamers were muscled out of patent rights in new tractors — these were some of the people who gave a tithe to Nicole, and as the whole system swayed and

13   Henry Adams, *The Education of Henry Adams*, Modern Library edition, New York, pp. 444—5.

thundered onward it lent a feverish bloom to such processes of hers as wholesale buying, like the flush of a fireman's face holding his post before a spreading fire. She illustrated very simple principles, containing in herself her own doom, but illustrated them so accurately that there was grace in the proceeding, and presently Rosemary would try to imitate them.[14]

Fitzgerald, like Adams, dwells on the fact of vast economic resources turned over to women so that they can create a social style. Even Nicole, in her fragile mental state, senses the reality of this power, and spends her money with a confidence to which Rosemary as yet can only aspire. Indeed, Nicole and Rosemary are simply individualized cases of the female tourists whom Adams pictures swarming over three continents. Like their prototypes, they have used their freedom, at best, for the production of an exquisite triviality. The toiling millions of the two Americas have given a tithe to Nicole merely so that she can pass a casual afternoon of graceful extravagance — making a tasteful selection of 'quality rather than quantity from the run of the world's bazaar.'

This scene has undertones, however, which are not to be found in the passage from Henry Adams. Their presence can be accounted for very largely by the fact that Fitzgerald was working in the intellectual and political climate of the 1930s. As well as being exposed to these diffused general influences, he had actually been studying Marx's writings during 1932 – 34, the exact period in which he composed the final draft of *Tender is the Night*. This is not of course to argue that it is a propaganda novel, but simply to observe that he was now inclined to see the social position of the American rich at least in part through images of exploitation, class struggle and incipient revolution. Nicole is 'the product of much ingenuity and toil', and there is a rising tide of condemnation in Fitzgerald's enumeration of the sources of the Warren fortune: in the first items, there is an ironic echo of the phrases used by politicians and boosters to glorify the achievements of trade and industry; with the factory girls and Brazilian natives, the reality of economic oppression begins to emerge; and the sordid catalogue reaches its climax with the swindling of inventors.

The theme of exploitation is one of the most important in the novel. It is not only a key element in Fitzgerald's understanding of society, but also affects his dramatic sense of the relations between individual people. In Baby Warren's behaviour, he shows how the evils of capitalist exploitation can add some distinctive variations to the commission of a much older sin. In the humane tradition of English and American literature, the sin of using other people as instruments to effect one's own practical purposes has often seemed the hardest to forgive. Iago and Edmund are the most detestable of Shakespeare's villains; and in *The Portrait of a Lady*, Isabel Archer's bitterest moment is the discovery that, for Madame Merle, 'she had been an applied handled hung-up tool, as senseless and convenient as mere shaped

14 *Tender is the Night*, BH2, pp. 127—8.

wood and iron.'[15] Baby uses people in the new way — as commodities: she acquires and disposes of them in the same fashion as her grandfather Sid Warren, the horsetrader, presumably dealt in horseflesh. She buys and sells doctors, husbands and psychiatric clinics with the same hard business sense she shows in her handling of real-estate and railroad investments. With complete unselfconsciousness, she informs Dick of her plan to buy a doctor for Nicole from a decent family on Chicago's South Side. Later, in Rome, she thanks him for what he has done as if he were a highly paid, confidential servant: it is not part of her scheme of ideas to suppose that he might have loved Nicole. At the end, when Nicole protests half-heartedly that Dick had been a good husband in the first years of their marriage, Baby retorts, 'That's what he was educated for.'

The element of pure hostility in Fitzgerald's attitude towards the American rich reaches a unique degree of intensity in his portrayal of Baby Warren, but she is no mere abstract embodiment of the moral failure of a class. She is a wholly convincing character, and her battles with Dick are due quite as much to a clash of personalities as to the operation of social forces. Her coldly aggressive and domineering temper gives her a decisive psychological advantage in the sustained campaign she wages against him: his warmth makes him easy to wound, her sterility makes her invulnerable. As a bitch she has no equal in American literature. She is hard — on one occasion she fulfilled an advantageous social engagement in the early stages of appendicitis with an ice-pack strapped under her evening gown. She is outrageously bullying and rude, as in the episode in Rome where she rouses American embassy officials at dead of night in order to get Dick out of jail. She is sexless and emotionally sterile: in the silence which follows Dick's final departure from Gausse's beach, her thoughts turn to her own marital prospects —

> [She was] considering whether or not to marry the latest candidate for her hand and money, an authenticated Hapsburg. She was not quite *thinking* about it. Her affairs had long shared such a sameness, that, as she dried out, they were more important for their conversational value than for themselves.[16]

There is an obvious vein of sardonic humour here, which colours Fitzgerald's whole treatment of Baby's character. It is vital to the success of the portrait, since it enables him to control his feelings towards her — to prevent his dislike from tipping over into hysteria or melodramatic exaggeration.

A subsidiary but important figure in Fitzgerald's analysis of upper-class attitudes is Tommy Barban. In some ways, he is a kind of male European counterpart to Baby Warren: if she represents an advanced stage in the evolution of the American woman, he is a relatively primitive European type — the aristocratic soldier of fortune. His fundamental impulses are

15   Henry James, *The Portrait of a Lady*, Bodley Head Henry James, Vol. 5, p. 586.
16   *Tender is the Night*, BH2, p. 403.

barbaric: he enjoys the physical excitement of danger, and he like to kill; he sees love as an alternative excitement to killing — the proper occupation for the intervals between battles; and he regards women frankly as camp-followers. He quickly grows scornful of the artificial serenity of the Divers' life. He uses people, but he is not a horsetrader: he regards them as inferior wretches who have been created merely to gratify his appetites. Unlike Baby, who imitates English snobbery without understanding it, he has a complex sense of style. This appears most strikingly during the dinner at the Villa Diana, when Albert McKisco tries to draw him into a political argument. McKisco, an absurdly complacent radical, imagines he can demolish Barban's reactionary position in a few well-rehearsed moves. Like many intellectuals, he can only argue from certain prepared positions, and he is comically disconcerted by the unadorned egotism of Barban's point of view. When the latter explains that he fought against the Soviets because they would take away his property, and against the Riff in Morocco because he is a European, McKisco is outraged but helpless: he is easily out-manoeuvred by that characteristic European mixture of barbaric simplicity and civilized complexity which the American mind, from Henry James onwards, has found to be either totally baffling or fascinatingly elusive.

Tommy also has a code of honour which is not to be discounted even if it is in some ways little more than a kind of formalized savagery. Baby Warren in her battle of wills with Dick Diver observes no rules, respects no decencies. Tommy on the other hand, according to his own lights, behaves in a perfectly honourable manner towards the Divers. Although he is in love with Nicole, he makes no move towards her for five years, waiting with the patience of a wild animal, and an aristocrat's sense of honour, until her marriage has manifestly broken down; and in fighting his duel with McKisco, although his primary motive is to protect Nicole's honour, he must realize that he is helping to sustain the Divers' marriage. In this, as in many other ways, he is by no means as repellent a figure as Baby — he is at least a man in a sense in which she certainly cannot be said to be a woman. Nevertheless he too plays his part in the complex process of Dick's ruin.

Although Nicole and Baby Warren and Tommy Barban play important parts in the destruction of Dick Diver, it would be a crude over-simplification of the novel to suggest that Dick is merely a victim of the rich or a martyr to capitalist exploitation. Through marrying Nicole, he finds himself entangled in a maze of compromises, a subtle process of corruption which undermines his moral will even more surely than the external pressures. With one part of himself he knows he must fight against the rich to preserve his own identity, but another, even stronger, side of his character drives him to compete with them, to try to beat them at their own game. His impulse to please, to charm, to entertain, and at the same time to dominate other people through a conscious use of these abilities, leads him to create a style, an aristocratic way of life, designed to surpass in its amenity and taste anything that the rich themselves are capable of. With the benefit of Rosemary's enraptured and uncritical gaze, we are able to do more than justice to the beautiful surface of the Divers' existence. When she joins them for a morning swim, she finds that it is no ordinary swim but a carefully arranged hedonistic adventure. They move 'from the heat to the cool with the gourmandise of a tingling curry eaten with a chilled white wine. The Divers' day was spaced like the day of the older civilizations to yield the utmost from the materials at hand, and to give all the transitions their full value.'[17] The dinner at the Villa Diana affects Rosemary even more deeply: the table itself seems to her to rise a little towards the sky in response to the powerful enchantment of Dick's charm.

Even in these beatific moments at the very beginning of the novel, Fitzgerald hints at disturbing undercurrents of which Rosemary is unaware. During the beach scene from which I have just quoted, he qualifies her enthusiasm with some severity:

> Her naiveté responded whole-heartedly to the expensive simplicity of the Divers, unaware of its complexity and its lack of innocence, unaware that it was all a selection of quality rather than quantity from the run of the world's bazaar; and that the simplicity of behaviour also, the nursery-like peace and good will, the emphasis on the simpler virtues, was part of a desperate bargain with the gods and had been attained through struggles she could not have guessed at. At that moment the Divers represented externally the exact furthermost evolution of a class, so that most people seemed awkward beside them — in reality a qualitative change had already set in that was not at all apparent to Rosemary.[18]

The style of living Dick has created, despite its exquisite serenity and charm, does not differ in essentials from the lives of other wealthy cosmopolitans. Furthermore, the special problems in the Divers' marriage introduce several more equivocal qualities into their way of life.

Dick's consummate social gifts always carry with them a faint but persistent aura of falsity, the sense that he is staging a performance in those very areas of human intercourse where sincerity and directness are most important. When Rosemary exclaims, 'Oh, we're such actors — you and I', at a moment of high emotion in her affair with Dick, she is remarking on this characteristic of his behaviour. Again and again, Fitzgerald expresses his sense of the suspect quality of Dick's charm through images of acting or entertaining. A particularly striking instance occurs in the scene at the Gare St Lazare, where Nicole, Rosemary and Mary North have gathered to see Abe off on the boat-train. Alarmed and helpless in face of Abe's condition of alcoholic stupor, they wait anxiously for Dick to arrive:

> Dick Diver came and brought with him a fine glowing surface on which the three women sprang like monkeys with cries of relief, perching on his shoulders, on the beautiful crown of his hat or the gold head of his cane.[19]

17　*Ibid.*, p. 91.
18　*Ibid.*
19　*Ibid.*, p. 158.

Although the image is not made clumsily over-explicit, it is clear that Dick is being presented here as a kind of social organ-grinder, and the image gains in force when one recalls the way in which Fitzgerald describes the party Dick had organized the night before:

> The party that night moved with the speed of a slap-stick comedy. They were twelve, they were sixteen, they were quartets in separate motors bound on a quick Odyssey over Paris. Everything had been foreseen. People joined them as if by magic, accompanied them as specialists, almost guides, through a phase of the evening, dropped out and were succeeded by other people, so that it appeared as if the freshness of each one had been husbanded for them all day.[20]

Dick has planned the party with the precision of a showman, bringing on people like performing animals, extracting a little entertainment from each, and then hurrying them once more into obscurity.

There is nearly always something of the mountebank or the impresario in Dick's social behaviour. When Rosemary first sees him on Gausse's beach, he is putting on a mysterious little performance for his friends which draws burst after burst of hilarious laughter from them. At the very end, on the same beach, he delivers a little lecture on acting which, while it may have very little to do with Rosemary's professional problems, tells us a great deal about Dick's social method. An actress, he says, must never respond emotionally to the situations she is involved in — the audience will do that for her — her business is to entertain. If, for instance, she has to play a scene in which she learns suddenly of the death of her lover, she will fail if she tries to imagine what her feelings would be in real life and portray them. Instead, she must do 'the unexpected thing' — something adroit and original enough to manoeuvre the audience's attention away from the shocking fact and back to herself.

Through most of the novel — certainly throughout the period of Dick's social reign on the Riviera and in Paris — his manners and his personal charm are the products of a conscious technique which is virtually identical with the acting method he recommends to Rosemary. In his relations with other people, he avoids responding directly and genuinely to their emotional demands: he tries instead to entertain, to captivate, to concentrate their attention upon himself. He himself is acutely aware of the many subtle insincerities involved in this proceeding. When Mrs Speers tells him that he and Rosemary are the politest people she knows, he replies that his politeness is simply 'a trick of the heart.' In conversation with Baby Warren, he reflects even more harshly on the falsity of the kind of good manners admired in the circles into which he has married:

> 'There's too much good manners ...
> 'Good manners are an admission that everybody is so tender that they have to be handled with gloves. Now, human respect — you don't call a man a coward or a

liar lightly, but if you spend your life sparing people's feelings and feeding their vanity, you get so you can't distinguish what *should* be respected in them.'[21]

Dick's bitterness is directed not only at Baby and her friends but at himself: he realizes that, in allowing good manners to become divorced from human respect in his own social contacts, he has fatally compromised his integrity. His courtesy and consideration have ceased to be a natural expression of his innate decency as a human being and become merely a collection of tricks.

This is why his exquisite manners and social tact are very close to the element of cruelty and violence in his character. His aristocratic style is a game he has learnt to play. At first it is a serious game played to protect Nicole from the abrasive contacts of everyday life; later, as in his affair with Rosemary, it is just a game, played for the sake of emotional excitement; later still, when he extricates Mary Minghetti and Lady Caroline Sibly-Biers from the consequences of their foolish prank, he plays the game in a purely mechanical way — to prove to himself that he can still remember the moves. It is inevitable that Dick's attitude to the social virtues should become fundamentally cynical and disbelieving, and that this attitude should in turn find expression in behaviour which is often perverse and cruel, sometimes violent. The dinner at the Villa Diana, which in Rosemary's eyes epitomizes the perfection of the Diver style, is given to gratify sinister impulses of which she has no inkling:

'I want to give a really *bad* party. I mean it. I want to give a party where there's a brawl and seductions and people going home with their feelings hurt and women passed out in the *cabinet de toilette*. You wait and see.'[22]

If that is what Dick wanted, the party is unquestionably a great success — a duel, a new crisis in Nicole's illness, and a lover's quarrel between Mr Campion and Mr Dumphry, can all be ascribed to his efforts. His cruelty on this and other occasions is, psychologically, a direct reversal of his social tact. Since he knows so perfectly how to do the right thing, it follows that when he decides to do the wrong thing his purposes take deadly aim. By the end of the novel, the only true feelings he has left are destructive ones. In a last conversation with Mary Minghetti, he tries in vain to sustain a note of emotional intimacy. He reminds her of shared memories, playing on her feelings shamelessly, 'but the old interior laughter had begun inside him and he knew he couldn't keep it up much longer.' For a moment they gaze into each other's eyes like lovers; then the cynical demonic laughter inside him becomes so loud that he is sure Mary must hear it too. Suddenly, he switches off the light — his last performance is over.

Fitzgerald's view of the rich in *Tender is the Night* is more sombre than in any earlier novel or story. He had always believed, if only theoretically, in the possibility of an aristocratic style which would be the ideal expression of

21   *Ibid.*, p. 261.
22   *Ibid.*, p. 97.

human life, but by now that confidence was almost gone. Dick Diver, who has more intelligence, moral integrity and self-awareness than any other character in Fitzgerald's fiction, is given the opportunity not merely to assimilate, but to create an aristocratic style. For him, however, the experience is purely destructive — a bewildering descent into falsity, corruption and cruelty.

Fitzgerald's conflicting feelings about what is desirable in human life are reflected most clearly in his sense of class. All the colour, excitement and beauty of existence are associated in his mind with the idea of an aristocracy. Even in *Tender is the Night*, for all its pessimism, there are haunting intimations of what might have been realized — moments on Gausse's beach, in the gardens of the Villa Diana, and in the streets and cafés of Paris.

In opposition to this, there is a provincial, puritanical, middle-class midwesterner in Fitzgerald, who not only scrutinizes the short-comings of the rich with uncompromising rigour, but finds the firmest moral ground in a version of the middle-class protestant ethic. Dick Diver's sense of dedication to the profession of medicine and to scientific discovery at the outset of his career can be seen only in these terms; his sense of morality is an extension of the ethics of his profession. Of all the acts of self-betrayal which contribute to his ruin, the abandonment of his proper work is probably the most serious in its effects. This is a largely unconscious process — a succession of compromises and equivocations which carry him insidiously into deeper and deeper moral confusion. Fitzgerald describes a significant stage in the process when he shows Dick returning to work after the first phase of his adventure with Rosemary is over. Dick's work-room is, to all appearances, a little temple of the sciences — a cottage in the grounds of the Villa Diana, well away from the house itself. Its shutters are closed against the glare, and no servant is ever allowed inside for fear of disturbing the 'ordered confusion' of his piles of notes. He takes stock of the vast research project which has occupied his mind for many years, and, without being aware of the full implications of what he is doing, in effect abandons it. Through a series of subtle rationalizations, he persuades himself that it would be better to summarize his ideas in a short book which he could finish quickly. He is stimulated by the feeling that he has put his thoughts in order, and the same impulse leads him to clean and tidy up his room. He rearranges his notes, sweeps the floor, disinfects his washroom, sends away for new books. Then, more than satisfied with his afternoon's work, he takes a modest drink of gin.

Fitzgerald's insight into the psychology of subtle evasion and self-deception here is incomparably sensitive and precise. He has been praised for many things, but the lucidity of perception and the sober penetrating intelligence, which are so evident in this and scores of other places in *Tender is the Night*, have never been adequately recognized. In this brilliantly observed little scene, we see how the manner of Dick's new life has gradually come to supplant the substance of the old. There is no sense here of real scientific work being done: the ritual of privacy and academic seclusion, the obligatory gestures which supposedly accompany deep thought, are mere play-acting, a charade as empty as the performances of Dick's social life — as meaningless as the games he plays to amuse and captivate the little circle on Gausse's beach. This game, however, is one he plays alone: the only audience it can possibly dazzle and bewitch is Dick himself. It is only much later, when the experiment of running a psychiatric clinic in partnership with Franz has also failed, that he grasps fully what has been happening to him: 'Not without desperation he had long felt the ethics of his profession dissolving into a lifeless mass'.

Dick's case is not an isolated one — indeed Fitzgerald sees it as in many ways typical of the age. *Tender is the Night* is, among other things, a historical novel, one which seeks not only to evoke the unique character of a particular period in time, but, in Georg Lukács' phrase, to trace 'the pre-history of the present'[23] to turn to the immediate past for some of the evidence needed to understand what is happening now. For Fitzgerald, it was the existence of the professions, and of the exacting sense of responsibility they embodied, which alone ensured the health of the nineteenth-century middle-class civilization he so much admired. It is therefore not surprising that Fitzgerald should regard the undermining of professional ethics as a key element in the moral chaos of the postwar decade.

In Dick's own personal development, there is a striking contrast between the way in which, before the War, his profession has a self-evident value for him, and the ease with which he loses himself afterwards. When he visits the Somme battlefields, he tells Rosemary that he sees in the slaughter both the apotheosis and the extinction of that 'middle-class love' which made for the only kind of moral sense he could understand.

Fitzgerald makes brilliant use of the clinic on the Zugersee to bring out the way in which professional work itself can lose its meaning in a decadent age. For one thing, it shows that Dick's choice between dedicating himself to the needs of the Warren family and working as a doctor at the clinic is not as simple as we had at first supposed. To give his life to the service of patients like the 'Queen of Chile', or the Australian alcoholic Von Cohn Morris is no different fundamentally from being bought by the Warrens. When he finds Devereux Warren, the author of Nicole's ruin, among the other 'rich ruins' in the hotel at Lausanne, the circle is complete — each alternative turns out to be merely a different version of the other. There can be no real sense of vocation in shoring up the wreckage of a civilization — in compounding the failure of a class.

Dick's partner Franz Gregorovious is a well-observed instance of the decline of the bourgeois tradition in Europe. His forebears were discoverers,

23 Georg Lukács, *The Historical Novel*, translated by Hannah and Stanley Mitchell, London, 1962, p. 53.

healers, men of science; he is nothing more than a canny businessman, hiding behind the respectability of a tradition in order to prey upon the carrion of the times.

Fitzgerald saw in the clinic at least some of the fictional possibilities which Thomas Mann explored in *The Magic Mountain*. (The connection between the two novels is probably no more than a coincidence, although, later, Fitzgerald came to admire Mann's work very much, and they actually met in Hollywood in 1938). A Swiss clinic for the wealthy — whether the patients were suffering from mental illness or tuberculosis — seemed to each writer to offer a dramatic focus for examining the decay of Western civilization.

Fitzgerald's sense of the all-pervading presence of this decay is conveyed in several ways besides his use of his medical and psychiatric material. One of the most important of these is his portrayal of rich American expatriates in Europe. From this point of view, *Tender is the Night* closely resembles his international short stories — indeed he ruthlessly pillaged 'The Rough Crossing', 'Babylon Revisited' and 'The Swimmers' for atmospheric and descriptive passages which he could incorporate into the novel. As in these earlier writings, he shows only an occasional passing interest in the contrasts between American and European manners: Tommy Barban and Baby Warren are differentiated as predatory aristocratic types; while Dick and Franz, in their professional roles, appear as representatives of two distinct cultures. In the main, however, Fitzgerald is concerned with that 'society in Europe which is merely a heterogeneous prolongation of American society.'[24] His expatriates are as effectively cut off from specifically European influences as if they had never left home. When they do have contact with Europeans of their own class, it is with figures like Lady Caroline Sibly-Biers, who are even more rootless than they. Often, as if by a curious effect of camera focusing, Europeans are kept out of the picture altogether. In the scene where Abe leaves on the boat-train, the Gare St Lazare seems as American as the Pennsylvania Station in *The Great Gatsby*; and the two French porters who discuss the shooting have the status of recent immigrants in New York rather than that of citizens in their own country.

The American rich bring with them to Europe the habits, the dissipations, the neuroses and the violence of the Jazz Age. The three lesbian girls whom Dick and Rosemary meet when they visit a bohemian salon, are not a part of the artistic life of Paris but a manifestation of the Boom; and their hostess, who has devised the whole bizarre occasion, is simply 'another tall rich American girl promenading insouciantly upon the national prosperity.' The hysteria and the anarchy of expatriate life are equally characteristic of the febrile rhythms of the postwar decade: 'everything they did had a purely nervous inspiration. They were very quiet and lethargic at certain hours and

24 'Majesty', BH5, p. 459.

then they exploded into sudden quarrels and breakdowns and seductions.'[25] Dick and Nicole believe they can create a civilized retreat within this wilderness, but in different ways they both fail. The tranquil Riviera summer life which Dick invented is overwhelmed and lost in an invasion of the strident, the raffish and the vulgar:

> Now the swimming-place was a 'club', though, like the international society it represented, it would be hard to say who was not admitted.
>
> ... few people swam any more in that blue paradise, children and one exhibitionistic valet who punctuated the morning with spectacular dives from a fifty-foot rock — most of Gausse's guests stripped the concealing pyjamas from their flabbiness for only a short hangover dip at one o'clock.[26]

The irony of Nicole's cure is that her nerves are finally strong enough to enable her to join the party. What prepares her psychologically for her affair with Tommy Barban is not so much Dick's solicitude, as her observation of the chaos around her: she is 'stimulated by watching people do exactly what they were tempted to do and pay no penalty for it.'

Nicole has reached the point where freedom becomes, not a positive, but a purely destructive condition: the money, the ease of movement, the lack of social friction, ensure that she need never commit herself to anything. Henry Adams had noted at the turn of the century how the liberation of the American woman tourist tended to trivialize the idea of freedom. Fitzgerald had not previously viewed the Jazz Age in this way: he preferred to work with the much larger dramatic elements of hope, orgy and catastrophe, and continued to do so in *Tender is the Night*. But in the conditions of expatriate life, he could not avoid the realization that triviality was an essential feature of the times. The emergence of this idea in *Tender is the Night* coincides with another important development: his willingness to treat sex more explicitly than he had ever done before. Through the combined effect of these innovations, the trivialization of sex becomes a key element in his understanding of the cultural decadence to which his characters are exposed, and of which they are a part. (I have already touched on this theme in discussing his posthumously published story, 'News of Paris — Fifteen Years Ago'.)

Nicole's affair with Tommy Barban is a striking illustration of the process, despite the fact that she tries to present it to herself in terms of high romance, with Tommy cast in the role of a *condottiere* or knight errant, bearing her off on his saddle bow. After her meeting with him on Golding's yacht, she begins to wonder whether a love-affair might not be good for her. Her attitude is not dissimilar to that of a woman Fitzgerald mentions in 'Echoes of the Jazz Age':

> I remember a perfectly mated, contented young mother asking my wife's advice

25   *Tender is the Night*, BH2, p. 146.
26   *Ibid.*, p. 369.

about 'having an affair right away,' though she had no one especially in mind, 'because don't you think it's sort of undignified when you get much over thirty?'[27]

Nicole's liaison with Tommy is clearly a diversion of this sort, not a grand passion. Fitzgerald brings out the essential emptiness of their relationship in the scene where they make love for the first time in a little Riviera hotel. They have scarcely had time to dress, when two whores rush through their room to the balcony outside, in order to wave good-bye to their departing clients — the sailors from an American warship anchored offshore. As a final gesture of affectionate farewell, the girls tear off their knickers and wave them frantically at the receding launch. Their salute is unexpectedly acknowledged with full naval ceremonial: 'at the battleship's stern arose in rivalry the Star-Spangled Banner.' The romantic pretensions of Nicole and Tommy are exposed to the same mockery as the patriotic bombast of the battleship and its flag.

What disturbs Fitzgerald most in expatriate life however — as in the Jazz Age generally — is its tendency to break out in arbitrary acts of violence or swift personal catastrophes. In *Tender is the Night*, the quality of such events is represented most clearly by the murder of the negro Peterson. A fortuitous chain of circumstances, which begins when Abe North is involved in a drunken dispute in a Montmartre bar, ends with the appearance of Peterson's corpse on Rosemary's bed. In its dramatic and psychological effect, the episode is shocking and unexpected, but in a more fundamental sense, it is typical — just as Abe's own death is appalling and yet predictable.

From the very beginning, Fitzgerald believed that the American adventure of the 1920s, through its lack of restraint and its absence of style, was bound to end in disaster. As early as 1920, in his short story 'May Day', Fitzgerald had tried to use the suicide of Gordon Sterrett as a way of expressing his sense of this tendency. One of the most urgent problems he faced as a historian of manners was that of finding the right image of disaster. It is this difficulty — far more than his drinking, Zelda's illness, or the need to write magazine stories for money — which explains why it took him nine years to write *Tender is the Night*. At first, he thought he had found what he was looking for in one of the celebrated murders of the decade — either the Leopold and Loeb case of 1924, or the Dorothy Ellingson case of 1925. Both murders were the result of an irresponsible following-through of impulse — one of the distinguishing faults of the age. Leopold and Loeb were two rich college boys who murdered another boy as a psychological experiment. Dorothy Ellingson was a sixteen-year-old San Francisco girl who murdered her own mother during the course of an argument about her wild conduct. In the earliest version of the *Tender is the Night* material, Fitzgerald tried to make the crime of matricide the climax of his plot, but he found this subject unsuited to his talents and eventually abandoned it. The

27 'Echoes of the Jazz Age', BH3, p. 334.

Crash of 1929, which might have offered him an alternative, did not affect his imagination nearly as deeply as the violence of the Jazz Age itself. (When he discussed the question of advance publicity with Maxwell Perkins late in 1933, he insisted that *Tender is the Night* should be presented as a novel of the Boom, not of the Depression.)[28] Zelda's mental breakdown, and Fitzgerald's own complex sense of failure, finally gave him a sufficiently precise knowledge of the mechanisms of disaster. This is not to say that *Tender is the Night* is an autobiographical novel, but merely to point out that a novelist can only use those parts of his observation and experience which are within the scope of his artistic talents. There was nothing in Fitzgerald's fictional methods that enabled him to deal with climactic acts of violence, but he was superbly fitted to evoke subtle psychological states and finely shaded social situations. In the final version of the novel, he discovered how to make violence part of an atmosphere, and personal catastrophe a matter of slow disintegration and hidden suffering.

Fitzgerald writes not only as a historian of the manners of his own time, but as a historical novelist in a more usual sense — as one who is concerned to trace certain elements in his hero's situation back to their origins in an earlier period. It is this which leads him to give so much importance to the First World War.

Dick did not actually take part in the War — even in 1917 he was already too valuable to be 'shot off in a gun' — but this does not mean that he escaped the catastrophe unscathed. When he returns to the clinic after the Armistice, Franz questions his cheerful assumption that, since he did not experience the War at first hand, he must necessarily be unaffected by it: ' "That doesn't matter — we have some shell-shocks who merely heard an air raid from a distance. We have a few who merely read newspapers." '[29] Almost a decade later, Dick is reminded of this equivocal sense in which one may miss, and yet perhaps not miss the War, by a disturbing dream experience which seems to link him with the psychological cases Franz describes. It is a 'dream of war' filled with 'symbols of disaster' — marching troops, fire engines, and a hideous uprising of the mutilated and deformed. Thoroughly awakened, Dick makes a record of it which concludes with the ironic comment, 'Non-combatant's shell-shock'. No one, it appears, really missed the War: whether a man suffers from non-combatant's shell-shock or has endured the real thing is a question merely of detail, of circumstances — his mental state is fundamentally the same. The War has maimed a whole generation: even if they escaped physical mutilation, their deepest visions are composed of 'symbols of disaster'.

Although the language of psychology gives Fitzgerald a striking set of images for describing the disintegrative effect of the War, he is more

28   *Letters*, p. 237.
29   *Tender is the Night*, BH2, p. 195.

interested in analysing the situation historically. When I discussed Dick's medical career, I pointed out the vast difference between his attitudes to his profession before and after the War. It is this sense of difference which Fitzgerald tries to capture — the sense of a stable civilization which the War destroyed, leaving only chaos in its place. He puts forward these ideas most explicitly in the scene in which Dick and his friends visit the battlefields of the Somme. Dick rhapsodizes, for Rosemary's benefit, and to the accompaniment of deflating, wisecracking interruptions from Abe North, on what the place means to him:

> 'This western-front business couldn't be fought again, not for a long time. The young men think they could do it but they couldn't. They could fight the first Marne again but not this. This took religion and years of plenty and tremendous sureties and the exact relation that existed between the classes.... You had to have a whole-souled sentimental equipment going back further than you could remember. You had to remember Christmas, and postcards of the Crown Prince and his fiancée, and little cafés in Valence and beer gardens in Unter den Linden and weddings at the *mairie*, and going to the Derby, and your grandfather's whiskers.'[30]

When Abe objects that the Somme was only a development of the kind of mass butchery invented by General Grant in the American Civil War, Dick disagrees. This, he maintains, was a 'love battle' — 'there was a century of middle-class love spent here.' 'All my beautiful lovely safe world blew itself up here with a great gust of high explosive love.'[31]

The 'tremendous sureties', 'the whole-souled sentimental equipment' of the nineteenth century were expended in the carnage of the Somme, with the result that the men of Dick Diver's generation suffer from a kind of moral exhaustion. They might be capable of a short gallant dash like the first Battle of the Marne, but they no longer have the resources for the sustained heroic effort needed to fight a battle like the Somme. (From this point of view, *Tender is the Night* is, in part, a belated Lost Generation novel and bears some relation to Hemingway's masterpiece *The Sun Also Rises*.)

The great interest of this passage, and of the whole episode it comes from, is not confined to the exposition of these ideas, however, and Dick certainly cannot be regarded as merely a mouthpiece for Fitzgerald. He is not a detached and objective student of history, but a victim — and at this stage an unconscious victim — of the malaise he describes. We are aware of this not only through our sense of context — our knowledge of the extent to which his character has already begun to deteriorate — but through the texture of the writing itself. The language Dick uses is deplorably sentimental, his posturings stagey and absurd: it is no wonder that Abe keeps up a constant fusillade of ridicule, horse-play and disagreement. What is most offensive about Dick's performance, however, is its partial insincerity: he exploits the

30   *Ibid.*, pp. 129—30.
31   *Ibid.*, p. 130.

feelings properly aroused by the suffering and destruction of the War in order to play on Rosemary's emotions. Nothing could demonstrate more convincingly the loss of that emotional wholeness and moral integrity which he associates with the prewar years. Consequently, everything he does has a suspect quality — even his kindness to the girl at the American cemetery who cannot find her brother's grave — isn't it just another brilliant improvisation in the charade? If so, it is completely successful — the girl and Rosemary weep together in the rain: 'altogether it had been a watery day'. By this time, the scene has taken on a broadly comic aspect; the rain itself seems almost to be a part of Dick's expert arrangements for the day. Even the knowledge of military history Dick draws upon as self-appointed guide to the battle-fields, is part of a plan to impress and dominate his friends: 'he had made a quick study of the whole affair, simplifying it always until it bore a faint resemblance to one of his own parties'.[32] Rosemary's reactions contribute an element of pure farce. She is the classic type of the sentimentalist — essentially hard and selfish, she loves the luxury of tears. She is very similar to those characters in Chekhov's comedies, whose immoderate weeping is as much a source of laughter as their ludicrous misadventures.

Fitzgerald put more of the complexity of Dick Diver's case into this episode than into any other single scene in *Tender is the Night*. What Dick says is, from a historical point of view broadly true: the War has largely destroyed the world in which his career would have had a meaning, and his life a purpose. But, in relation to his friends — and to his own truest feelings — he is deeply false: here, more than anywhere, we see the subtle insincerities of Dick the mountebank, the social organ-grinder. A man who is capable of being simultaneously so true and so false, so intelligent and so trite, is in the greatest danger: he must end by confusing himself so completely that none of his judgments is ever to be trusted.

Fitzgerald sees Dick Diver as both observer and victim of a broad historical process; he is a representative figure from a period in which Western civilization has become decadent and self-destructive: the rich, who might once have been the creators of civilization, have degenerated into rootless exploiters; middle-class professional life, once a creative moral force, is now venal and self-seeking; above all the War has destroyed order and sanity, bringing a chaos of violence, madness and vulgarity to take their place. The great positiveness with which Fitzgerald expresses these convictions suggests something more definite than a generalized response to the atmosphere of his times: it implies that clearly identifiable ideas about history and civilization are an important aspect of the meaning of *Tender is the Night*. By this I do not mean simply that Fitzgerald's intellectual faculties are actively engaged by his material — in his best fiction they

32   *Ibid.*, p. 132.

always are: what is unique about this novel is that for the first and only time in his career he successfully makes use of concepts drawn from the work of specific modern thinkers, in particular Spengler and Marx.

Fitzgerald's awareness of cultural decline was deeply affected by the Spenglerian ideas which were so fashionable between the wars. He actually read *The Decline of the West* in the late 1920s, and continued to be fascinated by the theory of history presented there for the rest of his life. He had been familiar since Princeton days with similar ideas in Henry Adams and Shane Leslie, but the greater intellectual authority of Spengler made him more conscious of the possible value of such views. It was the dramatic sense of collapse, rather than the detailed structure of Spengler's historical system, which stimulated his imagination. As he wrote to Maxwell Perkins in 1940, 'Spengler believed that the Western world was dead, and he believed nothing else but that.'[33]

In the same way, Fitzgerald took certain ideas from Marx: I have already referred to the Marxist undertones in the scene where Nicole and Rosemary go shopping in Paris; and suggested the importance of the theme of exploitation in his portrayal of Baby Warren. He was deeply interested in Marxism throughout the 1930s, and often spoke of himself as a Marxist or a Communist. Andrew Turnbull makes it clear that this was an especially prominent feature of his life at La Paix, where he completed the final version of *Tender is the Night* between 1932 and 1934. Turnbull recalls how a man used to come out from Baltimore a couple of times a week, and how he and Fitzgerald would box and read Marx together — an amusing collocation of activities.[34] Robert Sklar has shown that, during the same period, Fitzgerald even engaged in a limited amount of left-wing political activity.[35] In the 'GENERAL PLAN' for *Tender is the Night* which he drew up in 1932, he stated that Dick Diver was to be 'a Communist-liberal-idealist, a moralist in revolt'[36], and that after the collapse of his marriage, he was to have sent his son Lanier to be educated in Soviet Russia. Indeed, as Matthew Bruccoli points out, the novel might easily have been something of a Marxist tract.[37] That Fitzgerald should have abandoned this element in his original plan is in harmony with his own truest sense of the nature of Dick's predicament: his conviction that there is no single key — Marxist, Spenglerian, or whatever — to the interpretation either of his character or of the society in which he lives.

For the American novelist with a commitment to Marxism in the 1930s, there were pitfalls on every side. Even if he avoided the propaganda writing of James T. Farrell or the crude system-building of John Dos Passos, he was still exposed to many dangers. If, like Fitzgerald, he chose to mingle Marxist

33 *Letters*, p. 289.
34 Andrew Turnbull, *Scott Fitzgerald*, London, 1962, p. 206.
35 Robert Sklar, *F. Scott Fitzgerald: the Last Laocoon*, New York, 1967, p. 305.
36 Bruccoli, *op.cit.*, p. 77.
37 *Ibid.*, p. 83.

concepts with ideas drawn from other sources, he risked falling into intellectual incoherence or self-contradiction — faults which mar Hemingway's *For Whom the Bell Tolls* and Steinbeck's *The Grapes of Wrath*. In *Tender is the Night*, Fitzgerald succeeds where virtually all his contemporaries failed — not through some ingenious act of cerebration, the mere ability to reconcile potentially conflicting ideas — but as the result of a profoundly creative process, in which ideas become a part of the deeper workings of the imagination, so that their pressure is felt in the texture of the writing. A particularly clear instance of this occurs towards the end of his description of Nicole's shopping excursion, at the point where he wishes to suggest that her actions are not simply personal to herself, but are also an aspect of the economic system which supports her:

> ... as the whole system swayed and thundered onward it lent a feverish bloom to such processes of hers as wholesale buying, like the flush of a fireman's face holding his post before a spreading blaze. She illustrated very simple principles, containing in herself her own doom[38] ...

The passage hints at the possibility of revolution, and implies — though it does not state — the familiar Marxist dictum that capitalism will be destroyed by its own contradictions. These ideas are in themselves commonplace, even banal, and if Fitzgerald had paraded them as pieces of homiletic wisdom culled from the pages of the master, they would have seemed extraneous and crude. As it is, however, they have been re-imagined and transformed into an ominous metaphor of disaster, which is not imprisoned within the confines of ideology, as it would have been if Fitzgerald had indicated its source with programmatic simplicity. Instead, it becomes an integral part of the organic life of the novel, adding a fresh significance to that aura of destruction which always surrounds the figure of Nicole.

Here the idea is half buried, half visible, just beneath the surface of Fitzgerald's prose; but, in the main, ideas are even more completely assimilated by his imagination, and can be felt only as deep undercurrents or vibrations in the complex pattern of his thought. In this respect, he shows a quality of mind which T. S. Eliot characterizes felicitously in an early essay on Henry James:

> James's critical genius comes out most tellingly in his mastery over, his baffling escape from, Ideas; a mastery and an escape which are perhaps the last test of a superior intelligence. He had a mind so fine that no idea could violate it.[39]

Eliot distrusts ideas because they have no necessary connection with actual thinking — particularly the kind of thinking which is the principal business of the artist: 'instead of thinking with our feelings (a very difficult thing) we

38   See note 14.
39   T. S. Eliot, 'Henry James' (1918), reprinted in Philip Rahv, *Literature in America*, New York, 1957, p. 223.

corrupt our feelings with ideas.' Ideas, in this sense, are resistant to thought, and tend to take on a life of their own: in France (which Eliot refers to ironically as 'the Home of Ideas') they are carefully segregated, preserved and labelled like rare plants in a botanic garden; while in England they run wild like the rabbits which infest Australia. James does not succumb to the bad intellectual habits of either tradition: in his novels, he is more successful than any of his contemporaries 'in maintaining a point of view, a viewpoint untouched by the parasite idea.'

Fitzgerald, no less than James, possesses a fine and subtle intelligence of this sort, but, unfortunately for his reputation, no critic of Eliot's stature has as yet drawn attention to the fact. Indeed, his supposed intellectual inadequacy is one of the least questioned critical assumptions about his work — even among readers who profess to admire him. To trace this misconception to its source, it is probably necessary to go as far back as Edmund Wilson's 'Literary Spotlight' article of 1922. Wilson's argument throughout is that there is a wide discrepancy between Fitzgerald's natural talent as a writer, and his enfeebled mental powers. Fitzgerald, he maintains, is like a stupid old woman entrusted with a precious jewel: 'For he has been given imagination without intellectual control of it; he has been given a desire for beauty without an aesthetic ideal; and he has been given a gift for expression without many ideas to express.'[40] There was some excuse, perhaps, for writing in this way in 1922, but there is no clear evidence that Wilson ever substantially changed his mind on this point: he reprinted the article some thirty years later in *The Shores of Light*, and critics have continued to cite it with approval. Fitzgerald himself appears to concur with the general opinion when he refers to Wilson as his 'intellectual conscience'.

In reality, however, Fitzgerald and Wilson are classic examples of the two sorts of mind described by Eliot. Wilson, for all his brilliance as a literary journalist and critic, finds it difficult to recognize the existence of thinking which is not in some sense the manipulation of ideas; and he does not readily acknowledge the presence of an idea unless it is clearly ticketed with the maker's name. Fitzgerald cared less about ideas, but did more real thinking, and seems to have understood the nature of Wilson's mind better than Wilson understood his. For instance he foresaw, as Wilson did not, the disadvantages which would follow from the latter's conversion to Communism: 'A decision to accept Communism definitely,' he wrote to Maxwell Perkins, 'no matter how good for the soul, must of necessity be a saddening process for anyone who has ever tasted the intellectual pleasures of the world we live in.'[41] Wilson, by placing too high a value upon a particular system of ideas, has in Fitzgerald's view narrowed his range —

40 Edmund Wilson, 'Fitzgerald before *The Great Gatsby*', reprinted by Alfred Kazin, *F. Scott Fitzgerald: the Man and his Work*, Cleveland and New York, 1951, p. 77. (Originally appeared in *The Bookman*, New York, 1922.)
41 *Letters*, p. 230.

sacrificed the intellectual flexibility which the artist cannot do without. One of the most impressive things about *Tender is the Night* is Fitzgerald's capacity to be fully engaged, morally and emotionally, with his material, while remaining ideologically uncommitted. Wilson on the other hand over-committed himself to Marxism in the 1930s, and was then forced into a wasteful process of intellectual withdrawal when Stalin's excesses became clear. This, coupled with the random eclecticism of his later years, is striking evidence of his inability to maintain a point of view without the support of 'the parasite idea'.

Fitzgerald's achievement in *Tender is the Night* implies an unusually full understanding of the true role of ideas in fiction. Quite apart from the evidence of the novel itself, there is a note in his 'GENERAL PLAN' which shows how firmly he now grasped the nature of his own thought processes. He reminds himself of the method he should follow in using the psychological background material he has gathered on the subject of Nicole's schizophrenia: he should, he writes, 'not end with a novelized Kraft-Ebing — better Ophelia and her flowers.'[42] An idea, in other words, is of no value to a novelist unless it can be transformed into a dramatic image. Fitzgerald regarded ideas as an additional resource, not a strait-jacket. He took from Spengler and Marx (as from Krafft-Ebing and Jung) only what he could use as an artist: a more dramatic sense of economic relations and historical change; fresh metaphors of disaster; a confirmation and toughening of his own observation of manners.

Fitzgerald's success in *Tender is the Night* is no less complete than in *The Great Gatsby*. Almost all the criticism of his work has been bedevilled by the attempt to elevate the reputation of one novel at the expense of the other — a foolish proceeding, which has been a serious obstacle to the proper appreciation of his work. As he himself recognized, the two novels exemplify quite distinct approaches to the art of fiction: *Gatsby* uses the method of poetic concentration which Henry James — more than anyone else within the American tradition — had developed; *Tender is the Night* has the extended scope and the richness of detail which one associates with classic European realism. In both novels, Fitzgerald is equally successful in achieving complexity of meaning and artistic truth.

Note: The page numbers in the *Bodley Head Scott Fitzgerald*, Vol. 2 (BH2), refer to the first edition of 1959. The publishers have subsequently omitted other writings by Fitzgerald from the beginning of the volume, so that readers using more recent editions will find that the page numbers given here no longer apply. Since the earlier edition is more likely to be found in libraries however, it was felt that the practice adopted here would be more helpful. Any reader wishing to trace a reference in the current edition should simply subtract 62 from the page number given here.

42   Bruccoli, *op.cit.*, p. 81.

7

The crack-up and Hollywood

The astonishing period of creativity which began with the first unmistakable signs of talent in Fitzgerald's Princeton stories of 1917, and reached its climax with the publication of *Tender is the Night* in 1934, came confusedly to an end the following year. During the summer of 1935, he experienced what he called his crack-up, and for most of 1935 and 1936, he was prostrated by nervous exhaustion, physical illness, and a deep feeling of discouragement. He was brought to this condition by a combination of circumstances: the cumulative effect of years of over-work; the financial troubles which reached a point of crisis after the commercial failure of *Tender is the Night*; his alcoholism and the strain of Zelda's illness; and a pervading sense of personal and artistic failure. The crack-up not only changed the course of his life, but made a complete break in his career as a writer. He found it necessary to make an entirely new start: for a time, it seemed as if everything he had previously learnt about life and about the craft of fiction had lost its meaning. As I showed in chapter 4, he adopted an entirely new approach to the art of the short story; while the fact that he was able to begin writing *The Last Tycoon* in 1939 amounts to a kind of artistic rebirth. Some of his late stories are remarkably fine, and parts of *The Last Tycoon* are as good as anything he ever wrote, but he never fully regained his powers. He did not succeed in completing anything between the summer of 1934 and his death on 21 December 1940, which reflects the widest range of his genius.

Fitzgerald attempted to give an account of his collapse in three articles which appeared in *Esquire* between February and April 1936: 'The Crack-up', 'Handle With Care' and 'Pasting it Together'.[1] The importance of these pieces has been consistently overrated. This is partly because they first received serious attention, not when they originally appeared in *Esquire*, but when they were republished by Edmund Wilson in 1945. Their second appearance coincided with — and helped to foster — the revival of interest

1   When Edmund Wilson collected these essays in *The Crack-up*, New York, 1945, he transposed the titles of 'Handle With Care' and 'Pasting it Together'. I have kept to his title order here and elsewhere in this book, since his editorial decision has been followed in virtually all subsequent reprintings, and to return to the original *Esquire* titles would be likely to confuse the reader.

149

in Fitzgerald's work which followed years of neglect. The crack-up essays in this way came to acquire a somewhat factitious place in the history of his reputation. Their continued celebrity seems to depend, more than anything else, upon the present tendency to value highly — indeed to over-value — confessional writing. The essays certainly contain moments of penetrating insight, expressed with such brilliance and precision, that they are now among the most familiar of Fitzgerald's pronouncements (I have already quoted extensively from them in previous chapters). But, as in the case of similar touches in many of the short stories, these felicities cannot compensate for fundamental weaknesses in his conception and design.

One of the most striking characteristics of the crack-up essays is that they are artistically stunted and emotionally dead: Fitzgerald's fictional treatment of Dick Diver's disintegration is deeply harrowing, but his autobiographical account of his own collapse fails to move. In part, this is due to the very nature of his emotional state — to that brittle, empty, superannuated condition which he conveys so effectively in the image of the cracked plate: 'It can never again be warmed on the stove nor shuffled with the other plates in the dishpan; it will not be brought out for company, but it will do to hold crackers late at night or to go in the ice box under left-overs ...'[2] The dry crackers, the unappetizing left-overs, these are now the materials of his art no less than of his life. It is, as he remarks himself, 'all rather inhuman and undernourished'.

One of the most striking weaknesses of the crack-up essays is the unsatisfactory nature of Fitzgerald's analysis of his own psychological state — in particular, his theory of emotional bankruptcy. He argues that emotional vitality is like money in the bank: if a man squanders this fixed capital foolishly or too early in life, he will eventually find himself without resources to call on. Fitzgerald first put forward this idea as early as 1931, in one of the Josephine stories, to which he actually gave the title 'Emotional Bankruptcy'. Josephine Perry, having expended all her youthful freshness and spontaneity in a series of worthless intrigues, finds she has no feelings left when, at last, she wishes to fall in love. The story is psychologically unconvincing and Fitzgerald, significantly, did not include it with the other Josephine stories he collected in *Taps at Reveille*. Nevertheless, in 'The Crack-up' and 'Handle With Care', he expresses this idea with still more explicitness. In the latter essay, he speaks of 'an over-extension of the flank, a burning of the candle at both ends; a call upon physical resources that I did not command, like a man over-drawing at his bank'.[3] And as late as 1940, he wrote to Scottie that 'writing is a sheer paring away of oneself leaving always something thinner, barer, more meager'.[4]

While no one would deny the possibility of premature exhaustion — the

2 'Handle With Care', BH3, p. 394.
3 *Ibid.*, p. 397.
4 *Letters*, p. 70.

reality of Fitzgerald's collapse is all too apparent for that — the monetary metaphor he uses imposes a mechanical and largely false psychology upon his analysis. Human energies cannot be regarded as a fixed capital. Living can be a process of enrichment as well as one of exhaustion, and the element of resiliency — the power to recover from emotional shocks — can never be discounted. It is significant that in *Tender is the Night*, the theory of emotional bankruptcy is never once adduced as an explanation of Dick Diver's ruin.

Fitzgerald's extensive reliance upon it in the crack-up articles points to a distinct superficiality in carrying on the business of self-analysis. Indeed these essays, far from being rigorous exercises in self-scrutiny, are, rather, exercises in self-dramatization and self-pity. Confessional writing, like all other varieties of public confession, is a slippery form: in all such cases, whether it is the converted sinner testifying from the mourners' bench, or the criminal, courtesan, or film-star publishing memoirs in the Sunday papers, the aim is generally to create an impression rather than to tell the unvarnished truth. The element of bad faith, which is so apparent in these cruder manifestations, is almost invariably present to some degree even in the most sophisticated confessional writing: no literary convention uses the rhetoric of sincerity more insistently, and yet there is no mode of expression in which it is more difficult to be really sincere. Fitzgerald seems disconcertingly unaware of the problems created by this paradoxical situation, a fact which Alfred Kazin noted when he reviewed *The Crack-up and Other Writings* in 1946. (Kazin is virtually the only critic to have recognized fully the unsatisfactory nature of the crack-up articles.) He sees Fitzgerald's professions of unworthiness as a case of 'aggressive guilt', a stance which is merely the obverse of that most unattractive of all forms of self-dramatization, 'false humility'. Fitzgerald, far from being wholly candid, is making a half-unconscious, half-artful bid for attention — seeking, through his admissions, to 'command that authority which the unloved exercise by their suffering.'[5] It is the last resource of a man who feels he cannot obtain a hearing by any less desperate means.

The act of public confession makes it almost impossible for a writer to be honest with himself: it also places him in a false position with regard to his audience. No one can refuse to listen to a man who offers to unfold the innermost secrets of his heart, but these disclosures are rarely welcome: they are an abuse of intellectual hospitality, and generally produce an effect of resentment rather than sympathy. Confessional writing cannot be artistically worthwhile unless the author finds some way of showing the reader that he is conscious of the treacherous ground that lies between them. Dostoievsky, as Kazin points out, has an incomparable understanding of these matters, but

---

5 Alfred Kazin, 'An American Confession', reprinted in *F. Scott Fitzgerald: the Man and his Work*, Cleveland and New York, 1951, p. 174. (First appeared in the *Quarterly Review of Literature*, 1946.)

his position is very different from Fitzgerald's, since he does not address the reader directly, but uses confession as a fictional situation — even in the *Notes from Underground*. A much closer parallel is provided by the American confessional poets of the 1960s. Often they fail for the same reason that the crack-up essays fail — because they simply talk about themselves without showing any awareness of what this involves. Their successes are due not so much to the intrinsic interest of what they confess, as to the insight they occasionally reveal into the dubious role of confession itself. John Berryman, in his *Dream Songs*, makes use of a semi-comic *alter ego* called Henry, in order to express an ironic sense of the uneasy relations which must exist between himself and his readers. A still more interesting case is Sylvia Plath's 'Lady Lazarus': this poem has gained notoriety because of the extravagant unreserve with which she exposes her sufferings, but its real distinction lies elsewhere — in the intelligence and wit with which she dramatizes the difficulties of the confessional poet. Her decision to make a poem out of her own most private agonies turns her into a kind of indecent fairground attraction — 'the big strip-tease'; while her readers, by the same process, are forced into the position of 'the peanut-crunching crowd' — a gaping mob, avid for sensation, crying out for blood. Fitzgerald, by contrast, is entirely unaware of the complexities of the form he is using, and the relative artistic failure of the crack-up articles is the inevitable result.

There is another circumstance, involving biographical fact as well as critical judgment, which helps to account for the poor quality of these essays. When they are seen in the context of the actual sequence of events that made up Fitzgerald's breakdown, they appear to have been in many ways a form of therapy rather than art. In a letter of 24 February 1936, he is already inclined to see them in these terms:

> ... now that things seem a little brighter, or at least the intensity of that despair is fading, I can see that the writing of them was a sort of catharsis but at the time of writing them what I said seemed absolutely real. And may I add that this is no claim to being completely out of the woods except that I would not be inclined to write that way again under the present circumstances.[6]

The feelings he wanted to get rid of through this process of catharsis were those which had led to the first phase of his breakdown in 1935. Under such conditions, writing is not a process of artistic creation, but a kind of moral stock-taking, or, more accurately, an attempt to find what comfort may be derived from putting the case at its worst: if failure can be made a role — a romantic destiny — one may perhaps be able to live with it.

His attempt to cure himself by writing was soon proved to be a failure, and in the summer of 1936, he probably sank to an even lower point than during the previous year. He suffered a prolonged period of severe illness following an accident to his shoulder, but the worst blows were undoubtedly those

6   *Letters*, p. 532—3.

which resulted directly from the publication of the articles in *Esquire*. As Alfred Kazin notes, these were not 'meditated autobiography' but an instance of 'those facile canny professions of guilt which are so rife in our personal conversation and our love affairs, in appeals to God or the psychoanalyst to restore our lost innocence'.[7] These 'professions of guilt' are meant to elicit not assent but prompt contradiction — the assurance that we are by no means as unworthy as we make ourselves out to be, the assurance above all that we are loved and understood. It was in this spirit no doubt that Fitzgerald expected his readers to take the painfully embarrassing gestures of self-disparagement in 'Pasting it Together'. For the most part, these expectations must have been fulfilled by the large fan-mail he received, most of it friendly and sympathetic, but in a number of instances — crucial if the therapeutic experiment were to succeed — the essays failed to evoke the response he desired. Already, by the autumn of 1936, he was expressing pained surprise that certain readers had taken what he said literally. He must have found it galling enough to be the recipient of John Dos Passos's scoutmasterly admonitions;[8] it was worse to discover that in Hollywood, where he desperately needed to obtain a writing contract, he was widely considered to be a finished man incapable of serious work; worse still to find Hemingway using his name to epitomize a dead and forgotten era in 'The Snows of Kilimanjaro'.

As a result of this bitter experience, Fitzgerald, while continuing to believe that the crack-up essays had helped him to understand his own case, came to feel that, professionally, they had been a mistake. When Maxwell Perkins suggested an autobiographical book which would include them, he firmly refused, and he never again attempted confessional writing.

Looking back on the experience in 1939, Fitzgerald wrote that the crack-up had been not so much a 'nervous breakdown' as 'a spiritual "change of life" ', 'a protest against a new set of conditions which I would have to face'.[9] The new conditions were those imposed on him by Hollywood, and the change of life was profound. Up to 1934, the ground on which he considered the question how one should live in America, had been marked out for him by the American rich. After 1937, the question had to be thought about in the startlingly different circumstances of Hollywood. As a writer, he had new subject-matter to handle, and, as a man, he had a new style of living to learn.

The subject-matter was not entirely new, however: his interest in Hollywood went back almost to the beginning of his career, and all the themes of his late Hollywood fiction are anticipated in earlier novels and stories. The film industry makes its first significant appearance in his work

---

7 Kazin, *op.cit.*, p. 173.
8 Letter reprinted in Edmund Wilson, *The Crack-up*, New York, 1945, p. 311.
9 *Letters*, p. 589.

154   *F. Scott Fitzgerald and the Art of Social Fiction*

as far back as 'The Diamond as Big as the Ritz', where Percy Washington explains to John Unger that the spectacular Washington estate had been designed by 'a moving-picture fella' after more traditional artists — an architect, a landscape gardener, a stage designer and a decadent poet — had failed. 'He was the only man we found who was used to playing with an unlimited amount of money, though he did tuck his napkin in his collar, and he couldn't read or write.'[10] Fitzgerald saw from the beginning that there was a deep affinity between the Hollywood producer and the American rich of the Gilded Age: unlimited wealth gave them both the same boldness of conception, and in what they created one often feels the equivocal power of that 'vast, vulgar, and meretricious beauty' for which Fitzgerald found the perfect epitomizing phrase. Gatsby's parties exhibit many of the skills of the film director, and moving-picture people are a significant element among his guests; while Orson Welles's *Citizen Kane*, by a kind of mirror effect, takes the career of an unscrupulous man of fabulous wealth for its story.

Fitzgerald's fascination with Hollywood — like his fascination with the rich — was balanced by an equally strong sense of disapproval. He saw and admired such early masterpieces of the cinema as Griffith's *Birth of a Nation* and Eisenstein's *Battleship Potemkin*, and he enjoyed the slapstick comedies of Charlie Chaplin and Harold Lloyd, but he had the deepest misgivings about the rise of Hollywood. In 'Handle With Care', he is appalled to observe that the novel, 'the strongest and supplest medium for conveying thought and emotion from one human being to another, was becoming subordinated to a mechanical and commercial art that, whether in the hands of Hollywood merchants or Russian idealists, was capable of reflecting only the tritest thought, the most obvious emotion'.[11]

If one looks back at Fitzgerald's Hollywood — the period which began with the invention of sound in the late 1920s and ended, more or less, with America's entry into the Second World War — one is bound to share his mixed feelings. It is probable that no artistic enterprise (except perhaps Diaghilev's Russian Ballet) has brought so many talented people together in one place in a similarly short space of time: Erich von Stroheim, Fritz Lang, Ernst Lubitsch, John Ford and Orson Welles; Greta Garbo, Katharine Hepburn, Peter Lorre, Groucho Marx, W. C. Fields, Charles Laughton, and Vivien Leigh; Scott Fitzgerald, William Faulkner, Nathanael West and Aldous Huxley — to mention these names is only to suggest, not to exhaust, the range and variety of creative ability employed. Hollywood produced films in those years which have a unique place in the achievement of cinema as an art form — *All Quiet on the Western Front, Grand Hotel, A Night at the Opera, Trouble in Paradise, The Great Dictator, The Maltese Falcon, Stagecoach* and *Citizen Kane* — but the number of films of this quality is not large in proportion to the available resources. Many — perhaps most — of

10 'The Diamond as Big as the Ritz', BH5, pp. 66—7.
11 'Handle With Care', BH3, p. 397.

the films released were cheap and false, and, if the industry on occasion knew how to use resources as they had never been used before, it also wasted them as never before. Other American industries had squandered money, soil, forests, minerals; Hollywood wasted human creative powers. Only Hollywood could have turned away Eisenstein whom even Stalin didn't choose to silence; and only Hollywood could have reduced a great actor like Peter Lorre to the status of bit parts in Bob Hope comedies. No one knew this better than Fitzgerald as each of his film-scripts in turn was mutilated, rejected, or shelved.

It is worth noting, however, that *Three Comrades*, the one film for which Fitzgerald received a screen credit, is a distinguished piece of work. Aaron Latham has shown that, although Joseph Mankiewicz, the director, altered Fitzgerald's script in a number of places, a great deal of his work was used in making the picture.[12] The film itself, while it is not a great classic of the cinema, has a distinctive and unforgettable atmosphere. Mankiewicz and Fitzgerald have caught the flavour of life in Weimar Germany, and the romantic delicacy with which love and friendship are presented seems unmistakably Fitzgerald's.

He had already made two brief and unsatisfactory visits to Hollywood, however, before this final phase of his career began, and these experiences greatly strengthened that mingled sense of fascination and repugnance which is so characteristic of his attitude. He explores these feelings in the brilliant little scene in *Tender is the Night* where Rosemary arranges a private showing of her picture *Daddy's Girl* for the Divers and the Norths. This episode is especially interesting since it does not deal simply with the film industry as applied wealth, but examines film itself as an art form, even if it is a form in which Fitzgerald only half believes. *Daddy's Girl* is a trashy sentimental picture 'embodying all the immaturity of the race'; its plot incorporates a blatant incest motif; and it is full of tasteless absurdities like the weeping woman who appears in every sequence. And yet there are times when Rosemary's performance is genuinely moving, and her audience, critical as they are, find themselves irresistibly drawn to her image on the screen.

The whole paradoxical nature of cinema as Fitzgerald saw it, is suggested by this scene. He distrusted the capacity of film to produce images of great psychological and emotional power, because this capacity, in his view, was not accompanied by any corresponding degree of artistic control. As a novelist, he himself had slowly learnt how to define and qualify his own romantic impulses through language: the apparent lack of any such subtle medium in the cinema meant that he could never admire the new form unreservedly. In this respect he was no doubt unfair — film has its own modes of artistic sophistication, and among these language is only a minor

---

12 Aaron Latham, *Crazy Sundays: Scott Fitzgerald in Hollywood*, London, 1972, see the chapter 'Three Comrades'.

resource. Nevertheless, his attitude reflects his habitual insight into the character of his own work. Some novels seem naturally cinematic: *The Grapes of Wrath* is an especially interesting case, since John Ford's film is in many ways a better work of art than Steinbeck's novel — Ford's images and soundtrack often seem to do more for the original conception than Steinbeck's words. Fitzgerald's fiction, however, could not possibly be more unlike this, and it is significant that almost every attempt to adapt his work for film or television has resulted in failure. From this point of view, Jack Clayton's version of *The Great Gatsby* is particularly illuminating, since Clayton is a director of talent who has a genuine respect for the book he is filming. But the images and situations which he takes from the novel lose all their meaning and value when they cease to be expressed in Fitzgerald's own words: the green light becomes an absurd and arbitrary symbol, winking grossly at the spectator in order to secure his attention; and the relationship between Gatsby and Daisy, as soon as it is detached from the ironic inflections of Nick Carraway's voice, becomes simply and crudely sentimental. Nothing could illustrate more clearly the underlying reasons for Fitzgerald's misgivings about Hollywood.

On the other hand, his treatment of Dick Diver's reactions to *Daddy's Girl* shows how deeply he was aware of the power of those art forms like the film and the novel which have a broad popular basis. They are so closely entwined with the feelings and convictions of millions of ordinary people that the artists who create them çan tap sources of true emotion in the most unexpected ways. When Fitzgerald began to write, the novel had possessed this power to a unique degree. He himself had gained a great popular success with *This Side of Paradise* and his *Post* stories, and a *succès d'estime* with *The Great Gatsby*, and he continued to believe — at least until the publication of *Tender is the Night* — that it should be possible to obtain both with the same book. In this respect, his attitude to the novel has much in common with that of the great popular writers of the nineteenth century, Scott and Dickens, Balzac and Zola. It is therefore not surprising that he quickly recognized the power of the cinema, even while insisting that it was, when compared with the novel, a crude and debased art.

On a purely practical level, Fitzgerald had long admired Hollywood for its superb professionalism. This is a major theme in his best Hollywood story 'Crazy Sunday' (which I have already discussed), and it is the one quality that makes Rosemary Hoyt something more than a mere selfish, empty-headed, sentimental opportunist. Fitzgerald respected the high standards of technical competence which Hollywood brought to the craft of film-making, even when he was most contemptuous of the films produced. And, in the 1930s, Hollywood deserved his respect. To see the films of that period now is to be overwhelmed, again and again, with a sense of their sheer professionalism. Groucho Marx's range of performing skills is as amazing as his creative sense for the possibilities of a comic situation; Fred Astaire, in his dancing, brings faultless standards of execution to the most ephemeral of musicals; the bit players in their brief appearances are as accomplished as the stars, for example the Italian tenor who tries to .teach Citizen Kane's second wife to sing. Fitzgerald set himself the same high standards in his own work for the studios. When he learned that he was to write the script for a projected Joan Crawford picture, he ran off all her old films and made detailed notes on her facial expressions and gestures[13]: he knew that it was useless to create situations for the cinema unless they were founded upon a thorough knowledge of his star and her limitations. Sometimes he had a better grasp of what was involved than the film-makers themselves. This is clear from some of the alterations he made to the script of *Gone With the Wind*, which David O. Selznick asked him to revise. At the point where Scarlett winds a yellow sash round Ashley's waist, a previous writer had given him the line, 'It looks like gold.' Fitzgerald crossed this out, reminding Selznick in a marginal note that 'This is technicolor.'[14] He was well aware that this degree of attention to matters of craft was a vital pre-requisite for all creative achievement. Great art, for him, was never an inspired short-cut — it began where the purely professional skills left off. In his reconstruction of Monroe Stahr's day at the studio, he shows how necessary these skills are to the collaborative art of cinema.

These ideas were already in Fitzgerald's mind when he came to Hollywood in the summer of 1937, but it was some time before he was able to develop them in the light of his wider experience. As a script writer for MGM, he not only had to work hard, but was expected to keep normal office hours and to be available for emergency story conferences that might last far into the night. It was only when MGM failed to renew his contract in January 1939, and free-lance work became difficult to obtain, that he found the time and energy to write fiction. He put most of his resources into two enterprises: the seventeen Pat Hobby stories which appeared (five of them posthumously) in *Esquire* between January 1940 and May 1941; and the unfinished novel, *The Last Tycoon*.

The Pat Hobby stories, a series of farcical sketches about a seedy unsuc-cessful middle-aged script writer, are perhaps the most purely commercial of all Fitzgerald's writings. In their way, they are highly accomplished, and the best of them — 'A Man in the Way', 'Teamed with Genius', 'Boil Some Water, Lots of it', and 'Two Old Timers' — are extremely funny. But Pat's character is simplified down to a few blunt strokes, and his adventures are so formalized and predictable that they could easily be represented by the frames of a strip cartoon. Above all, one has a sense of Fitzgerald carefully rationing his material: he shows, as never before, a hard calculating awareness of the exact minimum of effort needed to satisfy his editor and readers. In this respect, these stories seem to be a hangover from the crack-up period,

13 *Ibid.*, pp. 156—7.
14 *Ibid.*, p. 216.

and to reflect that determination which he expresses so unattractively in 'Pasting it Together' never to give himself spontaneously or prodigally again. The reality of this connection is emphasized by the emotional undertone of anxiety and discouragement which runs through the whole series.

By contrast, *The Last Tycoon* seems anything but the work of a fatigued unhappy man; and there is a special poignancy in the fact that Fitzgerald's physical energies should have failed him at the very moment when his creative powers had been so strikingly restored. Even in its unfinished state, the novel has many outstanding qualities. It evokes the atmosphere of Hollywood — and, in particular, what it means to work for the movies — with a unique blend of wit and insight. Chapters III and IV, which follow Monroe Stahr through a typical day at the studio, give precision to the idea that cinema is both an art and an industry, and that a great producer has to be manager, financier, artist and technician all in one. Stahr imposes his notion of the kind of picture the public wants on a rebellious story conference; he creates the psychological pressures required to obtain the performance he needs from a fading evil-tempered actress; he excoriates a director and cameraman for photographing the top of Claudette Colbert's head instead of her beautifully expressive face in a scene that was supposed to be intimate and moving; he sets a whole team to scan a film in which the leading man appears briefly with his fly open, so that the offending footage can be identified and cut; he discusses the differences between cinema and the novel with a discontented writer whom he doesn't want to lose; and at the rushes, he picks out a sensitively observed moment in a film about children as an example of the kind of work for which the studio will be remembered. Although Fitzgerald introduces a great deal of naturalistic detail into these chapters, his writing has a lightness and brilliance one would never find in the Hollywood scenes of Dos Passos's *U.S.A.*

Fitzgerald is carried far beyond the limits of naturalism by his imaginative response to the kind of consciousness created by Hollywood. For those involved in film-making — and to a lesser extent for every picturegoer — the imaginary world of the cinema tends to invade the ordinary world of everyday objects: at one extreme, events on film become more real than life itself, while, at the other, the mind half-consciously conceives of experience as if it were a perpetual movie. Monroe Stahr almost always regards situations and people from this equivocal point of view. When the studio lot is shaken by earthquake and deluged by flood, the ensuing chaos, seen through his eyes, seems not so much a product of the destructive powers of nature, as an expression of the new phantasmagoric reality created by the film industry itself. When his love-affair with Kathleen begins, he catches himself looking at her as if she were an actress taking a screen test, wondering whether her beauty will vanish as she begins to move. In this atmosphere, the freakish and the odd acquire the status of normality: when Stahr picks up the telephone in his unfinished beach house, he is asked to stand by for a call from the President of the United States, only to find himself a moment later in conversation with an orang-outang. He is simply the victim of a practical joke, and yet the incident seems to epitomize the peculiar dislocations of experience which are so characteristic of the Hollywood scene. (It is interesting to note that this theme is central to the other major Hollywood novel of the period, Nathanael West's *The Day of the Locust*; and also to *Sunset Boulevard* — the most brilliant of all those films in which Hollywood tries to look at itself.)

Fitzgerald's greatest achievement in *The Last Tycoon*, however, is his conception of Monroe Stahr. The nature of the film industry enabled him to develop in the same character qualities which he had never been able to bring together satisfactorily before: Stahr is a leader of men who also possesses an artistic consciousness. This had not been possible in the cases of Jay Gatsby or Dick Diver: Gatsby's fine sensibilities are stultified by the banal images he is forced to use, and Diver finds that in expatriate society the roles of scientist and arbiter of taste are mutually exclusive. Fitzgerald found the germ of his idea in the figure of Irving Thalberg, a producer who had had a dazzling career at MGM in the 1920s and early 1930s. Thalberg did much to establish the enormous financial power of Metro-Goldwyn-Mayer, and was, at the same time, a man with a true understanding of the artistic possibilities of the cinema. *Grand Hotel*, one of those rare films in which Hollywood seems to draw on all its creative resources at once, emerged from his production unit. He died in 1936, and already, by the time Fitzgerald came out to Hollywood the following year, the character of the industry was changing as the film companies began to transform themselves from personal empires into modern bureaucratic corporations. The organization man was in process of replacing the tycoon. In this situation Fitzgerald had his principal character and his historical theme ready to hand.

Stahr is a true leader: his power flows from within — from unique qualities of character — and not from the mere ability to serve the corporation skilfully and unscrupulously (the qualities which, in Fitzgerald's plan for the novel, were to have enabled the lawyer Fleishacker to succeed him). In controlling the affairs of the studio, he does not use the power of the institution as a lever for getting his own way. For him, the exercise of power is a peculiarly personal matter which always involves him in direct relationships with other people: sometimes he gets what he wants by sheer force of character, as when he dismisses the weak director, Red Ridingwood; at other times he draws on magnetic, charismatic qualities so as, quite literally, to charm the right response from his subordinates. We see an example of this latter method at work in the scene where he brings a stale story conference to life by playing a game — organizing a competition to see who is best at flicking coins into a light-fitting overhead.

Fitzgerald sees clearly that Stahr's style of leadership is an anachronism in the age of the giant corporation, which exercises power impersonally through bureaucratic channels, and understands human relations, if it understands them at all, only as a problem of social engineering. There is almost always an elegiac note in the way Fitzgerald writes about Stahr. This is especially apparent in the scene in which Stahr organizes the cleaning up of the flooded studio lot and the salvaging of expensive sets and properties threatened by the effects of the earthquake. It is his last great moment, an occasion when he succeeds in dominating not only the studio but the physical terrors of the earth — earthquake and flood. As the studio hands stream past him on their way to repair the damage, they salute him as their hero: 'The old loyalties were trembling now, there were clay feet everywhere; but still he was their man, the last of the princes'. The older workers have an almost feudal sense of devotion of Stahr: they feel that they owe their employment through the Depression directly to him, and they greet him individually and by name in what amounts to a ritual act of homage. His lieutenant Robinson, on whose technical skill he depends for clearing up the mess, is himself a kind of American folk-hero, a man who began work by fixing telephone lines in Minnesota blizzards. Some men, by their actions, confer on Stahr what is virtually the power of life and death. The failed producer Manny Schwartz takes Stahr's rebuff as a death sentence, and he commits suicide just as the rejected follower of some Roman emperor might have done. When Pete Zavras, the blacklisted cameraman, tries to commit suicide from the balcony of Stahr's office, the latter reprieves him with a letter which has almost the force of a royal proclamation. In the manner of princes, too, Stahr can often appear — especially to his more 'practical' associates like Brady — to be whimsical and arbitrary, as when he announces his intention of making a quality picture that will lose money.

The burden of command has made him exhausted and ill. He feels he can never relax — that his power depends on his ability to communicate an unfaltering — an almost magical — sense of certainty to his subordinates. He explains what this means near the beginning of the novel:

> 'Suppose you were a railroad man,' he said. 'You have to send a train through there somewhere. [He is looking down from a plane at a wild landscape of mountain peaks.] Well, you get your surveyors' reports, and you find there's three or four or half a dozen gaps, and not one is better than the other. You've got to decide — on what basis? You can't test the best way — except by doing it. So you just do it. ...
> 'You choose some one way for no reason at all — because that mountain's pink or the blueprint's a better one.'[15]

Since Stahr is a prince in America, he is necessarily a merchant prince. In a half-bantering, half-serious argument with Wylie White, he calls himself a merchant, and seems willing to accept 'Gould, Vanderbilt, Carnegie, Astor' as his ancestors, but, as White insists, there is a difference. Stahr has qualities which these historical figures lacked, as did the tycoons in Fitzgerald's earlier fiction — the megalomaniac Braddock Washington in 'The Diamond as Big as the Ritz', and the half-absurd adventurer Dan Cody in

15   *The Last Tycoon*, BH1, p. 333.

The Great Gatsby. Monroe Stahr may be a merchant, but, thanks to the conditions of the film industry, he is also an artist and visionary. This is made most vivid in the image of flight with which Fitzgerald opens the novel, and with which he intended to bring Stahr's career to a close. In Chapter 1, the actual transcontinental flight which carries Stahr to California leads us unobtrusively to the metaphorical flight which enabled him to see what his destiny was to be; as he watches the lights of Los Angeles from the descending plane, we are made to imagine him figuratively surveying the field of his activities:

> He had flown up very high to see, on strong wings, when he was young. And while he was up there he had looked on all the kingdoms, with the kind of eyes that can stare straight into the sun. Beating his wings tenaciously — finally frantically — and keeping on beating them, he had stayed up there longer than most of us, and then, remembering all he had seen from his great height of how things were, he had settled gradually to earth.[16]

From Fitzgerald's notes, we know that he intended Stahr to die in a plane crash — a flight abruptly cut short by catastrophe — and this event was to coincide with the irretrievable wreck of his commanding position at the studio. The corporation men and the labour unions, even though they were at war on every other issue, were united in their determination to destroy the kind of personal power he exercised. For the benefit of those who still believe that Fitzgerald was a kind of natural writer who was incapable of thinking, it is perhaps worth pointing out that in *The Last Tycoon* he had already grasped ideas about the changing nature of power in America, which were not formalized by sociologists and political theorists like C. Wright Mills until well into the 1950s. He also contrived, in order to bring out the full complexity of Stahr's character, to combine poetic evocation with the use of naturalistic detail, more skilfully than ever before in his career.

The surviving fragment of *The Last Tycoon* is not entirely successful, however, and while it has qualities which suggest that the completed novel might have been as fine as *The Great Gatsby* and *Tender is the Night*, it has, equally, shortcomings which raise doubts as to whether Fitzgerald would have done full justice in the end to his sense of Hollywood and his conception of Stahr. His decision to use Cecilia Brady as a narrator seems little short of disastrous. Her empty selfish nature, and her callow hardness — the premature cynicism of an immature mind — make her quite unsuitable as a device for bringing out the essence of Stahr's complex activities and magnetic influence. To be conscious of her voice is to hear either the hard bright chatter of Fitzgerald's poorest flapper stories ('The Offshore Pirate', say) or the feeblest and most sentimental banalities of women's magazine fiction. The really fine things in the novel seem to come — indeed they do come — from a very different source: they are communicated through that fine and quiet tone of impersonal authorial narration which Fitzgerald had

16 *Ibid.,* p. 334.

developed in 'The Rich Boy', 'Babylon Revisited', and *Tender is the Night*.

There are fundamental reasons, quite apart from the unsatisfactoriness of Cecilia herself, why the use of a fictional narrator does not seem a good way of approaching the action and the central character of *The Last Tycoon*. Stahr's activities are so varied that it is not plausible that any other character should have first-hand knowledge of more than a small proportion of them. *The Last Tycoon* is not a novel of manners, and its characters cannot come together socially in the way that made it possible for Nick Carraway to function so successfully in *The Great Gatsby*. Nor is there any need for the kind of technical ingenuity Conrad showed in his use of Marlow in *Lord Jim*: Stahr is complex, but he is not an enigma; no detective work is needed to reconstruct the circumstances of his life, and his case, unlike Jim's, does not demand sympathetic special pleading. Fitzgerald in fact often has to drop Cecilia and resort to the authorial narration which would have been much the best method for telling the whole story.

One is bound to have reservations, too, about Fitzgerald's ability to carry through the ambitious political plot he had planned for the later sections of the novel. Stahr was to have found himself at the centre of a struggle between the Writers' Guild (a union in which Communists had some influence), and those studio chiefs like Brady and Fleishacker who saw cinema as a purely commercial enterprise. It was a situation Stahr could not dominate with his personal style of leadership: as he found himself forced increasingly to descend to the methods of his enemies, his character would deteriorate and his vision be largely lost. One's doubts about this scheme rest not so much on the fact that Fitzgerald had never attempted anything like it before, as on the actual failure of Chapter VI, the episode in which the political plot begins to unfold, Brimmer, the Communist who is introduced there, is absolutely unconvincing as a party member (and in every other way), and Fitzgerald does nothing to prepare for the abrupt change in Stahr's behaviour — his drunkenness, his stupid aggressiveness, his ugly loss of self-control. This chapter does not augur well for the future progress of the novel, and there is no hint in it of the political sophistication which enabled Norman Mailer to write so well about Hollywood anti-Communism in *The Deer Park*.

By this point, however, one is becoming involved in speculation rather than analysis. Fitzgerald commonly rewrote and revised so much during the course of composition, that he might well have entirely corrected these faults in what is, after all, only an unfinished draft. Even in its uncompleted form, *The Last Tycoon* occupies an important place in his *oeuvre*, and it is not altogether unreasonable to wonder — as some critics have done — whether it might not have proved to be his greatest novel. One's keen disappointment that he did not live to finish it is offset to some degree by the knowledge that he died, not as the 'rather inhuman and undernourished' man of the crack-up articles, but as a great artist working once more at the height of his powers.

Select Bibliography

Writings of F. Scott Fitzgerald

Since there are no definitive texts of Fitzgerald's novels and stories and no collected edition of his writings, I have listed below, for the convenience of the reader, his works in chronological order. Important collections of letters are included in this list. The best available collection of his writings in Britain is the *Bodley Head Scott Fitzgerald*, in six volumes, and I have referred to this whenever possible. This edition has the merit of printing the 1934 text of *Tender is the Night*, the only proper basis for an understanding of the novel.

This Side of Paradise, New York, 1920.
Flappers and Philosophers, New York, 1920.
The Beautiful and Damned, New York, 1922.
Tales of the Jazz Age, New York, 1922.
The Vegetable: or From President to Postman, New York, 1923.
The Great Gatsby, New York, 1925.
All the Sad Young Men, New York, 1926.
Tender is the Night, New York, 1934.
Taps at Reveille, New York, 1935.
The Last Tycoon, New York, 1941.
The Crack-up, edited by Edmund Wilson, New York, 1945.
Afternoon of an Author: a Selection of Uncollected Stories and Essays, edited by Arthur Mizener, Princeton, 1957.

The Pat Hobby Stories, New York, 1962.
The Letters of F. Scott Fitzgerald, edited by Andrew Turnbull, New York, 1963.
The Apprentice Fiction of F. Scott Fitzgerald, 1909—1917, edited by John Kuehl, New Brunswick, N.J., 1965.
Dear Scott/Dear Max: The Fitzgerald-Perkins Correspondence, edited by John Kuehl, New York, 1971.
As Ever, Scott Fitz-: Letters Between F. Scott Fitzgerald and His Literary Agent Harold Ober, 1919—1940, edited by Matthew J. Bruccoli, New York, 1972.
Bits of Paradise: 21 Uncollected Short Stories by F. Scott and Zelda Fitzgerald, edited by Matthew J. Bruccoli, New York, 1973.

The Price Was High: the Last Uncollected Stories of F. Scott Fitzgerald, edited by Matthew J. Bruccoli, New York, 1979.

Full-length studies and other books containing important essays or background material.

Marius Bewley, *The Eccentric Design: Form in the Classic American Novel,* London, 1959.
Malcolm Bradbury (ed.), *Stratford-upon-Avon Studies 13. The American Novel and the 1920s,* London, 1971.
Matthew J. Bruccoli, *Apparatus for F. Scott Fitzgerald's 'The Great Gatsby',* Columbia, S.C., 1974.
Matthew J. Bruccoli, *The Composition of 'Tender is the Night': a Study of the Manuscripts,* Pittsburgh, 1963.
Matthew J. Bruccoli, *F. Scott Fitzgerald: a Descriptive Bibliography,* Pittsburgh, 1972.
Matthew J. Bruccoli, *The Last of the Novelists: F. Scott Fitzgerald and 'The Last Tycoon',* Carbondale, Ill., 1977.
Matthew J. Bruccoli: *Scott and Ernest: the authority of failure and the authority of success,* London 1978.
Jackson R. Bryer, *The Critical Reputation of F. Scott Fitzgerald: a Bibliographical Study,* New York, 1967.
Malcolm Cowley, *Exile's Return: a Literary Odyssey of the 1920s,* New York, 1934.
Malcolm Cowley, *A Second Flowering: Works and Days of the Lost Generation,* London, 1973.
Zelda Fitzgerald, *Save Me the Waltz,* New York, 1932.
Sheilah Graham, *Beloved Infidel,* London 1959.
John A. Higgins, *F. Scott Fitzgerald: a Study of the Stories,* Jamaica, NY, 1971.
Frederick J. Hoffman, *The Twenties: American Writing in the Postwar Decade,* New York, 1955.
Alfred Kazin (ed.), *F. Scott Fitzgerald: the Man and his Work,* Cleveland and New York, 1951.
Aaron Latham, *Crazy Sundays: Scott Fitzgerald in Hollywood,* London, 1972.
Richard Lehan, *F. Scott Fitzgerald and the Craft of Fiction,* Carbondale, Ill., 1966.
Nancy Milford, *Zelda Fitzgerald: a Biography,* London, 1970.
James E. Miller, *The Fictional Technique of F. Scott Fitzgerald,* The Hague, 1957. Enlarged and revised as *F. Scott Fitzgerald: his Art and his Technique,* New York, 1964.
Arthur Mizener, *The Far Side of Paradise: a Biography of F. Scott Fitzgerald,* Boston, 1951.
Sergio Perosa, *The Art of F. Scott Fitzgerald:* Ann Arbor, Mich., 1965.

Henry Dan Piper, *F. Scott Fitzgerald: a Critical Portrait*, London, 1965.

Robert Sklar, *F. Scott Fitzgerald: The Last Laocoon*, New York, 1967.

Milton R. Stern, *The Golden Moment: the Novels of F. Scott Fitzgerald*, Urbana, 1970.

Calvin Tomkins, *Living Well is the Best Revenge: Two Americans in Paris, 1921—1933*, London, 1972.

Lionel Trilling, *The Liberal Imagination: Essays on Literature and Thought*, London, 1951.

Andrew Turnbull, *Scott Fitzgerald*, London, 1962.

Edmund Wilson, *The Shores of Light: a Literary Chronicle of the Twenties and Thirties*, New York, 1952.

Index

'Absolution' 4, 29, 32, 33, 77, 80–82, 93, 95.
Adams, Henry viii, 2–3, 6–7, 22–5, 31–3, 37, 45, 113, 130–31, 140, 145.
'Afternoon of an Author' 76, 96–7.
Age of Innocence, The 46.
'Alcoholic Case, An' 97.
Alger, Horatio 100.
Allen, Frederick Lewis 63.
Ambassadors, The 29, 87.
American, The 35.
American Mercury, The 70.
American Scene, The 14, 31–2, 44, 58.
Anderson, Sherwood 2, 72, 95.
aristocracy and the aristocratic ideal. 2–3, 5–7, 16–18, 19, 31, 33–8, 51–2, 84–7, 88, 101–3, 104, 113, 116–7, 129, 132–7, 139, *see also* rich (the American).
Astaire, Fred 156–7.
Awkward Age, The 98–100.
Axel's Castle 15.

Babbitt 70.
'Babylon Revisited' 15, 75, 90–92, 96, 139, 162.
Balzac, Honoré de 34–5, 43–4, 156.
'Basil and Cleopatra' 79–80.
Beautiful and Damned, The 11, 23, 38, 49, 60, 64–7, 71, 77.
'Bernice Bobs her Hair' 3, 11, 56–7, 61, 67, 80.
Berryman, John 152.
Bewley, Marius vii, 71.
Bible 70.
Bishop, John Peale 17, 52.
Blackmur, R. P. 23.

Blithedale Romance, The 58.
Bostonians, The 44.
'Bowl, The' 9, 74–5, 77.
Boyd, Ernest 65.
Brooke, Rupert 52–4.
Bruccoli, Matthew J. 124–5, 145.
Burckhardt, Jakob 18.
Burke, Kenneth 16.
Byron, George Gordon, Lord 16, 52.

'Camel's Back, The' 72.
Castiglione, Baldassare 34–5.
Cather, Willa 24.
Catholicism 4, 6–7, 81.
Chaplin, Charlie 154.
Chekhov, Anton 76, 95, 144.
Citizen Kane 114–5, 154, 157.
Clayton, Jack 156.
Conrad, Joseph 21, 23, 24–5, 77, 162.
Cooper, James Fenimore vii, 35, 44.
Cowley, Malcolm x, 9, 12, 15–16, 122, 124–5.
crack-up ix, 16, 75, 84, 95–7, 124, 149–53, 157.
'Crack-up, The' xi, 19, 63, 96, 149–53, 162.
Crane, Hart 9–10, 13, 17, 62.
Crane, Stephen 62.
Crawford, Joan 157.
'Crazy Sunday' 15, 18, 75, 93–5, 156.
Crockett, Davy 111.
Custom of the Country, The 46–7, 58, 84–5.

'Daisy Miller' 23, 58, 77.
Davis, Jefferson 7.
Death in Venice 15, 77.

'Débutante, The' 59–60.
Diaghilev's Russian Ballet 154.
'Diamond as Big as the Ritz, The' vii, 2, 9, 67–71, 129, 154, 160.
Dickens, Charles 19, 61, 67, 111–3, 156.
Dos Passos, John vii, 9, 145, 153, 158.
Dostoievsky, Fyodor 151–2.
Dreiser, Theodore vii, 2, 43, 62, 64, 101, 123.

'Echoes of the Jazz Age' 10–15, 62, 77–8, 140–1.
Eisenstein, Sergei 154, 155.
Eliot, George 122.
Eliot, T. S. 22–3, 87, 104, 146–8.
Ellingson, Dorothy 141.
'Emotional Bankruptcy' 150.
Esquire 95, 149, 153, 157.
Ethan Frome 22, 77.
Europeans, The 27–8, 29, 30–3, 44, 58, 69.
Exile's Return 9, 15.

Falstaff 40, 61, 112–3, 116.
Farrell, James T. 145.
Faulkner, William x, 35, 63, 72, 154.
Fay, Sigourney Webster 6–7, 23, 36.
'Financing Finnegan' 96–7.
Fitzgerald, Edward (FSF's father) 3, 5–7, 36, 52.
Fitzgerald, Frances (Scottie) 5, 18, 20, 23, 26, 27, 88, 150.
Fitzgerald, Mollie McQuillan (FSF's mother) 4, 17.
Fitzgerald, Zelda Sayre ix, 5, 11, 17–8, 27, 72, 141–2, 149.
flapper 10–11, 57–61, 67, 82–3, 129, 161, *see also* women in America.
Flappers and Philosophers 49.
Flaubert, Gustave 106–7.
For Whom the Bell Tolls, 146.
Ford, Ford Madox 17, 23.
Ford, John 154, 156.
France, Anatole 21.
Franklin, Benjamin 100.

Galsworthy, John 21.

Gilded Age 2, 37, 68, 85, 87, 100, 129, 154.
Goethe, Johann Wolfgang von 16.
Golden Bowl, The 40.
Gone With the Wind (film) 157.
Graham, Sheilah 20.
Grand Hotel 154, 159.
Great Gatsby, The vii, viii, 2, 8–9, 11, 13, 16, 22, 23, 24, 29, 31, 33, 36, 38, 40–2, 43, 44, 47, 52, 55, 56, 60, 62, 63, 65, 67, 71, 77, 79, 80, 82, 85, ch. 5, 127, 129, 139, 148, 154, 156, 159, 160–1, 162.
Great Gatsby, The (film) 156.
Grant, Ulysses S. 143.
Grapes of Wrath, The 103, 146, 156.
Griffith, D. W. 154.

'Handle with Care' 149–50, 154.
Harding, D. W. 119.
Harding, Warren G. 12.
Hawthorne, Nathaniel 22, 25, 58.
Heart of Darkness 24.
Hemingway, Ernest 2, 8, 9–10, 19, 63, 72, 87, 92, 95, 143, 146, 153.
Henry, O. 76.
Hill, James J. 2.
history of manners 12, 25, 43–8, 50, 56–63, 141, 142.
Hollywood vii, ix, 1, 11, 18, 31, 69, 73, 93–5, 114, 139, 153–62.
Hoover, Herbert H. 92.
House of Mirth, The 22, 37, 46, 58, 84.
'How to Live on Practically Nothing a Year' 88.

Ibsen, Henrik 10–11.
'Ice Palace, The' 2, 55–6, 68, 69, 80.
'I Didn't Get Over' 97.
In Our Time 19.

James, Henry viii, x, 2–3, 14, 17, ch. 2, 58, 65, 69, 77, 87, 98–100, 101, 113, 133, 146–7, 148.
Jazz Age viii, xi, 1, 9–15, 19, 21, 31, 36, 37, 44–5, 46, 47, 50, 63, 78–9, 82–3, 86, 87–92, 95, 104, 138–42.
Jefferson, Thomas 35.
'Jelly-Bean, The' 58, 60–1.

'Jolly Corner, The' 44−5.
Josephine stories 129, 150.
Joyce, James 4, 9, 76, 95.

Kazin, Alfred 151, 153.
Keats, John 50, 52, 54.
King, Ginevra 3, 4.
Krafft-Ebing, Richard von 148.

Lampedusa, Guiseppe di 34.
Lardner, Ring 8.
'Last of the Belles, The' 61, 75, 80, 82−4, 93.
Last Tycoon, The 15, 18, 38, 42, 43, 73−4, 77, 92, 94, 149, 157−62.
Latham, Aaron x, 155.
Lawrence, D. H. vii.
Leopold and Loeb 141.
Leslie, Shane 6, 53, 145.
'Lesson of the Master, The' 40.
Lewis, Sinclair 2, 9, 70.
Lincoln, Abraham 5.
Lloyd, Harold 154.
Lord Jim 162.
Lorre, Peter 154, 155.
'Lost Decade, The' 96−7.
'Love in the Night' 105.
Lukács, Georg 138.

Mackenzie, Compton 22, 52.
Madame Bovary 16, 106−7.
Magic Mountain, The 139.
Magnificent Ambersons, The (film) 3.
Mailer, Norman 162.
'Majesty' 45−6, 61, 72.
Man and Superman 16.
Mankiewicz, Joseph 73, 75, 155.
Mann, Thomas 17, 77, 139.
Marx, Groucho 154, 156.
Marx, Karl 24, 131, 145−6, 147−8.
Matthiessen, F. O. 38−9.
Maupassant, Guy de 76.
'May Day' 15, 49, 56, 67−8, 77−9, 84, 95, 141.
Melville, Herman 22, 38.
Mencken, H. L. 9−10, 16, 23, 64−6, 70, 110, 125.
Metro-Goldwyn-Mayer 157, 159.
Middle West vii, 2−5, 9, 15, 25, 29,
47, 50, 55−6, 62, 67, 80−1, 84, 85, 101, 117, 137.
Milford, Nancy 1.
Miller, James E. 23.
Mills, C. Wright 161.
Mizener, Arthur ix, 1.
Moveable Feast, A 92.
Murphy, Gerald & Sara 36, 88.
'My Lost City' 1, 10−5, 16, 62, 96.

Nassau Literary Magazine 49, 59.
Nathan, George Jean 64.
'News of Paris — Fifteen Years Ago' 92, 96, 97, 140.
Nietzsche, Friedrich Wilhelm 16.
'Night at the Fair, A' 3, 32−3.
Norris, Frank 64, 68.
Nostromo 25, 106.

Ober, Harold 75, 95.
Octopus, The 68.
'Offshore Pirate, The' 59, 161.
'One Hundred False Starts' 4.
'One Trip Abroad' 77, 89−90.
Orwell, George 16.
Othello 94.

'Pasting it Together' 16, 149, 153, 158.
Pat Hobby stories 157−8.
Pater, Walter 52.
Perkins, Maxwell 22−3, 27, 29, 106, 142, 145, 147, 153.
Petronius 115−6.
Picture of Dorian Gray, The 16, 52−3, 66.
Piper, Henry Dan 1, 62.
Plath, Sylvia 152.
Poe, Edgar Allan 52.
Pope, Alexander 37.
'Popular Girl, The' 60.
Porter, Cole 26.
Portrait of the Artist as a Young Man, 4, 15.
Portrait of a Lady, The 3, 23, 26, 29, 30, 35−6, 39−40, 58, 69, 87, 131−2.
Pound, Ezra 17, 22, 87.
Princeton ix, 8, 9, 16−7, 49−55, 59, 66, 74, 145, 149.

'Princeton' 8.
Prohibition 12–4, 50, 56, 60, 88, 99.
Puritanism 3–5, 12, 25–30, 56, 58, 65–6, 116–7, 137–8.

'Reade, Substitute Right Half' 74.
rich (the American) vii, 1, 8–9, 23, 25, 32, 36–8, 46, 50, 51–2, 67–70, 84–7, 88–92, 99, 100–3, 104, 109, 116, 128–37, 139–41, 153, 154, *see also* aristocracy and the aristocratic ideal.
'Rich Boy, The' 8, 26–7, 38, 47–8, 52, 77, 84–7, 129, 162.
Roderick Hudson 23, 25–6.
Romantic Egotist, The 49–50.
Rothstein, Arnold 38.
'Rough Crossing, The' 42, 75, 88–9, 90, 139.

Sacco and Vanzetti 12.
Saturday Evening Post 72, 73, 75, 95, 156.
'Scandal Detectives, The' 3.
Schulberg, Budd x.
Scott, Sir Walter 61, 156.
Seldes, Gilbert 125.
Selznick, David O. 157.
Shakespeare, William 16, 17, 116, 131.
Shaw, George Bernard 10, 16.
Shores of Light, The 147.
Sister Carrie 64, 123.
Sklar, Robert 24, 145.
Smart Set, The 64.
Smith, Grahame 111–2, 113.
'Snows of Kilimanjaro, The' 153.
Spender, Stephen 3.
Spengler, Oswald 145, 148.
Stalin, Joseph 148, 155.
Stallman, R. W. 24.
Steinbeck, John 146, 156.
Stendhal 9, 34–5, 107, 122.
Sun Also Rises, The 143.
Sunset Boulevard 69, 159.
Suratt, Mrs 5.
Swanson, Gloria 69.
'Swimmers, The' 139.
Swinburne, Algernon Charles 52.

Tales of the Jazz Age 49, 72.
Taney, Chief Justice 5.
Taps at Reveille 150.
Tarkington, Booth 22.
'Tarquin of Cheepside' 16–7.
Taylor, Cecilia (Cousin Ceci) 5.
Tender is the Night x, 8, 9, 11, 13, 15, 18, 20, 30, 36, 38, 39–40, 42, 43, 48, 60, 62, 63, 65, 67, 77, 79, 85, 87–8, 89, 92, 95, ch. 6, 149, 150, 151, 155–6, 159, 161, 162.
Thalberg, Irving 18, 159.
This Side of Paradise 5, 6, 9, 10, 11, 19, 38, 48, ch. 3, 77, 103, 129, 156.
Three Comrades 73, 155.
'Three Hours between Planes' 80, 84, 92, 96.
Tolstoy, Leo 122.
Trilling, Lionel 34–5, 43.
Trimalchio 111, 115–6.
Turgenev, Ivan 9.
Turnbull, Andrew ix, 1, 145.

Updike, John 97.

Vandover and the Brute 64.
Vanity Fair 106.
Vegetable, The 49, 71.

Wall Street Crash xi, 9, 12, 14–15, 90–2, 96, 142.
Welles, Orson 3, 114, 154.
West, Nathanael 154, 159.
Wharton, Edith viii, 3, 19–20, 22–5, 31, 37, 46–7, 58, 62, 77, 84–5, 87, 101, 110, 112.
What Maisie Knew 23, 40–2.
Wilde, Oscar 16, 52–3, 66.
Williams, William Carlos vii, 128.
Wilson, Edmund 3, 15, 23, 24, 40, 71, 147–8, 149.
Wilson, Woodrow 34.
Wings of the Dove, The 40, 58.
'Winter Dreams' 80.
women in America 10–11, 57–61, 62, 129–32 *see also* flapper.
World War I 4, 10, 12, 14, 20, 34, 49, 50, 66, 78, 82–3, 100, 117, 120, 138, 142–4.

Yeats, W. B.   17, 34–5.
'Youth'   24–5, 77.

Zola, Émile   156.